WOMEN AND CITIZENSHIP

STUDIES IN FEMINIST PHILOSOPHY
Cheshire Calhoun, *Series Editor*

WOMEN AND CITIZENSHIP

EDITED BY

Marilyn Friedman

OXFORD
UNIVERSITY PRESS

2005

OXFORD

UNIVERSITY PRESS

Oxford University Press, Inc., publishes works that further
Oxford University's objective of excellence
in research, scholarship, and education.

Oxford   New York
Auckland   Cape Town   Dar es Salaam   Hong Kong   Karachi
Kuala Lumpur   Madrid   Melbourne   Mexico City   Nairobi
New Delhi   Shanghai   Taipei   Toronto

With offices in
Argentina   Austria   Brazil   Chile   Czech Republic   France   Greece
Guatemala   Hungary   Italy   Japan   Poland   Portugal   Singapore
South Korea   Switzerland   Thailand   Turkey   Ukraine   Vietnam

Library of Congress Cataloging-in-Publication Data

Women and citizenship / edited by Marilyn Friedman.
   p.   cm.—(Studies in feminist philosophy)
Papers presented at a conference held at Washington University in St. Louis in April 2002.
Includes bibliographical references and index.
ISBN-13 978-0-19-517534-9; 978-0-19-517535-6 (pbk.)
ISBN 0-19-517534-4; 0-19-517535-2 (pbk.)
1. Women's rights—Congresses. 2. Women—Government policy—Congresses.
3. Women in politics—Congresses. 4. Women—Social conditions—Congresses.
5. Citizenship—Congresses. 6. Feminist theory—Congresses.
I. Friedman, Marilyn, 1945– II. Series.

HQ1236.W6326 2005
323.3'4—dc22   2005047749

9 8 7 6 5 4 3 2 1

Printed in the United States of America
on acid-free paper

For Larry

Contents

Contributors

MARTHA ACKELSBERG is Professor of Government and Women's Studies at Smith College. Her research has centered around the nature and structure of political communities, patterns of power, urban politics, social movements, and feminist and democratic theory. She has focused particularly on the anarchist movement in Spain and the subordination and emancipation of women within the anarchist project, and on the involvement in or exclusion of minority women from communal life and their responses to their marginality. She is the author of *Free Women of Spain: Anarchism and the Struggle for the Emancipation of Women* (1991) and is currently at work on *Making Democracy Work: (Re)Conceiving Politics Through the Lens of Women's Activism* (forthcoming).

SANDRA BARTKY is Professor Emerita of Philosophy and of Gender and Women's Studies at the University of Illinois in Chicago. She is the author of *Femininity and Domination: Studies in the Phenomenology of Oppression* (1990) and of *"Sympathy and Solidarity" and Other Essays* (2002). She has also coedited *Revaluing French Feminism* with Nancy Fraser (1992). Her particular interests are in feminist social and political theory, feminist ethics, critical theory, phenomenology, and poststructuralism.

MARILYN FRIEDMAN is Professor of Philosophy at Washington University in St. Louis. She has published numerous writings in the areas of feminist philosophy, ethics, and social and political philosophy. Her authored books include *What Are Friends For? Essays on Feminism, Personal Relationships, and Moral Theory* (1993), *Political Correctness: For and Against* (coauthored, 1995), and *Autonomy, Gender, Politics* (2003). She has also coedited *Feminism and Community* (1995), *Mind and Morals: Essays on Ethics and Cognitive Science* (1995), and *Rights and Reason: Essays in Honor of Carl Wellman* (2000).

AÍDA HURTADO is Professor of Psychology at the University of California, Santa Cruz. Her main areas of expertise are in the study of social identity (including ethnic identity) and feminist theory. She is the author of *The Color of Privilege: Three Blasphemies on Race and Feminism* (1996); *Voicing Chicana Feminisms: Young Women Speak Out on Sexuality and Identity* (2003); and *Chicana/o Identity in a Changing U.S. Society: Quien Soy, Quienes Somos* (coauthored with Patricia Gurin, 2004).

ALISON M. JAGGAR is Professor of Philosophy and Women's Studies at the University of Colorado at Boulder. Her books include *Feminist Frameworks*, coedited with Paula Rothenberg (3rd ed., 1993); *Feminist Politics and Human Nature* (1983); *Living with Contradictions: Controversies in Feminist Ethics* (1994); and *The Blackwell Companion to Feminist Ethics*, coedited with Iris Young (1998). Currently she is working on *Sex, Truth and Power: A Feminist Theory of Moral Justification*. Jaggar was a founding member of the Society for Women in Philosophy. She works with a number of feminist organizations and sees feminist scholarship as inseparable from feminist activism.

SUAD JOSEPH is Professor of Anthropology and Women and Gender Studies at the University of California, Davis, and Director of the Middle East/South Asia Studies Program. Her research has focused on her native Lebanon, on the politicization of religion, on women in local communities, on women, family and state, and on questions of self, citizenship, and rights. She is General Editor of the *Encyclopedia of Women and Islamic Cultures*, volume 1 of which appeared in 2003, volume 2 in 2004, and the remaining four volumes are to appear in 2005–2006. Her edited books include *Gender and Citizenship in the Middle East* (2000), *Intimate Selving in Arab Families* (1999), *Building Citizenship in Lebanon* (1999), and, coedited with Susan Slyomovics, *Women and Power in the Middle East* (2001). She is founder and first president of the Association for Middle East Women's Studies and founder and facilitator of the Arab Families Working Group.

MARTHA C. NUSSBAUM is the Ernst Freund Distinguished Service Professor of Law and Ethics at the University of Chicago. She has written on a wide variety of topics, including ancient Greek and Roman philosophy, moral understanding through literature, love, virtue, character, practical reason, sexuality, lesbian and gay rights, women and human capabilities, cosmopolitanism, religion and women's human rights, and patriotism. Her extensive publications include numerous authored books, edited books, journal articles, and book chapters. Among the authored books are: *Sex and Social Justice* (1999), *Women and Human Development: The Capabilities Approach* (2000), *Upheavals of Thought: The Intelligence of Emotions* (2001), *Hiding from Humanity: Disgust, Shame, and the Law* (2004), and *Global Justice and Fellowship: Disability, Nationality, Species Membership* (forthcoming), and *The Cosmopolitan Tradition* (forthcoming). Nussbaum has received many awards and fellowships, most recently the Grawemeyer Award in Education for her book *Cultivating Humanity: A Classical Defense of Reform in Liberal Education* (1997).

JOAN WALLACH SCOTT is Harold F. Linder Professor of Social Science at the Institute for Advanced Study. She is the author of *Gender and the Politics of History* (2nd ed., 2000) and *Only Paradoxes to Offer: French Feminists and the Rights of Man* (1996). She is the editor of *Feminism and History* (1996) and the coeditor with Judith Butler of *Feminists Theorize the Political*. Her book *Parité: The French Movement for Sexual Equality in Politics* is forthcoming.

JOAN TRONTO is Professor of Political Science at Hunter College and the Graduate Center, City University of New York. She is former director of the Women's Studies Program. She is the coeditor of *Women Transforming Politics: An Alternative Reader*. She is the author of *Moral Boundaries: A Political Argument for an Ethic of Care* and of numerous articles on using a care perspective as a framework for public policy decisions.

AMINA WADUD is Professor of Philosophy and Religious Studies at Virginia Commonwealth University. Her main research interests are in profaith, gender-sensitive interpretations of Islam's primary sources, especially the Qur'an, and in all aspects of social justice and moral agency. The goal of this research is to find the theological basis for social and legal reforms for equality in Islam. She is most well known for her book *Qur'an and Woman: Re-Reading the Sacred Text from a Woman's Perspective* (1992), now in six translations, and for extensive travel nationally and internationally as a profeminist Muslim theologian. She is currently working on a book-length manuscript about the ideological and strategic struggles for justice in Islam and modernity, tentatively titled, *Inside the Gender Jihad.*

IRIS MARION YOUNG is Professor of Political Science at the University of Chicago. She is a member of the faculty boards of the Center for Gender Studies and the Human Rights Program. Her research interests are in contemporary political theory, feminist social theory, and normative analysis of public policy. Her books include *Justice and the Politics of Difference* (1990), *Throwing Like a Girl and Other Essays in Feminist Philosophy and Social Theory* (1990), *Intersecting Voices: Dilemmas of Gender, Political Philosophy, and Policy* (1997), and *Inclusion and Democracy* (2000). Young has held visiting fellowships at several universities and institutes around the world, including Princeton University, the Institute for Human Sciences in Vienna, Australian National University, and the Human Sciences Research Council of South Africa.

WOMEN AND CITIZENSHIP

Introduction

Marilyn Friedman

Citizenship is multiple and various. It can be an identity; a set of rights, privileges, and duties; an elevated and exclusionary political status; a relationship between individuals and their states; a set of practices that can unify—or divide—the members of a political community; and an ideal of political agency. It can be all these things and more.

In recent decades, citizenship has attracted multidisciplinary attention and analysis. Changing political boundaries, resurgent nationalisms, ethnic hostilities, increased migrations, and the global realignment of military power are among the many recent developments that have destabilized citizenship and impelled states and peoples to reassess longstanding citizenship practices (Beiner 1995). Western European countries have admitted large influxes of immigrants from their respective former colonies. Western countries generally have been engaged for some time now with the presence of non-Western cultural traditions, languages, and identities (Honig 2001; Kymlicka and Norman 2000). Some of those developments followed the collapse of the Soviet Union and the apparent triumph of liberal democracy. Some followed the end of Western colonialism and the frequent repudiation of liberal democracy.

The economic sphere has been equally instrumental in stimulating interest in citizenship. Western capitalism has become ever more aggressively global, as information technology has encircled the earth, the transnational movement of capital has soared, and multinational corporations have accelerated their searches for cheaper and cheaper labor markets (Held 1995). These trends, too, have destabilized identities, languages, boundaries, and traditions. All of these developments have directed both practical and theoretical attention to the nature of citizenship and to what it means to be, as T. H. Marshall defined it, a full member of a community (Marshall 1950).

At the same time that the practices, conditions, and meanings of citizenship were coming under these pressures in many parts of the world, gender was also undergoing intense scrutiny. The identities, categories, boundaries, and traditions that comprise gender practices have also shifted, attracting their own practical engagement and theoretical attention. Transformations in citizenship and those in gender are mutually relevant in a variety of ways. This is no surprise. Citizenship is one of many sets of social practices in which differentiation by gender is ancient and stubbornly persistent.

Throughout most of human history and in all regions of the globe, women of all classes, races, ethnicities, and religions were, and often continue to be, denied state citizenship of even the lowest rank. So exclusively male has this status been for nearly all of human history that it is a singular development of women's movements in the twentieth century to have ended this exclusion in many places. Substantial numbers of women have made enormous political headway in the past century. In many states, however, women do not yet have a citizenship status equal to that of their male counterparts. In any given state, still today, women and men are likely to differ in the political rights and privileges of citizenship that affect them, and differ in ways that are linked systematically to gender categories as well as categories such as race and class (Collins 1998; Hirschmann and DiStefano 1996; Nussbaum 2000; Okin 1989, 1999).

Issues of women and citizenship, however, are not merely about the deprivation of political rights to women. Also important is the gendered nature of the practices and contexts of political citizenship itself. The public and political realms in which citizenship is paradigmatically conceptualized and practiced are realms based largely on modes of living as well as attributes that are stereotypically male — the role of wage-earner, for example. This means that even when the rights and privileges of political citizenship are made available to women, practical and conceptual obstacles may make it difficult for women to avail themselves fully of these options. How we understand women (and men) as citizens is, in turn, dependent on these differentiated political elaborations (Landes 1998; Phillips 1998; Young 1997).

At the same time, citizenship is not confined to the public or political spheres. The citizenship practices of the public and political spheres are themselves related to conditions in other social spheres, such as those of family and civil society. Gender is generally salient to the meanings and practices of citizenship in these other social realms as well. These nonstate realms of citizenship practice provide options for women's political agency that may circumvent the restrictions of the political sphere, for example, agency based on women's traditional roles as nurturers (Kittay 1999; Ruddick 1989). If citizenship is about full membership in one's community, then these additional realms of culture and society are necessary contexts and conditions for its practice. Gender and citizenship thus intersect and engage each other in a variety of ways, often through the mediation of other social institutions.

The essays in this collection explore a number of these various political and cultural dimensions of citizenship and their relevance to women and gender. These essays were presented at a conference on "Women and Citizenship" at Washington University in St. Louis, Missouri, in April 2002 (see the acknowledgments at the end of this introduction). Some of these essays take account of contexts and practices of citizenship in the United States (Young, Bartky, Ackelsberg,

Jaggar, Hurtado, and Tronto) while the other essays focus on contexts and practices of citizenship elsewhere (Scott, Joseph, Wadud, and Nussbaum). Together, these studies survey a variety of ways in which citizenship—full membership in the community—has been politically and culturally en-gendered, for better and worse, yet is open to transformation through women's agency.

1. Citizenship, Government, and Law

Iris Marion Young's essay, "The Logic of Masculinist Protection: Reflections on the Current Security State," draws attention to practices of citizenship that can arise under a government at war. However, in contrast to literature that explains war in terms of stereotypically masculine tendencies toward violence (see the overview in Goldstein 2001), Young instead explores the logic of the masculine role of protector. A government acting in accord with this role protects its members in an overly aggressive fashion from external dangers as well as from internal dissension. This role, which Young calls the "security regime," threatens to undermine democratic practice. A state acting as a security regime expects to be rewarded by its population with uncritical obedience and submissiveness. A security regime plays a role toward its citizens that is analogous to that played by a protective family patriarch toward the women and children of his family. Young argues that adult citizens do not accept this sort of political relationship with their government. Even from a protective government, what adult citizens want instead are relationships that respect their autonomy and equality.

The question of whether women should be formally included in representative numbers in their respective legislative assemblies has been a part of the citizenship debates for some time now (Phillips 1995). In "French Universalism in the Nineties," Joan W. Scott brings out the complex nature of the processes that enacted this requirement in France in 2000. The *parité* law, enacted that year, calls for equal numbers of women and men to serve in various elected assemblies at all levels of government. The law challenged a theory of representation that was attributed to the French Revolution and that took the abstract individual to be the unit of citizenship. Although this notion of the individual was meant to be neutral (without religious, social, or economic identity), in fact it was consistently taken to be masculine. Even when women were granted the vote, the typical representative chosen for political office was a man.

The *parité* movement sought to rectify discrimination against women in political office by insisting that the individual also be abstracted from any association with sex. In order to do this, they drew a distinction between anatomical duality (an abstract notion) and sexual difference (an attribution of meaning to sexed bodies). The abstract individual, they argued, came in two sexes, but this had nothing to do with cultural ideas about gender. In the course of the debates about *parité* (and they were many and fierce), the original distinction between anatomical duality and sexual difference was lost. The law that passed seemed to implement an essentialist vision, when in fact that was not the intention of its first supporters. The strategy of "sexing" the abstract individual was, thus, both fruitful and dangerous. Scott believes this tension in the support for *parité* is an unre-solvable feature of the nature of representation in liberal or, like France, liberal republican states.

Sandra Bartky, in "Battered Women, Intimidation, and the Law," highlights features of legal institutions that obstruct women's attempts to use the law to reduce domestic violence. A large literature has dealt with domestic violence for several decades (Cardarelli 1997; Yllö and Bograd 1990). Bartky's analysis brings out some less remarked dimensions of the law's resistance to women's use of it to end do-mestic battery. One of these dimensions is the material embodiment of law; law is practiced in buildings of intimidating size and scale. In addition, law is practiced in forms of language that are inaccessible to ordinary women. Furthermore, judges and lawyers may abuse their power, intimidate the women who seek their help, and collude with each other in virtue of gender or class connections that the women do not share. Insofar as women are unable to gain redress from the legal system for the domestic violence they suffer, they fall outside the citizenship protection of the Social Contract, argues Bartky, and are effectively returned to the state of nature.

2. Practices of Citizenship in Culture and Civil Society

Citizenship is exercised in a variety of domains, not simply those of government and law. Civil society is a particularly important sphere for practices of citizenship (Walzer 1991). The practices of citizenship available to women in the realms of culture and civil society interweave in important ways with those of the political sphere (Benhabib 2002). The next four essays deal with culture and civil society and those important interconnections.

Martha Ackelsberg's essay, "Women's Community Activism and the Rejection of 'Politics': Some Dilemmas of Popular Democratic Movements," investigates the participation of certain women in a voluntary, activist association. As the public, political sphere undergoes changes that permit the greater participation of women, the challenge for women is to participate in policy-making in ways that incorporate differences while avoiding the exclusions of the past (Hirschmann and DiStefano 1996). According to Ackelsberg, the National Congress of Neighborhood Women (NCNW), a Brooklyn association established in 1974–75, is a model of such dem-ocratic civic engagement. The association aimed to assist poor and working-class women to organize to better meet their needs and those of their communities. The NCNW arose as a result of the discrimination and suppression that its members experienced when they attempted to engage in political work both in their com-munities and beyond. In working with each other, the women found right away that they needed to address issues of diversity. The programs they created to help build bridges across differences helped facilitate their successful activism while simulta-neously broadening their understanding of what constitutes "politics."

Alison Jaggar, in "Arenas of Citizenship: Civil Society, the State, and the Global Order," explores some of the feminine and feminist practices of citizenship that occur in nongovernmental associations. She recounts the optimism of recent years, as expressed in Ackelsberg's essay, that these and other groups in civil society offer greater hope than do public and political relationships for the development of social virtues such as egalitarianism, diversity, tolerance, democracy, and the empowerment of previously marginalized people (Young 2000).

Jaggar, however, finds problems that face women's activities in civil society. Some nongovernmental organizations (NGOs), for example, have come to depend over the years on governmental or business support. In order to obtain this support, NGOs may have to forego the more progressive or far-reaching activities in which they might otherwise have engaged. Obtaining this support also requires organizational staff to become professionalized fund-raisers, thus creating a gap in experience and understanding between them and the less well educated clients they serve. Jaggar also notes that the emergence of civil societal social services may prompt governments to cease providing those services, some of which are critically important for survival. Women and children are especially dependent on government provision for some of these services, such as nutrition, healthcare, and education. Civil society activism cannot attain the level of such services that a government could provide in an affluent nation, so this shift in service provision will lead to an overall decline in services for women and an increase in specifically female poverty.

Aída Hurtado's essay, "Multiple Subjectivities: Chicanas and Cultural Citizenship," uses the writings of Chicana feminists and other feminists of color (Pérez 1999) as a springboard for reconceptualizing citizenship in terms that incorporate diversity. Hurtado focuses on Chicana women who live in the cultural "borderlands" between on the one hand U.S. society, into which they do not completely assimilate, and on the other hand Mexican society, to which they retain an ambivalent connection. Chicanas do not utilize the individual rights or interest group politics of U.S. society. At the same time, they also resist the patriarchy and images of female betrayal from Mexican culture. For Chicanas, the project of defining their cultural citizenship takes place especially in the domains of language and space. Claiming discourse is crucial to claiming the power to construct themselves. Land, culture, language, ethnic and racial specificity, universality, and social justice all help to shape the contours of Chicana cultural citizenship.

In "Care as the Work of Citizens: A Modest Proposal," Joan Tronto explores a growing trend in civil society and domestic life today that impinges on the lives of both citizens and noncitizens and on the extent to which either of them can exercise their rights. This trend is the "care crisis" that now pervades advanced industrial societies. As women do more paid work, they do less of the care work of civil society (Sevenhuijsen 1998). Tronto urges that advanced industrial societies rethink who is responsible for care and recognize the role that government should play in ensuring that care is provided for those who need it. Unfortunately, citizenship has traditionally been defined in ways that make no provision for responsibilities to care for others.

Tronto observes that "privatizing" care by relegating it to the marketplace does not provide a solution to the care crisis, since paid care work is subject to exploitation, partly because it is often done by illegal immigrants from Third World countries. Despite expecting privatization to be the likely solution to the problem, Tronto nevertheless recommends regarding care work as a governmental responsibility in order to make it more valued publicly. She also suggests giving credits toward citizenship to those noncitizens who perform care work.

3. Grounds of Citizenship in Culture and Civil Society

The opportunities for women to engage in citizenship practices and the specific forms that practices of citizenship take in any society are grounded in a variety of cultural conditions. These cultural conditions are subject to change over time. Improvements in women's citizenship practices may require dramatic cultural transformation. It is therefore crucial to understand the underlying cultural conditions and the ways in which they interact with and sustain particular citizenship practices. The final three essays in this collection deal with some cultural grounds of citizenship.

Suad Joseph's essay, "The Kin Contract and Citizenship in the Middle East," builds on her prior work in this area (Joseph 2000). In this essay, Joseph develops ideas emerging from her work on family, citizenship, and state in Lebanon to develop an argument about the ways in which ideas about family and family idioms, relationships, and practices ground and intersect with formal governmental policies and practices. She argues that families and kinship are politically privileged in most Middle Eastern states. Women and men are committed to their families in Lebanon in a manner that Joseph calls the "kin contract," a commitment reinforced by familial care and structured by submission to patriarchal family control. In the Middle East in general, Joseph argues, the citizen-subject is embedded in kinship relationships rather than being an autonomous self. The gendered nature of the citizen-subject emerges thus from the implicit and legally encoded kin contract, which reinscribes patriarchal kinship with the force of state and religious institutional and practical backing. Families themselves, in turn, are regulated by state and religious institutions in Middle Eastern countries. This mutual support further bolsters patriarchy and male control over women.

In "Citizenship and Faith," Amina Wadud analyzes a form of citizenship that contrasts with that of modern secular nation states, namely, citizenship in theocratic states governed by *shari'ah*, or Islamic law (Barakat 1993). Wadud thus explores the formalities of citizenship in a type of society in which government is itself ruled and regulated by religious forces. Islamic states do not traditionally envisage the equality of women. Wadud argues, however, against such theocratic systems, that the canonical Islamic tradition of jurisprudence is open to reinterpretation in light of changing conditions in Muslim societies. According to Wadud, the Qur'an does not restrict agency on the grounds of gender. The gender disparity that has developed in Islamic tradition and theory denies women the means of completing their duties before Allah. Wadud calls upon all Muslims, female and male, to reform their societies so as to implement the equality inherent in the "tawhidic" Islamic paradigm, which stresses unity and harmony.

Martha Nussbaum's essay, "Women's Education: A Global Challenge," defends literacy and education for women as a crucial condition for lessening many of the problems that women face worldwide and that restrict women's capacities to engage in citizenship practices (Nussbaum and Glover 1995). Nussbaum's proposal extends to secondary as well as higher education and particularly urges the development of women's critical faculties and imagination. Among many other things, literacy helps women get better jobs, leave abusive marriages, enter the political process, improve their health, and gain in self-respect. In order for women to gain greater access to education globally, however, poorer nations and states must commit energy and resources to this project, and wealthy nations, as well as their citizens and corporations, must also commit resources to it.

At present, globally speaking, these commitments are far from sufficient to serve the need that exists. Female education is sometimes opposed on the grounds that it destroys nonliterate cultures that have their own values. Nussbaum argues in reply that such cultures may not be as idyllic as the objection suggests. They may harbor misery and injustice, and the women in the cultures may even oppose their own cultural norms. Nussbaum suggests that if governments cannot improve female education, nongovernmental organizations may be able to take on the responsibility.

Acknowledgments

This book grew out of a conference on "Women and Citizenship" held at Washington University in St. Louis, Missouri, on April 12–13, 2002. The conference was multidisciplinary and included speakers from political science, philosophy, history, anthropology, religious studies, and psychology. The conference marked a new plateau in the development of the Women's Studies Program (now the Women and Gender Studies Program) at Washington University. Susan E. and William P. Stirritz had recently endowed the program with a chair in women's studies and had provided it with a generous challenge grant, without which the conference would not have been possible. Abundant thanks are owed to the Stirritzes, especially Susan. Linda Nicholson came to Washington University as the first holder of the Susan E. and William P. Stirritz Distinguished Chair in Women's Studies (and as professor of history). Nicholson also became coordinator of the women's studies program, replacing Helen Power, who had directed the program for the previous decade. Women's studies at Washington University has thus grown substantially over the years since its creation in the 1970s by Joyce Trebilcot, the program's first coordinator.

In addition to the Stirritz Challenge Grant, numerous campus units and individuals at Washington University helped the Women and Gender Studies Program to support the "Women and Citizenship" conference. On behalf of the Women and Gender Studies Program, I gratefully acknowledge the support of the Women's Society of Washington University, the Philosophy Department, the Faculty of Arts and Sciences, the Political Science Department, the Office of Development, the History Department, and the Program in Social Thought and Analysis. Thanks are also due to Helen Power for giving the go-ahead to begin planning the conference in the last year of her tenure as Women's Studies Coordinator. Thanks to Linda Nicholson for numerous good ideas and practical help in organizing the conference. The following people provided welcome assistance in either planning or running the conference or both, and I extend my gratitude to them: Ben Alex, Kathy Atnip, Emily Austin, Willem Bakker II, Lisa Baldez, Stephanie Bauer, Tamara Casanova, Jim Davis, Sophie Fortin, James Harold, Frances Henderson, Kimberly Mount, Liz Peterson-Schmidt, Eric Rovie, Ken Shockley, Clerk Shaw, Sarit Smila, and Jennifer Stiff. Finally, abundant thanks to Kathy McCabe in the Women's Studies Program, who provided extensive and invaluable assistance with the project in all its aspects and stages.

In the time period between the "Women and Citizenship" conference and the publication of this volume, five of the essays in this collection were published elsewhere. I thank the following journals and publishers for permission to reprint those essays here: Iris Marion Young, "The Logic of Masculinist Protection: Reflections on the Current Security State," *Signs: Journal of Women in Culture and Society* 29, no. 1 (autumn 2003): 1–28, © 2003 by the University of Chicago, all rights reserved; Joan W. Scott, "French Universalism in the Nineties," *differences: A Journal of Feminist Cultural Studies* 15, no. 2 (2004): 32–53; Sandra Bartky, "Battered Women, Intimidation, and the Law," under the title "Intimidation," in *Moral Psychology: Feminist Ethics and Social Theory*, ed. Peggy DesAutels and Margaret Walker (Lanham, Md.: Rowman and Littlefield, 2004); Alison Jaggar, "Arenas of Citizenship: Civil Society, State, and the Global Order," *International Feminist Journal of Politics* 7 (March 2005): 1–24, available at: http://www.tandf. co.uk/journals; and Martha C. Nussbaum, "Women's Education: A Global Challenge," *Signs: Journal of Women in Culture and Society* 29, no. 2 (2004): 325–357, © 2004 by the University of Chicago, all rights reserved.

One poignant memory from the "Women and Citizenship" conference must be noted. Susan Moller Okin was a featured speaker at that conference, just two years before her untimely death. Because her paper had been previously committed for publication in the Oxford Amnesty Lectures series, we made no arrangement to include it in this volume of conference proceedings. Although she is absent from this volume, Susan is not absent from our work or our thoughts. Her influence over feminist cultural and political theory has been enormous and groundbreaking. Both as a scholar and as a passionate human being, she fought to promote women's well-being in social and political life. Our status as citizens is more secure today because Susan Okin championed our cause. She will be deeply missed.

Bibliography

Barakat, Halim. *The Arab World: Society, Culture and State*. Berkeley: University of California Press, 1993.

Beiner, Ronald, ed. *Theorizing Citizenship*. Albany, N.Y.: State University of New York Press, 1995.

Benhabib, Seyla. *The Claims of Culture: Equality and Diversity in the Global Era*. Princeton: Princeton University Press, 2002.

Cardarelli, Albert P. *Violence Between Intimate Partners*. Boston: Allyn and Bacon, 1997.

Collins, Patricia Hill. *Fighting Words: Black Women and the Search for Justice.* Minneapolis: University of Minnesota Press, 1998.

Goldstein, Joshua S. *War and Gender.* Cambridge: Cambridge University Press, 2001.

Held, David. *Democracy and the Global Order: From the Modern State to Cosmopolitan Governance.* Stanford: Stanford University Press, 1995.

Hirschmann, Nancy, and Christine DiStefano, eds. *Revisioning the Political: Feminist Reconstructions of Traditional Concepts in Western Political Theory.* Boulder, Colo.: Westview Press, 1996.

Honig, Bonnie. *Democracy and the Foreigner.* Princeton: Princeton University Press, 2001.

Joseph, Suad. *Gender and Citizenship in the Middle East.* Syracuse, N.Y.: Syracuse University Press, 2000.

Kittay, Eva Feder. *Love's Labor: Essays on Women, Equality, and Dependency.* New York: Routledge, 1999.

Kymlicka, Will, and Wayne Norman, eds. *Citizenship in Diverse Societies.* Oxford: Oxford University Press, 2000.

Landes, Joan B. *Feminism, the Public and the Private.* Oxford: Oxford University Press, 1998.

Marshall, T. H. *Citizenship and Social Class.* Cambridge: Cambridge University Press, 1950.

Nussbaum, Martha C. *Women and Human Development: The Capabilities Approach.* Cambridge: Cambridge University Press, 2000.

Nussbaum, Martha C., and Jonathan Glover, eds. *Women, Culture, and Development: On Human Capabilities.* Oxford: Clarendon Press, 1995.

Okin, Susan Moller. *Justice, Gender, and the Family.* New York: Basic Books, 1989.

Okin, Susan Moller, with respondents. *Is Multiculturalism Bad for Women?* Edited by Joshua Cohen, Matthew Howard, and Martha C. Nussbaum. Princeton: Princeton University Press, 1999.

Pérez, Emma. *The Decolonial Imaginary: Writing Chicanas into History.* Bloomington: Indiana University Press, 1999.

Phillips, Anne, ed. *Feminism and Politics.* Oxford: Oxford University Press, 1998.

———. *The Politics of Presence.* Oxford: Oxford University Press, 1995.

Ruddick, Sara. *Maternal Thinking: Toward a Politics of Peace.* New York: Ballantine Books, 1989.

Sevenhuijsen, Selma. *Citizenship and the Ethics of Care.* London: Routledge, 1998.

Walzer, Michael. "The Civil Society Argument." In *Dimensions of Radical Democracy: Pluralism, Citizenship, and Community,* edited by Chantal Mouffe. London: Routledge, 1992, pp. 89–107. Originally published under the title "The Idea of Civil Society," *Dissent* (spring 1991): 293–304.

Yllö, Kersti, and Michele Bograd, eds. *Feminist Perspectives on Wife Abuse.* Newbury Park, Calif.: Sage, 1990.

Young, Iris Marion. *Inclusion and Democracy.* Oxford: Oxford University Press, 2000.

———. *Intersecting Voices: Dilemmas of Gender, Political Philosophy, and Policy.* Princeton: Princeton University Press, 1997.

I

Citizenship, Government, and Law

1

The Logic of Masculinist Protection: Reflections on the Current Security State

IRIS MARION YOUNG

"My most important job as your President is to defend the homeland; is to protect American people from further attacks."

George W. Bush, March 29, 2002

"Every man I meet wants to protect me. I can't figure out what from."

Mae West

The American and European women's movement of the late 1970s and early 1980s contained a large segment that organized around issues of weapons, war, and peace. Creative civil disobedience actions wove webs of yarn at entrances to the Pentagon and set up colorful camps on cruise missile sites in England's Greenham Common. Writings of the women's peace movement tried to make theoretical connections between male domination and militarism, between masculine gender and the propensity to settle conflicts with violence, and these echoed some of the voices of the women's peace movement earlier in the twentieth century. By the early 1990s the humor and heroism of the women's peace actions had been all but forgotten.

Organized violence, led both by states and by nonstate actors, has certainly not abated in the meantime and has taken new and frightening forms (Kaldor 1999).

Earlier versions of this essay were presented at conferences at Washington University in St. Louis and Lancaster University in England, and I have benefited from discussions on both occasions. I am grateful to David Alexander, Gopal Balakrishnan, Neta Crawford, Tom Dumm, Samantha Frost, Susan Gal, Sandra Harding, Anne Harrington, Aaron Hoffman, Jeffrey Isaac, Patchen Markell, John McCormick, Linda Nicholson, Sara Ruddick, Lora Viola, Laurel Weldon, Alexander Wendt, and an anonymous reviewer for *Signs* for comments on earlier versions. Thanks to Anne Harrington and Kathy McCabe for research assistance.

Thus there are urgent reasons to reopen the question of whether looking at war and security issues through a gendered lens can teach lessons that might advance the projects of peace and democracy. In this chapter I analyze some of the security events and legal changes in the United States since the fall of 2001 by means of an account of a logic of masculinist protection.

Much writing about gender and war aims to explain bellicosity or its absence by considering attributes of men and women (Goldstein 2001). Theories adopting this approach attempt to argue that behavioral propensities of men link them to violence and those of women make them more peaceful and that these differences help account for the structure of states and international relations. Such attempts to connect violence structures with attributes or behavioral propensities that men or women supposedly share, however, rely on unsupportable generalizations about men and women and often leap too quickly from an account of the traits of persons to institutional structures and collective action. Here I take a different approach. I take gender not as an element of explanation but rather of interpretation, a tool of what might be called ideology critique (see Cohn 1993). Viewing issues of war and security through a gender lens, I suggest, means seeing how a certain logic of gendered meanings and images helps organize the way people interpret events and circumstances, along with their positions and possibilities for action within them, and sometimes provides some rationale for action.

I argue that an exposition of the gendered logic of the masculine role of protector in relation to women and children illuminates the meaning and effective appeal of a security state that wages war abroad and expects obedience and loyalty at home. In this patriarchal logic, the role of the masculine protector puts those protected, paradigmatically women and children, in a subordinate position of dependence and obedience. To the extent that citizens of a democratic state allow their leaders to adopt a stance of protectors toward them, these citizens come to occupy a subordinate status like that of women in the patriarchal household. We are to accept a more authoritarian and paternalistic state power, which gets its support partly from the unity a threat produces and our gratitude for protection. At the same time that it legitimates authoritarian power over citizens internally, the logic of masculinist protection justifies aggressive war outside. I interpret Thomas Hobbes as a theorist of authoritarian government grounded in fear of threat and the apparent desire for protection such fear generates.

Although some feminist theorists of peace and security have noticed the appeal to protection as justification for war-making (Stiehm 1982; Tickner 1992, 2001), they have not elaborated the gendered logic of protection to the extent that I try to do here. These accounts concentrate on international relations, moreover, and do less to carry the analysis to an understanding of the relation of states to citizens internally. My interest in this essay is in this dual face of security forms, those that wage war outside a country and conduct surveillance and detention inside. I notice that democratic values of due process, separation of powers, free assembly, and holding powerful actors accountable come into danger when leaders mobilize fear and present themselves as protectors.

Since the attacks of September 11, 2001, I argue, the relation of the leaders of the United States to its citizens is well illuminated by interpreting it under the logic of masculinist protection. The Bush administration has mobilized the language of fear and threat to gain support for constricting liberty and dissent inside the United States and waging war outside. This stronger U.S. security state offers a bargain to its citizens: obey our commands and support our security actions, and we will ensure your protection. This protection bargain between the state and its citizens is not unique to the United States in this period but rather often legitimates authoritarian government. I argue that the bargain is dangerous in this case, as in most others. The essay concludes with a gendered analysis of the war against Afghanistan of the fall of 2001. While the Bush administration initially justified the war as a defensive action necessary to protect Americans, its rhetoric quickly supplemented this legitimation with an appeal to the liberation of Afghan women. I suggest that some of the groundwork for this appeal may have been laid by feminist campaigns concerning the Taliban, which the Bush administration chose at this moment to exploit. The apparent success of this appeal in justifying the war to many Americans should trouble feminists, I argue, and prompt us to examine whether American or Western feminists sometimes adopt the stance of protector in relation to some women of the world whom we construct as more dependent or subordinate.

Masculinism as Protection

Several theorists of gender argue that masculinity and femininity should not be conceptualized with a single logic but rather that ideas and values of masculinity and femininity, and their relation to one another, take several different and some-times overlapping forms (Brod and Kaufman 1994; Hooper 2001). In this spirit, I propose to single out a particular logic of masculinism that I believe has not received very much attention in recent feminist theory: that associated with the position of male head of household as a protector of the family, and by extension with masculine leaders and risk-takers as protectors of a population. Twenty years ago Judith Stiehm called attention to the relevance of a logic of masculinist pro-tection to analysis of war and security issues, and I will draw on some of her ideas (Stiehm 1982). Her analysis more presupposes than it defines the meaning of a masculine role as protector, so this is where I will begin.

The logic of masculinist protection contrasts with a model of masculinity assumed by much feminist theory, of masculinity as self-consciously dominative. On the male domination model, masculine men wish to master women sexually for the sake of their own gratification and to have the pleasures of domination. They bond with other men in comradely male settings that gain them specific benefits from which they exclude women, and they harass women in order to enforce this exclusion and maintain their superiority (MacKinnon 1987; May 1998, chaps. 4–6).

This image of the selfish, aggressive, dominative man who desires sexual capture of women corresponds to much about male-dominated institutions and the behavior of many men within them. For my purposes in this essay, however, it is important to recall another more benign image of masculinity, more associated with ideas of chivalry. In this image, real men are neither selfish nor do they seek to enslave or overpower others for the sake of enhancing themselves. Instead, the gallantly masculine man is loving and self-sacrificing, especially in relation to women. He faces the world's difficulties and dangers in order to shield women from harm and allow them to pursue elevating and decorative arts. The role of this courageous, responsible, and virtuous man is that of a protector.

The "good" man is one who keeps vigilant watch over the safety of his family and readily risks himself in the face of threats from the outside in order to protect the subordinate members of his household. The logic of masculinist protection, then, includes the image of the selfish aggressor who wishes to invade the lord's property and sexually conquer his women. These are the bad men. Good men can only appear in their goodness if we assume that lurking outside the warm familial walls are aggressors who wish to attack them. The dominative masculinity in this way constitutes protective masculinity as its other. The world out there is heartless and uncivilized, and the movements and motives of the men in it are unpredictable and difficult to discern. The protector must therefore take all precautions against these threats, remain watchful and suspicious, and be ready to fight and sacrifice for the sake of his loved ones (Elshtain 1987, 1992). Masculine protection is needed to make a home a haven.

Central to the logic of masculinist protection is the subordinate relation of those in the protected position. In return for male protection, the woman concedes critical distance from decision-making autonomy. When the household lives under a threat, there cannot be divided wills and arguments about who will do what or what is the best course of action. The head of the household should decide what measures are necessary for the security of the people and property, and he gives the orders they must follow if they and their relations are to remain safe. As Stiehm puts it: "The protector cannot achieve status simply through his accomplishment, then. Because he has dependents he is as socially connected as one who is dependent. He is expected to provide for others. Often a protector tries to get help from and also control the lives of those he protects — in order to 'better protect' them" (Stiehm 1982, 372).

Feminine subordination, in this logic, does not constitute submission to a violent and overbearing bully. The feminine woman, rather, on this construction, adores her protector and happily defers to his judgment in return for the promise of security he offers. She looks up to him with gratitude for his manliness and admiration for his willingness to face the dangers of the world for her sake. That he finds her worthy of such risks gives substance to her self. It is only fitting that she should minister to his needs and obey his dictates.

Hobbes is the great theorist of political power founded on a need and desire for protection. He depicts a state of nature in which people live in small families where all believe some of the others envy them and desire to enlarge themselves by stealing from or conquering them. As a consequence, everyone in this state of nature must live in a state of fear and insecurity, even when not immediately under attack. Each household must live with the knowledge that outsiders might wish to attack them, especially if they appear weak and vulnerable, so each must construct defensive fortresses and be on watch. It is only sensible, moreover, to conduct preemptive strikes against those who might wish to attack, to try to weaken them. But each knows that the others are likely to make defensive raids, which only adds to fear and insecurity. In Hobbes's state of nature, some people may be motivated by simple greed and desire for conquest and domination. In this state of nature, everyone has reason to feel insecure, however, not because all have these dominative motives but because they are uncertain about who does and understand his or her own vulnerability.

In her contemporary classic *The Sexual Contract*, Carole Pateman interprets Hobbes along the lines of contemporary feminist accounts of men as selfish aggressors and sexual predators. In the state of nature, roving men take advantage of women encumbered by children and force them to submit to sexual domination. Sometimes they keep the women around as sexual servants; thus arises marriage. These strong and aggressive men force other men to labor for them at the point of a sword. On Pateman's account, this is how the patriarchal household forms, through overpowering force (Pateman 1988, chap. 3).

One can just as well read Hobbes's ideas through the lens of the apparently more benign masculinity of protection. Here we can imagine that men and women get together out of attraction and feel love for the children they beget. On this construction, families have their origin in a desire for companionship and caring. In the state of nature, however, each unit has reason to fear the strangers who might rob or kill them; each then finds it prudent at times to engage in preemptive strikes and to adopt a threatening stance toward the outsiders. On this alternative account, then, patriarchal right emerges from male specialization in security. The patriarch's will rules because the patriarch faces the dangers outside and needs to organize defenses. Female subordination, on this account, derives from this position of being protected. As I will discuss in the next section, however, Hobbes does not think that it is a good idea to leave this armed power in the hands of individual male heads of household. Instead, the sovereign takes over this function.

Both Pateman's story of male domination and the one I have reconstructed depict patriarchal gender relations as upholding unequal power. It is important to attend to the difference, however, I think, because in one relation the hierarchical power is obvious and in the other it is more masked by virtue and love. Michel Foucault argues that power conceived and enacted as repressive power, the desire and ability of an agent to force the other to obey his commands, has receded in importance in modern institutions. Other forms of power that enlist the desire of those over whom it is exercised better describe many power relations both historically and today. One such form of power Foucault calls pastoral power. This is the kind of power that the priest exercises over his parish and by extension that many experts in the care of individuals exercise over those cared for (Foucault 1988, 1994). This power often appears gentle and benevolent both to its wielders and those under its sway, but it is no less powerful for that reason. Masculinist protection is more like pastoral power than dominative power that exploits those it rules for its own aggrandizement.

The State as Protector and Subordinate Citizenship

The gendered logic of masculinist protection has some relevance to individual family life even in modern urban America. Every time a father warns his daughter of the dangerous men he fears will exploit her and forbids her from "running around" the city, he inhabits the role of the male protector. Nevertheless, in everyday family life and other sites of interaction between men and women, the legitimation of female inequality and subordination by appeal to a need for protection has dwindled. My purpose in articulating a logic of masculinist protection is not to argue that it describes private life today but rather to argue that we learn something about public life, specifically about the relation of a state to its citizens, when state officials successfully mobilize fear. States often justify their expectations of obedience and loyalty—their establishment of surveillance, police, intimidation, detention, and the repression of criticism and dissent—by appeal to their role as protectors of citizens. I find in Hobbes a clever account of authoritarian rule grounded in the assumption of threat and fear as basic to the human condition, and thus a need for protection as the highest good.

Hobbes tells a story about why individuals and families find it necessary to constitute a sovereign, a single power to rule them all. In response to the constant fear under which they live, families may join confederations or protection associations. Such protection associations, however, no matter how large and powerful, do not reduce the reasons for fear and insecurity. As long as the possibility exists that others will form protective associations larger and stronger than their own, the nasty state of war persists. As long as there is a potential for competition among units, and those units hold the means to try to force their desires on one another, they must live in fear. Without submission to a common power to which they yield their separate forces, moreover, members of a protective association are liable to turn on one another during times when they need to rely on one another from protection from others (Hobbes [1668] 1994, chap. 17, par. 3, 4; see Nozick 1974, chap. 2). So Hobbes argues that only a Leviathan can assure safety, quell the fear and uncertainty that generate a spiral of danger. All the petty protectors in the state of nature give up their powers of aggression and defense, which they turn over to the sovereign. They make a covenant with one another to live in peace and constitute civil society under the common rule of an absolute authority who makes, interprets, and enforces the laws of the commonwealth for the sake of the peace and security of the subjects.

Readers of Hobbes sometimes find in the image of Leviathan a mean and selfish tyrant who sucks up the wealth and loyalty of subjects for his own aggrandizement. Democratic values and freedoms would be much easier to assert and preserve in modern politics if the face of authoritarianism were so ugly and easy to recognize. Like the benevolent patriarch, however, Leviathan often wears another aspect, that of the selfless and wise protector, whose actions aim to foster and maintain security. What I call a security state is one whose rulers subordinate citizens to ad hoc surveillance, search, or detention and repress criticism of such arbitrary power, justifying such measures as within the prerogative of those authorities whose primary duty is to maintain security and protect the people.

The security state has an external and an internal aspect. It constitutes itself in relation to an enemy outside, an unpredictable aggressor against which the state needs vigilant defense. It organizes political and economic capacities around the accumulation of weapons and the mobilization of a military to respond to this outsider threat. The state's identity is militaristic, and it engages in military action, but with the point of view of the defendant rather than the aggressor. Even when the security regime makes a first strike, it justifies its move as necessary to preempt the threatening aggressor outside. Security states do not justify their wars by appealing to sentiments of greed or desire for conquest; they appeal to their role as protectors.

Internally, the security state must root out the enemy within. There is always the danger that among us are agents who have an interest in disturbing our peace, violating our persons and property, and allowing outsiders to invade our communities and institutions. To protect the state and its citizens, officials must therefore keep a careful watch on the people within its borders and observe and search them to make sure they do not intend evil actions and do not have the means to perform them. The security regime overhears conversations in order to try to discover conspiracies of disaster and disruption and prevents people from forming crowds or walking the streets after dark. In a security regime, there cannot be separation of power or critical accountability of official action to a public. Nor can a security regime allow expression of dissent.

Once again, Hobbes explains why not. It is necessary that the sovereign be one. The commonwealth can secure peace only if it unites the plurality of its members into one will. Even if the sovereign consists of an assembly of officials and not only one ruler, it must be united in will and purpose. It is the mutual covenant that each man makes to all the others to give over his right of governing his own affairs to the sovereign, on condition that all others do the same, that gives the sovereign both its power and unity of will (Hobbes [1668] 1994, chap. 17, par. 13). Sovereign authority, then, must be absolute, and it cannot be divided. The sovereign decides what is necessary to protect the commonwealth and its members. The sovereign decides what actions or opinions constitute a danger to peace and properly suppresses them.

> The condition of man in this life shall never be without inconveniences; but there happeneth in no commonwealth any greater inconvenience, but what proceeds from the subject's disobedience and breach of these covenants from which the commonwealth hath its being, and whosoever, thinking sovereign power too great, will seek to make it less, must subject himself to the power that can limit it, that is to say, to a greater. (Hobbes [1668] 1994, chap. 20)

Through the logic of protection, the state demotes members of a democracy to dependents. State officials adopt the stance of masculine protector, telling us to entrust our lives to them, not to question their decisions about what will keep us safe. Their protector position puts the citizens and residents who depend on their strength and vigilance in the position of women and children under the charge of the male protector (see Berlant 1997). Most regimes that suspend certain rights and legal procedures declare a state of emergency. They claim that special measures of unity and obedience are required in order to ensure protection from unusual danger. Because they take the risks and organize the agency of the state, it is their prerogative to determine the objectives of protective action and their means. In a security state, there is no room for separate and shared powers or for questioning and criticizing the protector's decisions and orders. Good citizenship in a security regime consists of cooperative obedience for the sake of the safety of all.

The authoritarian security paradigm, I have argued, takes a form analogous to the masculine protector toward his wife and the other members of his patriarchal household. In this structure, I have suggested, masculine superiority flows not from acts of repressive domination but from the willingness to risk and sacrifice for the sake of the others (Elshtain 1987, 1992). For her part, the subordinate female in this structure neither resents nor resists the man's dominance but rather admires it and is grateful for its promise of protection.

Patriotism has an analogous emotive function in the constitution of the security state. Under threat from outside, all of us, authorities and citizens, imagine ourselves as a single body enclosed on and loving itself. We affirm our oneness with our fellow citizens and together affirm our single will behind the will of the leaders who have vowed to protect us. It is not merely that dissent is dangerous; worse yet, it is ungrateful. Subordinate citizenship does not merely acquiesce to limitation on freedom in exchange for a promise of security; the consent is active, as solidarity with the others uniting behind and in grateful love of country.

The United States as a Security State

A security state is what every state would have to be if Hobbes were right that human relations are always on the verge of disorder and violence, if only an authoritarian government that brooks no division of power or dissent can keep the peace, and if maintaining peace and security is unambiguously the highest value. Democratic theory and practice, however, question each of these Hobbesian assumptions. Democrats agree that a major purpose of government is to keep peace and promote public safety, but we deny that unquestioning obedience to a unified sovereign is the only means to achieve this, and we question that values of freedom and autonomy must be traded against the value of security. In a nonideal world of would-be aggressors and states having imperfect procedural justice, transparency, accountability, and lax rights enforcement, every state exhibits features of a security state to some extent. It seems to me, however, that in recent months the United States has slipped too far down the authoritarian continuum. The logic of masculinist protection, I suggest, provides a framework for understanding how government leaders who expand arbitrary power and restrict democratic freedom believe they are doing the right thing, and why citizens accept their actions. It also helps explain this state's righteous rationale for aggressive war.

A marauding gang of outsiders attacked buildings in New York and Washington with living bombs, killing thousands in barely an instant and terrifying large numbers of people in the country. Our government responded with a security alert, at home and abroad. Many were frightened, and the heads of state stepped up to offer us protection. Less than a week after the attacks, the Bush administration announced the creation of an Office of Homeland Security to centralize its protection efforts. "Our nation has been put on notice: We are not immune from attack. We will take defensive measures against terrorism to protect Americans" (George W. Bush speech, September 14, 2001).

The events of September 11, 2001, are certainly a turning point for U.S. politics, for the relation of the government to its citizens and to the rest of the world. Americans learned that "oceans no longer matter when it comes to making us safe" (George W. Bush speech, March 15, 2002), that we are just as vulnerable as persons elsewhere who have long lived with the awareness that some people have the motive and means to kill and wound randomly. Several years later, it appears that little has changed, either in the fear some Americans say they have of another attack or the material ability of law enforcement to predict or prevent one (Firestone 2002). Much has changed in the letter and application of the law in the United States, however, and in the environment of democracy. The Bush administration has repeatedly appealed to the primacy of its role as protector of innocent citizens and liberator of women and children to justify consolidating and centralizing executive power at home and dominative war abroad.

It is arguable that before September 11, airports and other public places in the United States were too lax in their security screening protocol. I welcome more thorough security procedures; this essay is not an argument against public officials taking measures to try to keep people safe. The key questions are how much power should officials have, how much freedom should citizens have, how fair are the procedures, how well do they follow due process, and how easily can citizens review official policies and actions to hold them accountable. With respect to these questions there have been very large and damaging changes in the United States since the fall of 2001, although a direction toward some of them had been enacted by legislation and judicial action in the years before.

The U.S. security state has expanded the prerogative of the executive and eroded the power of the legislative or judicial branches to review executive decisions or to be independent sources of decision-making. In the week after the September 11 attacks, for example, Congress passed a resolution effectively waiving its constitutionally mandated power to deliberate and decide on whether the state shall go to war. Months later, again with virtually no debate, Congress approved the largest increase in the military budget in twenty years. Since the war on terrorism has no declared ending, the executive may have been granted permanent legal discretion to do what it wants with U.S. military personnel and equipment, at current taxpayer expense of nearly $400 billion per year.

Drafted quickly and passed with almost no debate, the USA-Patriot Act, signed on October 26, 2001, severely reduces the power of courts to review and limit executive actions to keep organizations under surveillance, limit their activities, and search and seize or detain individuals. Under its provisions, individuals and organizations have had their records investigated, their assets seized, or their activities and correspondence monitored. The citizen access to government files and records that took so much struggle to achieve in the 1970s has been severely reduced, with no fanfare and thus no protest (Rosen 2002). Thousands of people have been detained, interrogated, or jailed at the discretion of law enforcement or immigration officials, and hundreds remain in jails without being charged with any crime. Few are allowed access to lawyers. Many foreign residents have been deported or threatened with deportation, sometimes without time to arrange their lives. Laws with similar purposes have been passed in other supposedly liberal democratic states, such as the United Kingdom and Australia.

The U.S. executive has taken other steps to enlarge and centralize its power and put itself above the law. In November 2002, Congress approved the creation of a Department of Homeland Security, which merged twenty-two existing federal agencies. The Bush administration has flouted principles of a rule of law at the international level by holding captured citizens of many countries prisoner and declaring its prerogative to bring any or all of them before secret tribunals.

These and other legal and policy changes have far-reaching implications. The most ordinary and fundamental expectations of due process have been undermined when search and surveillance do not require court approval, when persons can be jailed without charge, and when there is no regularity or predictability to the process a person in custody will undergo. The basic American principle of the separation of power has been suspended, with no reversal in sight. Legislatures and judiciaries at federal and more local levels have been stripped of some formal powers and decline to use much of what they have left to question, criticize, or block executive action. Most citizens apparently register approval for the increased policing and war-making powers, and the ability for those who do not to organize, criticize publicly, and protest in public streets and squares has been seriously curtailed, not only by fear of peer and employer disapproval but directly by official repression and intimidation.

How can citizens and their representatives in a democracy allow such rapid challenge to their political principles and institutions, with so little discussion and protest? The process of limiting civil liberties, due process, and deliberation about war has itself been deeply undemocratic, a bold assertion of dictatorial power. One part of the answer lies in a conviction that most people believe that their own rights and freedoms will not be threatened. Aliens will be subject to surveillance and deportation, and these enemies who have infiltrated deserve to be routed out by any means, and we can leave it to the discretion of police officers, immigration officials, and military personnel to determine who they are. Already many of those whose records have been seized or who have been detained without charge are U.S. citizens, however, and the new legislation and guidelines do not make any citizen immune. Well, then, many of us tell ourselves, the ones whose privacy is invaded or freedoms limited by government action must be doing something wrong and deserve what they get. Since I am not doing anything wrong, I am protected. The move from a relatively free society to one over which the state exercises authoritarian domination often occurs by means of just this logic; citizens do not realize how easily they may find themselves under suspicion by authorities over whose decisions there is no public scrutiny. The principle of trial by a jury of peers in which the accused is presumed innocent is an important protection any person has from false charge and arbitrary power. The slippery slope from the fearsome outsiders, to the aliens within, to the bad fellow citizens is likely to end at my brother's front door.

The deeper explanation for why people who live in what promotes itself as one of the most enlightened democracies in history so easily allow and even support the erosion of basic rights lies in the mobilization of fear. John Keane (2002) challenges the opinion that democracies privatize fear. On the contrary, he claims, contemporary commercial communications media in democratic societies often exploit and incite fear. Although freedom of speech and press make possible such public accumulation of fear, the process threatens to shut down civic freedom. "Fear is indeed a thief. It robs subjects of their capacity to act with or against others. It leaves them shaken, sometimes permanently traumatized. And when large numbers fall under the dark clouds of fear, no sun shines on civil society. Fear saps its energies and tears and twists at the institutions of political representation. Fear eats the soul of democracy" (Keane 2002, p. 235).

Public leaders invoke fear, then they promise to keep those living under them safe. Because we are afraid, and our fears are stirred by what we see on television or read in the newspaper, we are grateful to the leaders and officers who say they will shoulder the risk in order to protect us. The logic of masculinist protection works to elevate the protector to a position of superior authority and demote the rest of us to a position of grateful dependency. Ideals of democratic equality and accountability go by the wayside in the process. Although some researchers claim to have noticed a shift in the acceptability of women occupying positions of authority since the fall of 2001 (O'Connor 2002), in the contemporary United States the position of protector and the position of those protected does not correspond to that of men and women. A few of the most security-minded leaders are women, and many of those who accept the promise of protection are men. What matters, I believe, is the gendered meaning of the positions and the association of familial caring they carry for people. It also matters that this relationship carries an implicit deal: forego freedom, due process, and the right to hold leaders accountable, and in return we will make sure that you are safe.

Is It a Good Deal?

I discussed earlier how the logic of masculinist protection constitutes the "good" men who protect their women and children by relation to other "bad" men liable to attack. In this logic, virtuous masculinity depends on its constitutive relation to the presumption of evil others. Feminists have much analyzed a correlate dichotomy between the "good" woman and the "bad" woman. Simply put, a "good" woman stands under the male protection of a father or husband, submits to his judgment about what is necessary for her protection, and remains loyal to him. A "bad" woman is one unlucky enough not to have a man willing to protect her, or who refuses such protection by claiming the right to run her own life. In either case, the woman without a male protector is fair game for any man to dominate. There is a bargain implicit in the masculine protector role: either submit to my governance or all the bad men out there are liable to approach you, and I will not try to stop them.

I have argued so far that the position of citizens and residents under a security state entails a similar bargain. There are bad people out there who might want to attack us. The state pledges to protect us but tells us that we should submit to its rule and decisions without questioning, criticizing, or demanding independent review of the decisions. Some of the measures in place to protect us entail limitation on our freedom and especially limitation of the freedom of particular classes of people. The deal is: you must trade some liberty and autonomy for the sake of the protection we offer. Is it a good deal?

Some years ago, Susan Rae Peterson likened the state's relation to women under a system of male domination to a protection racket. The gangland crowd offers protection from other gangs to individuals, their families, and businesses for a fee. If some people decline their services, the gangsters teach them a brutal lesson and by example teach a lesson to others who might wish to go their own way. Thus those who wish to break free of the racketeer's protection discover that they are most in danger from him. Insofar as state laws and policies assume or reinforce the view that a "good" woman should move under the guidance of a man, Peterson argued, the state functions as a protection racket. It threatens or allows men to threaten those women who wish to be independent of the individualized protection of husbands or boyfriends. Not only do the protectors withhold protection from the women who claim autonomy but they may become attackers (Peterson 1977; see Card 1996).

The security state functions as a similar protection racket for those who live under it. As long as we accept the state's protection and pay the price it exacts, not only in taxpayer dollars but also in reduction on our freedom and submission to possible surveillance, we are relatively safe. If we try to decline these services and seek freedom from the position of dependence and obedience in which they put us, we become suspect and thereby are threatened by the very organization that claims to protect us.

Current forms of "homeland security" in the United States look like a protection racket. As long as we are quiet and obedient, we can breathe easy. If we should step out of the bounds of "good" citizens, however, we may find ourselves unprotected and even under attack by the protector state. If we publicly criticize the state's policies, especially the war or foreign policy, we may land on lists of unpatriotic people that are published to invite our neighbors or employers to sanction us. We may find that we are no longer allowed to assemble in some public places, even when we wish to demonstrate about issues other than war and the security regime, and that we are subject to arrest if we try. When we are able peaceably to protest, government officials nevertheless threaten us with horses and tear gas canisters and cameras taking our pictures. Organizations we support may appear on lists of terrorist organizations at the discretion of bureaucrats, and we won't even know that they are monitoring our e-mail or tapping our phones.

Some citizens become defined as not good citizens simply because of their race or national origin. Although public opinion only recently claimed to disapprove of policy and security practices that use racial or ethnic profiling, many now accept the state's claim that effective protection requires such profiling. Residents who are not citizens, especially those from places defined as sources of danger, lose most of the protection they may have had from attack by neighbors or arbitrary and punitive treatment by state agents.

The United States is by no means unique in enacting such measures and justifying them by appeal to protective emergency, nor is this the first time in the past century when such logic has been apparent. This is not the first time either that citizens have applauded the threatening and surveillance activities of the security regime because they are anxious for protection and believe that such measures will only apply to others—the terrorists, the foreigners, and the disloyal citizens—and not to themselves. We endanger democratic practice, however, when we consent to this bargain. When we fail to question a legal distinction between the good citizen and the bad citizen that affords less legal protection to the latter, and when we allow the rhetoric of fear to label any foreigners as enemies within, increasing numbers of us are liable to find that our attributes or activities put us on the wrong side of the line. If we allow our fear to cow us into submission, we assume the position of subordinates rather than democratic citizens equal to and not above our neighbors, equal to and not beneath our government.

There is little evidence that the way the United States has chosen to conduct its war on terrorism has in fact made itself or others in the world any safer. Indeed, it may have put Americans at even greater risk. When U.S. planes began bombing Afghanistan in October 2001, officials publicly admitted that the action put Americans inside and outside the country at greater risk from retaliating attackers. It is plausible to suggest that the stances of increased belligerence between India and Pakistan that emerged in the summer of 2002 resulted in part from U.S. military actions, and it seems that the government of Israel has been emboldened by the U.S. example to conduct its own brutal war on terrorism. The Bush administration has buried the Cold War doctrine of deterrence and announced its willingness to make preemptive strikes against what it decides are terrorist threats. The United States has prosecuted a war in Iraq that seems to have fomented greater instability there and that may contribute to destabilizing other countries or regions. Many Americans believe, moreover, that the likelihood of terrorist attacks against Americans has increased because of the Iraq war (Longworth 2002). The claimed desire to protect by means of guns generates a spiral of danger and uncertainty (see Tickner 1992, 51–53).

The logic of masculinist protection positions leaders, along with some other officials, such as soldiers and firefighters, as protectors and the rest of us in the subordinate position of dependent protected people. Justifications for the suspension of due process or partial abrogation of privacy rights and civil liberties, as well as condemnation of dissent, rest on an implicit deal: that these are necessary tradeoffs for effective protection. The legitimacy of this deal is questionable, however, not only because it may not be effective in protecting us but also because it cheapens and endangers democracy. Subordinate citizenship is not compatible with democracy. The relation of leaders to citizens under democratic norms ought to be one of equality, not in the sense of equal power but in the sense that citizens have an equal right and responsibility with leaders to make policy judgments, and thus that leaders entrusted with special powers should be held accountable to citizens. Institutions of due process, public procedure and record, organized opposition and criticism, and public review both enact and recognize such equal citizenship. Trading them for protection puts us at the mercy of the protectors.

War and Feminism

The logic of masculinist protection, I have argued, helps account for the rationale leaders give for deepening a security state and its acceptance by those living under their rule. There are two faces to the security state, one facing outward to defend against enemies and the other facing inward to keep those under protection under necessary control. So far I have concentrated on describing recent legislative and executive actions of the U.S. government in terms of the inward-looking face. Now I shall turn to the outward-looking face, the United States as war-maker.

In the fall of 2001 the United States led a bombing campaign against Afghanistan. Even though that state had not taken aggressive action against the United States, the United States justified the war as a defensive reaction to the attacks of September 11. Perhaps because the claim that the state of Afghanistan actively supported al-Qaeda was weak, the United States quickly repackaged the war as a case of humanitarian intervention to liberate the Afghan people. The logic of masculinist protection appears in the claimed relationship of the United States to people outside the West, particularly in Islamic countries, ruled by brutal dictatorships. The United States will fight and sacrifice to save them. The Bush administration has used the same discourse to justify the war against Iraq. The United States not only defends itself in this scenario but all the world's people, whom the Bush administration claimed were threatened by weapons of mass destruction that have not been found. By saving ourselves, we also save the Iraqi people from domination. So the United States is the protector of the world. Through this logic, the American people and others who choose to identify with the actions of the United States can put themselves into the role of the protector, even as the state restricts our freedom for our own good.

Packaging the war against Afghanistan as a humanitarian war to protect the Afghan people from domination was particularly effective because the Bush administration and journalists focused on women (see Tickner 2002). The women of Afghanistan constituted the ultimate victims, putting the United States in the position of ultimate protector. Use of the rhetoric of women's rights by the Bush administration during and after the war against Afghanistan should make feminists very uncomfortable. I wonder whether some seeds for such cynical appeals to the need to save women might not have been sown by some recent North American and European feminist discourse and practice that positioned itself as protector of oppressed women in Asia and Africa.

On November 17, 2001, Laura Bush became the first First Lady to give the president's Saturday morning radio address, which was devoted to condemning what she called the Taliban's war on women and justifying the U.S. war as an effort to free Afghan women. After the overthrow of the Taliban regime, the Bush administration repeatedly invoked women's liberation to justify the war. In his 2002 State of the Union address, for example, George W. Bush said, "The last time we met in this chamber the mothers and daughters of Afghanistan were captives in their own homes, forbidden from working or going to school. Today women are free, and are part of Afghanistan's new government" (George W. Bush, speech, January 29, 2002). On International Women's Day, Laura Bush again spoke to the UN Commission on the Status of Women, linking the terrorist attacks with the oppression of women and thus, by implication, the war on terrorism with the liberation of women.

> The terrorist attacks of September 11 galvanized the international community. Many of us have drawn valuable lessons from the tragedies. People around the world are looking closely at the roles women play in their societies. Afghanistan under the Taliban gave the world a sobering example of a country where women were denied their rights and their place in society. Today, the world is helping Afghan women return to the lives they once knew. Women were once important contributors to Afghan society, and they had the right to vote as early as the 1920s. . . . This is a time of rebuilding—of unprecedented opportunity–thanks to efforts led by the United Nations, theUnited States, the new Afghan government, and our allies around the world. (Laura Bush, speech to United Nations Commission on the Status of Women, March 8, 2002)

Years before the attacks of September 2001, U.S. feminists mounted a campaign directed at saving the women of Afghanistan from the Taliban. Although they lobbied the Clinton administration to put pressure on the Taliban government regarding women's rights, neither Clinton nor Bush evinced any concern for the situation of women under the Taliban before the war. Appeal to women's rights was thus a cynical attempt to gain support for the war among the citizens of the United States and other liberal countries. Some feminists jumped onto the war bandwagon. Shortly after the war began, for example, Eleanor Smeal, leader of the Feminist Majority, chatted cordially with U.S. generals. "'They went off about the role of women in this effort and how imperative it was that women were now in every level of the Air Force and Navy,' said Smeal, who found herself cheered by the idea of women flying F16s. 'It's a different kind of war,' she says, echoing the President's assessment of Operation Enduring Freedom" (Lerner 2001).

Certainly the Taliban should have been condemned for its policies, as should all the world's governments that perpetrate or allow systematic and discriminatory harms to and subordination of women. The Taliban stood with only a few other governments of the world in the degree of legally enforced restriction of women's freedom and horrible punishments. Even before the war, it seemed to me, however, and still seems to me, that feminist focus on women under the Taliban constructed these women as exoticized others and paradigmatic victims in need of salvation by Western feminists, and it conveniently deflected attention from perhaps more intractable and mundane problems of gender-based violence, domination, and poverty in many other parts of the world, including the enlightened West. What is wrong with this stance, if it has existed, is that it fails to consider the women as equals, and it does not have principled ways of distancing itself from paternalist militarism.

The stance of the male protector, I have argued, is one of loving self-sacrifice, with those in the feminine position as the objects of love and guardianship.

Chivalrous forms of masculinism express and enact concern for the well-being of women, but they do so within a structure of superiority and subordination. The male protector confronts evil aggressors in the name of the right and the good, while those under his protection submit to his order and serve as handmaid to his efforts. Colonialist ideologies have often expressed a similar logic. The knights of civilization aim to bring enlightened understanding to the further regions of the world still living in cruel and irrational traditions that keep them from developing the economic and political structures that will bring them a good life. The suppression of women in these societies is a symptom of such backwardness. Troops will be needed to bring order and guard fledgling institutions, and foreign aid workers to feed, cure, and educate, but all this is only a period of tutelage that will end when the subject people demonstrate their ability to gain their own livelihood and run their own affairs. Many people living in Asian, African, and Latin American societies believe that not only U.S. military hegemony but also international trade and financial institutions, and many Western-based nongovernmental development agencies, position them in this way as feminized or infantilized women and children under the protection and guidance of the wise and active father.

In its rhetoric and practice, according to some scholars, the British feminist movement of the late nineteenth and early twentieth centuries aligned itself with the universal humanitarian civilizing mission that was invoked as the justification for the British Empire. Feminists endorsed male imperial leaders' assessment of the status of women in other nations as a measure of their level of moral development. Such interest in the status of women was useful to feminists in pointing out the hypocrisy of denying women's rights in the center as one fought for them in the periphery. Providing services for Indian women and other oppressed women in the empire also offered opportunities for the employment of middle-class professional women (Burton 1994).

Some contemporary feminists have worried that Western feminism today has had some tendency to express and act in similar ways in relation to non-Western women. In a well-known essay, Chandra Mohanty, for example, claims that Western feminists too often use an objectified general category of Third World women, who are represented as passive and victimized by their unenlightened cultures and political regimes (Mohanty 1991). Uma Narayan claims that much feminist discussion of the situation of women in Asian and African societies, or women in Asian immigrant communities in Western societies, "replicates problematic aspects of Western representations of Third World nations and communities, aspects that have their roots in the history of colonization" (Narayan 1997, 43).

Assuming that these criticisms of some of the discourse, attitudes, and actions of Western feminists have some validity, the stance they identify helps account for the ease with which feminist rhetoric can be taken up by today's imperialist power and used for its own ends. It also helps account for the support of some feminists for the war against Afghanistan. Sometimes feminists may identify with the stance of the masculine protector in relation to vulnerable and victimized women. The protector-protected relation is no more egalitarian, however, when between women than between men and women.

According to some recent reports, the lives of women in Afghanistan have changed little since before the war, except that some of them have lost their homes, their relatives, and what little livelihood they had (Reilly 2002). The oppression of most of them remains embedded in social structure, custom, and a culture of warlord anarchism. I would not argue that humanitarian reasons can never justify going to war against a state. I think, however, that such protectionist grounds for military intervention must be limited to situations of genocide or impending geno-cide and where the war actually makes rescue possible (Young 2003). Even if the U.S. government is sincere in its conviction that its military efforts are intended to save the world from evil, its political and military hegemony materially harms many poor and defenseless people of the world and positions most of the world in a position of subordination that nurtures resentment.

Democratic Global Citizenship

The contemporary security state in the United States, like many security states, has two faces, one looking outward and the other inward. Each aspect reinforces the other. Both threaten democratic values, in the institutions and practices of the United States, as well as globally. Citizens and residents who accept the security state because they fear attack allow themselves to be positioned as women and children in relation to the paternal protector-leaders. At the same time, to the extent that we identify with a rhetoric of war for the sake of saving the victims of tyranny, we put ourselves in a position superior to those we construct as in need of our aid. Whether looking outward or inward, adopting a more democratic ethos entails rejecting the inequality inherent in the protector-protected logic.

When leaders promulgate fear and promise to keep us safe, they conjure up childish fantasies and desires. We are vulnerable beings, and we want very much to be made safe by a being superior in power to all that might threaten us. Demo-cratic citizens, however, should resist leaders' attempts to play father over us. We should insist that government do its job to promote security without issuing guar-antees it cannot redeem or requiring subordination from the people it promises to protect.

Democratic citizenship should first involve admitting that no state can make any of us completely safe and that leaders who promise that are themselves suspect. The world is full of risks. Prudence dictates that we assess risks, get information about their sources, and try to minimize them, and we rightly expect our gov-ernment to do much of this for us. In a democracy, citizens should not have to trade this public responsibility for submission to surveillance, arbitrary decision, and the stifling of criticism.

In making this claim, I am extending recent feminist arguments against a model of citizenship that requires each citizen to be independent and self-sufficient in order to be equal and fully autonomous. Feminist theorists of care and welfare have argued that the rights and dignity of individuals should not be diminished just because they need help and support to enable them to carry out their chosen pro-ject (Kittay 1999; Tronto 1994). Persons who need care or other forms of social support ought not to be forced into a position of subordination and obedience in relation to those who provide care and support; not only should they retain the rights of full citizens to choose their own way of life and hold authorities accountable but they ought to be able to criticize the way in which support comes to them (Hirschmann 2002, chap. 5; Sevenhuijsen 1998; Young 2003). This feminist argument rejects the assumption behind a notion of self-sufficient citizenship that a need for social support or care is more exceptional than normal. On the contrary, the well-being of all persons can be enhanced by the care and support of others, and in modern societies some of this generalized care and support ought to be organized and guaranteed through state institutions. The organization of reasonable measures to protect people from harm and make people confident that they can move and act relatively safely is another form of social support. Citizens should not have to trade their liberty of movement or right to protest and hold leaders accountable in return for such security.

Democratic citizenship thus means ultimately rejecting the hierarchy of protector and protected. In the article I cited earlier, Judith Stiehm argues that rejection of this hierarchy implies installing a position of defender in place of both that of the protector and the protected. A society of defenders is "a society composed of citizens equally liable to experience violence and equally responsible for exercising society's violence" (Stiehm 1982, 374). Modern democracies, including U.S. democracy, are founded partly on the principle that citizens should be able to defend themselves if they are also to defend the republic from tyranny. In the twenty-first century, in a world of organized and less organized military institutions and weapons capable of unimaginable destruction, it is hard to know what it might mean for world citizens to exercise collective self-defense. It certainly does not mean that every individual should amass his or her own weapons cache. Nor does it mean whole groups and nations engaging in arms races. The distinction between defender and protector invokes an ideal of equality in the work of defense, and today this may have at least as much to do with political processes that limit weapons and their use as with wielding arms.

The United States claims to use its arms to do this, much as a policeman does in domestic life. In a democratic relationship, however, the policeman-protector comes under the collective authority of the people whose neighborhood he patrols. Democratic citizenship at a global level, then, would constitute a relationship of respect and political equality among the world's peoples in which none of us thinks that he or she stands in the position of the paternal authority who knows what is good for the still-developing others. To the extent that global law enforcement is necessary, it is only legitimate if the world's peoples together have formulated the rules and actions of such enforcement (see Archibugi and Young 2002).

References

Archibugi, Daniele, and Iris Marion Young. 2002. "Envisioning a Global Rule of Law." *Dissent* (Spring): 27–37.

Berlant, Lauren. 1997. "The Theory of Infantile Citizenship." In *The Queen of America Goes to Washington City: Essays on Sex and Citizenship*. Durham, N.C.: Duke University Press, 25–54.

Brod, Harry, and Michael Kaufman, eds. 1994. *Theorizing Masculinities*. London: Sage.

Burton, Antoinette. 1994. *Burdens of History: British Feminists, Indian Women, and Imperial Culture, 1865–1915*. Chapel Hill: University of North Carolina Press.

Card, Claudia. 1996. "Rape Terrorism." In *The Unnatural Lottery: Character and Moral Luck*. Philadelphia: Temple University Press, 97–117.

Cohn, Carol. 1993. "Wars, Wimps, and Women: Talking Gender and Thinking War." In *Gendering War Talk*, ed. Miliam Cooke and Angela Woollocott . Princeton: Princeton University Press, 227–248.

Elshtain, Jean Bethke, 1987. *Women and War*. Chicago: University of Chicago Press.

———. 1992. "Sovereignty, Identity, Sacrifice." In *Gendered States: Feminist (Re)visions of International Relations Theory*, ed. V. Spike Peterson. Boulder, Colo.: Rienner, 141–154.

Firestone, David. 2002. "Are You Safer Today Than a Year Ago?" *New York Times*, November 17, sec. 4, p. 1.

Foucault, Michel. 1988. "Technologies of the Self." In *Technologies of the Self: A Seminar with Michel Foucault*, ed. Luther Martin, Huck Guttman, and Patricia Hutton. Amherst: University of Massachusetts Press, 19–49.

———. 1994. "*Omnes et Singulatim*: Toward a Critique of Political Reason." In *The Essential Works of Foucault*, vol. 3, *Power*, ed. James D. Faubion. New York: New Press, 298–325.

Goldstein, Joshua S. 2001. *War and Gender: How Gender Shapes the War System and Vice Versa*. Cambridge, England: Cambridge University Press.

Hirschmann, Nancy J. 2002. *The Subject of Liberty: Toward A Feminist Theory of Freedom*. Princeton: Princeton University Press.

Hobbes, Thomas. [1668] 1994. *Leviathan*. Indianapolis: Hackett.

Hooper, Charlotte. 2001. *Manly States: Masculinities, International Relations, and Gender Politics*. New York: Columbia University Press.

Kaldor, Mary. 1999. *New and Old Wars: Organized Violence in a Global Era*. Stanford: Stanford University Press.

Keane, John. 2002. "Fear and Democracy." In *Violence and Politics: Globalizations' Paradox*, ed. Kentor Worcester, Sally Avery Birmansohn, and Mark Ungar. New York: Routledge, 226–44.

Kittay, Eva Feder. 1999. *Love's Labor: Essays on Women, Equality, and Dependency*. New York: Routledge.

Lerner, Sharon. 2001. "Feminists Agonize over War in Afghanistan: What Women Want," *Village Voice*, October 31–November 6.

Longworth, R. C. 2002. "The Ball Is Rolling Toward Iraq War," *Chicago Tribune*, December 22, sec. 2, 1, 6.

MacKinnon, Catharine. 1987. *Feminism Unmodified: Discourses on Life and Law*. Cambridge: Harvard University Press.

May, Larry. 1998. *Masculinity and Morality*. Ithaca, N.Y.: Cornell University Press.

Mohanty, Chandra Talpade. 1991. "Under Western Eyes: Feminist Scholarship and Colonial Discourse." In *Third World Women and the Politics of Feminism*, ed. Chandra Talpade Mohanty, Ann Russo, and Lourdes Torres. Bloomington: Indiana University Press, 51–80.

Narayan, Uma. 1997. "Restoring History and the Politics of 'Third World Traditions': Contesting the Colonialist Stance and Contemporary Contradictions of *Sati*." In *Dislocating Cultures: Identities, Traditions and Third World Feminism*. New York: Routledge, 41–80.

Nozick, Robert. 1974. *Anarchy, State, and Utopia*. New York: Basic Books.

O'Connor, Karen. 2002. "For Better or for Worse? Women and Women's Rights in the Post 9/11 Climate." In *American Government in a Changed World: The Effects of September 11, 2001*, ed. Dennis L. Dresang et al. New York: Longman, 171–191.

Pateman, Carole. 1988. *The Sexual Contract*. Stanford: Stanford University Press.

Peterson, Susan Rae. 1977. "Coercion and Rape: The State as a Male Protection Racket." In *Feminism and Philosophy*, ed. Mary Vetterling-Braggin, Frederick A. Elliston, and Jane English. Totowa, N.J.: Littlefield Adams, 360–371.

Reilly, Kristie. 2002. "Left Behind: An Interview with Revolutionary Afghan Women's Association's Shar Saba," *In These Times*, 26, 11: 16–18.

Rosen, Ruth. 2002. "The Last Page." *Dissent* (spring).

Sevenhuijsen, Selma. 1998. *Citizenship and the Ethics of Care: Feminist Considerations on Justice, Morality and Politics*. New York: Routledge.

Stiehm, Judith. 1982. "The Protected, the Protector, the Defender." *Women's Studies International Forum* 5, 367–376.

Tickner, Ann. 1992. *Gender in International Relations: Feminist Perspectives on Achieving Global Security*. New York: Columbia University Press.

———. 2001. *Gendering World Politics: Issues and Approaches in the Post-Cold War Era*. New York: Columbia University Press.

———. 2002. "Feminist Perspectives on 9/11." *International Studies Perspectives* 3: 333–350.

Tronto, Joan. 1994. *Moral Boundaries: A Political Argument for an Ethic of Care*. New York: Routledge.

Young, Iris Marion. 2003. "Autonomy, Welfare Reform, and Meaningful Work." In *The Subject of Care: Feminist Perspectives on Dependency*, ed. Eva Feder Kittay and Ellen Feder. Lanham, Md: Rowman and Littlefield, 40–60.

2

French Universalism
in the Nineties

Joan Wallach Scott

This chapter tells a story about a French feminist attempt to refigure universalism in the 1990s in a movement for gender equality in politics that they called *parité*. It is a story that addresses a set of questions much debated by philosophers and psychoanalysts, to say nothing of feminists: What is the relationship between anatomical difference and its symbolic representation? Is sexual difference (understood as a psychic, not an anatomical, reality) a fixed or mutable phenomenon? These questions are at the heart of countless theoretical debates, and for many feminists they have required "an obligatory detour via philosophy (Schor 17). My story, following the hunch of the *parité* movement as well as my own disciplinary inclination, takes a different route, seeking its insights not so much in philosophy as in history.

French politics in the 1990s was full of debates about universalism. Whatever the issue—citizenship for North African immigrants, greater access to political office for women, or domestic partnership for homosexual couples (to take only the most prominent)—its proponents and critics framed their arguments as critiques of, appeals to, or defenses of a universalism thought to be distinctively French. And not just French but republican. Universalism was taken to be the defining trait of the French republic, its most enduring value, its most precious asset. To accuse someone of betraying universalism was tantamount to accusing them of treason.

It is important to note that the debates about universalism in the 1990s were not confined (as they were in that period in the U.S.) to lofty academic circles or arcane theoretical texts. They were instead at the very center of politics: they resounded in the National Assembly and filled the pages of daily newspapers. Nor was universalism just a slogan; it was a serious (if disputed) philosophical concept. For many

This essay was given as the first annual Naomi Schor Memorial Lecture at Yale University on September 24, 2003. Thanks to Debra Keates and James Swenson for help with translations from the French. It was published in *differences*, 15:2 (summer 2004), pp. 32–53.

Americans, the high level of French political discourse is surprising, and the key role intellectuals can play in the articulation of public policy is enviable. There is no less corruption or dishonesty there than here, but there is a lot more intelligent reflection, and political strategy is more often formulated with an eye to its philosophical implications, since these are a recognized part of the political stakes.

The story I want to tell here centers on a feminist movement that sought to refigure the terms of universalism in order to increase the numbers of women in elected office. The point was not to press for antidiscrimination or affirmative action measures but to guarantee an equal number of seats for women and men. The partial realization of that goal came with the law of June 6, 2000, which requires (with typically complex variations) that half of all candidates for political office be women. The argument for *parité* was neither essentialist nor separatist; it was not about the particular qualities women would bring to politics, nor about the need to represent a special women's interest. Instead—and this is what has intrigued me since I began reading about it—the argument for *parité* was rigorously universalist.

Before I begin to tell the story of this compelling movement, however, I think it is necessary to define universalism. And I will do that with a look at its history.

French universalism in the 1990s—at least in the realm of politics—was a mythologized restatement of the principles of 1789. Those who vociferously defended the values and ideals of the Republic against the threat of what was most often described as American multiculturalism saw themselves as protectors of a distinctively French conception of political representation. This conception rested on two related abstractions: that of the individual and that of the nation. The nation was the expression of the people's will, articulated by its representatives. These representatives were not (as had been the case under the Old Regime) spokesmen for various corporate interests; instead, each stood for the collectivity as a whole. Unlike the American system, articulated at the same time (most famously by James Madison in the Federalist Papers), which saw legislatures as arenas of conflicting interests and defined representatives as voices for particular social and economic groups (or factions), the French system took the abstraction of the nation as the referent for representation. Representatives did not reflect some already existing, competing entities; instead they constituted, through their actions, the singular body of the nation. And it was a nation "one and indivisible."

The ability of any citizen to stand for (to represent) the nation came from the fact that political individuals were understood to be abstracted from their social attributes (wealth, family, occupation, religion, profession). The Abbé Sièyes put it succinctly: "Democracy requires the complete sacrifice of the individual to the *res publica*, that is the sacrifice of the concrete being to the abstract being" (quoted in Rosanvallon 48–49). Abstract individuals were commensurable and interchangeable units, possessing in common only that independent rationality upon which political life was thought to depend. The nation they constituted was equally abstract: not a reflection of the disparate and divisive realities of society but a fictional entity—a unified totality, the embodiment of a disembodied "peuple."

The abstractions of individual and nation were the key to a distinctively French concept of universalism. They allowed the revolutionaries to substitute political equality for the corporate hierarchies of the Old Regime and republican unity for the rule of kings. And they held out a promise of universal inclusion in political life. Abstraction, after all, meant disregarding the attributes that distinguished people in their ordinary lives; by this measure, any and all individuals could be considered citizens. Indeed, as Étienne Balibar has pointed out, abstract individualism understands itself to be a *fictitious* universality, "not the idea that the common nature of individuals is given or already there, but rather the fact that it is produced inasmuch as particular identities are relativized and become mediations for the realization of a superior and more abstract goal" (58). In this sense, universality does not rest on the exclusion of the particular but on (socially or politically) agreed-upon indifference to certain particularities. The abstract must always take the social into account (if only to discount it) and so becomes the site of arguments about whether there can be limits to abstraction and of what these limits consist. Jacques Rancière puts it another way. Democracy, he argues, rests on a necessary tension between the abstraction of "the people" and the social reality such abstraction obscures. Democratic politics is the adjudication of the claims by various constituencies to represent or be represented as the people ("Post-Democracy" 171–178).

The tensions between the abstract and the social were present in political debate from the Revolution on. In the 1790s, Jews were admitted to citizenship only when they relinquished allegiance to their "nation" and became individuals for whom religion was a private matter. Clermont-Tonnerre's is the classic formulation of this principle: "We must deny everything to the Jews as a Nation, in the sense of a constituted body, and grant them everything as individuals" (quoted in Birnbaum 242). Slaves, wage-earners, and women were initially ruled out of active citizenship because they were considered dependents, and autonomy was a prerequisite for individuality. Even when dependency was redefined, when slaves were freed and wage-earners enfranchised (in 1848), women remained unacceptable as citizens. This was, I argue, because the difference of sex was not considered to be susceptible to abstraction; it was irreducible, symbolic of a fundamental division or antagonism that could not be reconciled with the notion of an indivisible nation. Whenever the revolutionaries discussed women's place in the public sphere, they inevitably used corporeal imagery to justify exclusion—the body seemed to offer undeniable, common-sense evidence of unbridgeable difference. "Since when is it permitted to give up one's sex?" thundered the Jacobin Pierre-Gaspard Chaumette. "Is it to men that nature confided domestic cares? Has she given us breasts to feed our children?" (quoted in Levy, Applewhite, and Johnson 15). Pierre-Joseph Proudhon echoed this view years later, in 1849, when he objected to the feminist Jeanne Deroin's attempt to run for office. A female legislator, he quipped, made as much sense as a male wet nurse. Her reply—Show me which organ is required for the functions of the legislator, and "I will concede the debate"—exposed the symbolic investments of his argument: well beyond any logical criteria or substantive discussion of the real capabilities and capacities of women, sexual difference stood for difference itself (quoted in Tixerant 86). Not just any difference but one so primary, so rooted in nature, so visible, that it could not be subsumed by abstraction.

There were, of course, objections to this view from feminists and other advocates of women's citizenship. There were bound to be objections. First of all, sexual difference is a site of struggle over meaning, not a set of fixed oppositions. Second, the virtue of abstract individualism is that it allows for debate about what counts as irreducible difference. But there were also alterations in the doctrine of republican universalism, which might have changed (but did not) the arguments that could be made about women. During the Third Republic, class was acknowledged to be a divisive force in the body politic, and (in part under the influence of the new discipline of sociology) the play of interests was admitted as a legitimate motive for choosing representatives.[1] Put in other terms, the social was now represented in the political sphere. The emergence of a workers' party and the triumph of its candidates in local and national elections called into question the founding fathers' notion of a seamless "general will," but—as the defeat of attempts to institute proportional representation for political parties indicated—the nation was not reimagined as a reflection of preexisting social divisions. Even if representatives were elected by constituencies with particular interests, the nation they represented was still conceived as a singular, coherent body. And one of the marks of this singular coherence, as of the interchangeability of its individual representatives, was masculinity. When the suffragist Hubertine Auclert issued a call to arms for women to organize, as workers had, to assert their interest by attaining the right not only to vote but to serve as representatives, a furious journalist impugned her motives in terms that revealed his belief in the masculinity of citizenship: "Is it our resignation as men that dame Hubertine asks of us? Let her say it frankly" (Villemot).

Women were granted the vote in 1944 and thus presumably designated abstract individuals. At the time, de Gaulle used the franchise as a way of repairing national unity after the divisions of the Occupation and the disgrace of the collaborationist Vichy regime. The inclusion of women signaled a return to universalist principles; differences, even the most intractable of them, now seemed amenable to incorporation. Simone de Beauvoir warned a few years later that the vote had been only a partial victory: "abstract rights . . . have never sufficed to assure to woman a definite hold on the world; true equality between the sexes does not exist even today" (150). But even the issue of abstract rights was not fully resolved; indeed, the "true equality" Beauvoir sought was elusive precisely because the difference of sex seemed to pose a limit to abstraction.

Giving women the vote recognized them as individuals, but not quite. Although the constitution of the Fifth Republic considered them eligible for office, it was extremely difficult for women to clear the hurdles political parties put in their path. It was one thing to cast a ballot (to be a citizen), it seemed, quite another to represent the nation (to be a representative). The pressure to keep women out of the body of the nation (to refuse to allow it to be divided symbolically) was enormous and effective. In the years from 1945 to 1997, women never constituted more than 6 percent of the deputies in the National Assembly or 3 percent of the Senate. And despite feminist agitation for quotas during the 1970s and 1980s (especially within the Socialist Party), politicians seemed unable to find a way to

---

1. On these developments, see Rosanvallon.

correct the persistent discrimination women experienced.[2] (Those women who did dare to run for office recounted the opposition they faced within their own parties. It was like declaring war, one reported. Others told of receiving obscene threats and insults from those who were supposed to be their comrades. Another confided that she was never treated like a "real" deputy because she was a woman. Many more took the hint and stayed away [Sineau 54–55].) Feminist protest in these years called for politicians to live up to the promises of de Gaulle's constitution—"the law guarantees to women equal rights with men in all spheres"—but the difference of sex continued to be held against them. It became increasingly clear that this was not just a matter of male politicians protecting their monopoly—or quasi monopoly—of elective office at a moment when it was publicly called into question but a problem with the way in which the underlying principle of universalism was understood. If women were to become abstract individuals, fully interchangeable with men as representatives of the nation, then the issue of sexual difference had to be directly addressed. Instead of allowing it to stand for that which had to be excluded (antagonism, division, difference)—in this way functioning as what Slavoj Zizek calls universalism's "obscene underside"—differences of sex had to become a characteristic of universalism itself ("*Da Capo*" 220).

The exploration of this possibility took place in a context in which—on the eve of the bicentennial of the first revolution—the original universalist principles were being turned to ever more conservative uses. Indeed, the vehement reassertion of republican universalism began in the 1980s as a response to the emergence of what are usually called the "new social movements"—precursors to the identity-based politics of the 1990s. The questions of difference, and discrimination based upon it, loomed large, despite a national policy of studious ignorance: among other things, statistics were not kept on minorities in the population (published census data contains no ethnic classification, only information about whether a person's grandparents were not French born) or on the results of elections by gender. (In this way the illusion of national unity is preserved by counting everyone only as individuals.) Unlike the United States, where affirmative action was the policy offered to end years of discrimination based on gender and race, France resisted "differentialism" in the name of republican universalism. An antidiscrimination law was passed in the 1970s to punish racist utterances, but the turn to positive action was firmly resisted in the name of universalism. Public debate prevented any measures taken in favor of immigrants, and a decision by the Constitutional Council in 1982 ruled out special treatment of women as a way of correcting discrimination against them. The classification of individuals as members of groups was impermissible, the Council ruled, citing (in the case of quotas for women candidates in elections) both the constitution of 1958 and article 6 of the Declaration of the Rights of Man and Citizen (1789), which reads, "All citizens are equal before the law and are equally admissible to all offices, places and public employments, according to their capacity and without other distinction than that of their virtues and talents" (full text cited in Marques-Pereira 174).

2. See Jenson and Sineau.

The problem was, of course, that social distinctions *did* prevent some individuals from enjoying equal access to "all offices, places, and public employments." There were two groups for whom equal access was particularly difficult: those of North African origin or Islamic affiliation who were designated "immigrants," though many were several generations removed from any "immigrant" experience, and women. What these two groups had in common was a difference that was deemed irreducible (not susceptible to assimilation or abstraction). North African "immigrants" by definition were outside French cultural boundaries; even if they were born in France, even if they were secular, they were outsiders because of a presumed association with Islam. Women signified internal difference and irreparable antagonism. In both cases, these qualities were taken as antithetical to universalism. How could those exhibiting such qualities be capable of speaking in the name of the general will? What would it take for North Africans and women to be incorporated into the body politic without fracturing its unified representation?

The answer to the immigrant question offered by politicians in the early 1990s set the context within which feminists articulated their demands for *parité*. The immigrant question was particularly fraught because of the arrival on the political scene in 1983 of Jean-Marie Le Pen and his ultranationalist Front National. (Le Pen's continued electoral success—he won 14 percent of the vote in the presidential election of 1988 and more than that in 2002—was taken to be symptomatic of a "crisis of representation." The discussion of this crisis provided an important opening for parity.) Le Pen's position was that North Africans should be sent back to their countries of origin, and he managed (and manages increasingly) to acquire impressive electoral support. Among those who opposed him were advocates of a more multicultural approach, one that would recognize the complex ethnic composition of France, and those—the majority—who insisted that universalism could accommodate, could integrate, the troubling challenge posed by the growing North African population. The official doctrine of *intégration* was articulated in 1993 in revisions of the nationality code and in a set of laws that came to be known as the Pasqua Laws (named for the right-wing minister of the interior). *Intégration* was premised, not surprisingly, on abstract individualism. To become a citizen, a report from the Haut Conseil à l'Intégration argued in 1993, meant enjoying full freedom of private communal association, while rejecting "the logic of there being distinct ethnic or cultural minorities, and instead looking for a logic based on the equality of individual persons" (quoted in Favell 70). France might be culturally diverse—liberty of association guaranteed this—but politically, it was homogeneous—individuals were equal before the law, their rights conferred and protected by the laws of the state. *Intégration* did not hold up the old standard of cultural assimilation (according to which one had to embrace not only the values of secular universalism but speak, eat, dress and "look" French), but it did demand a singular national identification. For purposes of politics, only one collective identity was admitted: that of being French (Favell 17).[3]

3. See also Rancière, "Citoyenneté" 55.

This scheme of integration actually did little to solve the problem of "immigrants" in French society. In fact, it drew attention away from the social and economic realities faced by North Africans living in France and made difficult any representation of their collective fate. Those who spoke for the group were seen as advocating a "multiculturalism" at odds with universalism. And others who simply went about their own business were still subject to discrimination. Even as citizens, North Africans are treated as strangers by virtue of their ethnicity (dubbed "Islamists" even if they are secular); they are assumed to be foreigners whose interests are tangential, irrelevant, or dangerous to the collective interest of "France." Needless to say, such people can hardly be considered eligible to represent the nation. As in the case of women, even after they were granted citizenship, North Africans were not counted as fully individual. They continue to be associated with a difference that cannot be abstracted.

The reaffirmation of the principles of republican universalism in the context of the immigration question did not finally address the problem of the relationship of France's increasing cultural diversity to national unity; it served instead to deny the existence of discrimination. For if all individuals were equal, how could there be discrimination? Yet, if there were discrimination (based on attributions of group identity), how could it be rectified if these attributions could not be taken into account? For those concerned with the relationship between the social and the political, this raised troubling issues: Had the principles of 1789 outlived their usefulness in the 1990s? Or was there a way to adapt them to new exigencies without losing the very desirable equalizing effect abstraction could have? Was there some way to change the notion of the individual, expanding its capacity for abstraction to include differences once thought to be irreducible? It was on the terrain of sexual difference that feminists tried to grapple with these questions.

The movement for parity began formally in 1992, with the publication of a manifesto by Françoise Gaspard, Claude Servan-Schreiber, and Anne LeGall entitled *Au Pouvoir, citoyennes! Liberté, Egalité, Parité*. The authors were veterans of the feminist attempts in the 1980s to improve women's position in the political sphere. They were also outspoken partisans of greater representation for immigrants and their families. Gaspard and Servan-Schreiber had coauthored a book in 1984, *La Fin des immigrés*, arguing for a more pluralist definition of French culture and politics. Gaspard had been the mayor of Dreux until she was unseated by the National Front, and a Socialist Party deputy from the department of Eure-et-Loir (see Gaspard, *Une petite Ville*). Servan-Schreiber was a journalist, Le Gall a feminist activist. Their long experience made them skeptical of the capacity of male politicians to voluntarily accommodate feminist demands. What was needed, they believed, was a law that would both force such accommodation and change the terms that defined what representation was. Law had the power not only to overcome the resistance of politicians but also to alter the symbolic structures upon which social organization rested. Law had the power to replace what was deemed a false universalism with a true one.

Parité was conceived entirely within the terms of the discourse of abstraction so critical to French republicanism. If the abstract individual was supposed to be without physical or social marking, then why was it that [white] men made up more than 90 percent of those representing the nation? This was not, parity advocates maintained, an accident of history but the result of the fact that universality and masculinity were taken to be synonymous. Or, as the historian Michelle Perrot put it, the universal "is in fact a fig leaf that only covers over the masculinity that has served to exclude women from the government of the polity." Since all humans come in two sexes, the consistent exclusion of one sex was a sign of discrimination. And if there was discrimination, the individual was not a universal figure. The republican theory of representation (which these feminists granted) was based on the idea that individuals were interchangeable units, made identical by their capacity for reason; no other traits mattered. Women's ability to reason had long been established (in laws granting equal education at the end of the nineteenth century and in enfranchisement in 1944), but they had yet to be deemed worthy of representing the electorate, and by extension the nation. They were not, in other words, considered identical to all other individuals, not universal enough to transcend the difference of their sex. The exclusion of women suggested there might be other exclusions too, since the representative individual turned out to be a set of particularities. The absence of women serving as representatives, then, indicated a corruption of republican universalism; the representatives of the nation were not only financially corrupt (as various scandals in 1988 and 1989 had revealed) but—through the practice of discrimination, which introduced the difference of sex as a criterion for holding office—they had corrupted the principle of representation itself.

If women were to achieve the status of individuals, nothing less than full equality was required. Dismissing quotas as inadequate, the *paritairistes* called initially for a fifty-fifty division of seats. Fifty-fifty was not a quota, they argued, but a reflection of the fact that, whatever other qualities they might have, individuals were always sexed. Anatomical difference was universal, but the meanings attributed to it were social and cultural. These meanings were the source of inequality. Until now, the *paritairistes* reasoned, the universal abstract individual had been figured in terms of symbols that associated reason and abstraction with masculinity, passion and the concrete with femininity. In order to extend the possibility of abstraction to women, anatomical difference had to be separated from its symbolizations. The way to do this was to insist on the *duality* of the human (not the *difference* of the sexes): the universal individual was man *and* woman.

This was not the same as the nature/culture, sex/gender argument that American feminists first used and then deconstructed, because no inherent meaning (upon which gender was constructed or to which it could be referred) was attributed to anatomical duality (indeed, biology was also understood to be "cultural"—it was a discourse attempting to account for and to resolve the brute "fact" of the anatomical difference of sex). Servan-Schreiber put it clearly in a discussion of parity with the feminist group Dialogue des femmes.[4] First, she refuted the idea

---

4. Dialogue des femmes was a group that met regularly in the early 1990s to which speakers were invited. Their minutes were circulated as mimeographed typescripts. Copies from some sessions are at the Bibliothèque Durand in Paris in the parité files.

that parity was a way to recognize "the true nature" of women, their essential "difference." The point was not to defend any special "women's interest" or to bring a uniquely feminine capacity to law-making ("We would fall here into a differentialist discourse that I myself in no way share" [9]), but rather to make women plausible representatives of the nation. Insisting on the duality of the human was a way of claiming the equal right of women to represent humanity. "Human kind is an entity that stands on two legs—two legs which are part and parcel of a single body and yet not interchangeable; in light of this, what we want is the political recognition of such duality." While "difference" came laden with all sorts of cultural assumptions about the inescapably biological capacities and characteristics of women and men, Servan-Schreiber thought, "duality" avoided those associations. Women and men were not, in one sense, interchangeable; if they were, women would be subsumed and thus effaced by dominant males. The argument against such obliteration (and thus against discrimination) required that women be distinctly visible. Equality implied a recognition of difference—in this case that the human was man and woman—in order to qualify women as individuals and eliminate their sex as a consideration. Only by insisting on the necessary duality of the human could a truly inclusive individualism (one in which sex no longer mattered) exist. "It is paradoxical, but interesting to argue," commented the philosopher Françoise Collin, "that it was universalism that best maintained the sexualization of power, and that parity attempts, by contrast, to desexualize power by extending it to both sexes. Parity would thus be the true universalism" (103).[5]

Duality was not an argument about complementarity, nor was it about the necessary heterosexual foundation of society. Rather, men and women simply existed as two human types; laws that attributed necessary meanings to the abstraction of this duality had prevented women from acting as representatives in elected assemblies. This was a violation not of nature—nature had nothing to do with it—but of the principles of democracy. For the authors of *Au Pouvoir, citoyennes,*

> democracy is a universal aspiration; universality encompasses women and men. There is, therefore, no representative democracy if representation is not equal (paritaire). Today, the under-representation of women in elected assemblies is so constant in its disproportion that it reveals a deficit of thought and consequently of law. Because of this disproportion, a new democratic contract is needed. The word "contract" presumes equality between the contracting parties. Only the adoption of a parity law will insure that this equality is real. (Gaspard et al. 130)

Anticipating objections from those who saw *parité* as the tip of a differentialist or communitarian iceberg *à l'américaine*, the authors denied that they were treating women as a "class" or a "social group." There was no "women's interest" at

---

5. *Projets féminists* published a special double issue in 1996 containing transcriptions of a year-long seminar devoted to parity. Sessions consisted of brief presentations by several speakers followed by questions and discussion.

stake, because women cut across all interest groups. Electing women would not mean introducing a separate, unified element into the legislatures; women could be expected to be found in every party, on all sides of contested issues. It was "pernicious," they said, to put women on the same plane as classes, social categories, or ethnic communities:

> Women are not a minority. They are everywhere. They are found in every class, in all social categories. They are Catholic, Protestant, Jewish, Muslim, agnostic. They cannot be compared to pressure groups...demanding better representation....Women are neither a corporate entity nor a lobby. They constitute half of the sovereign people, half of the human race. (166)

Blandine Kriegel also rejected the equation of women with a minority group. "Femininity is a universal," she wrote, "and just as when one is masculine one is considered human, so when one is feminine one is human" (*Le Monde*). The law on parity was meant to implement not a fixed relationship of sexual difference (now rendered irrelevant), but the abstract, hence universalist, principles of democracy.

For the parity movement, passage of a law was critical for achieving this end, since only a law would provide the conditions within which a resymbolization of the relations between women and men would become possible. As Gaspard put it:

> Social and political prejudices deduced from differences based on anatomical sex persist in relations of power (to men's benefit) and are expressed, notably, in politics. In the field of political decision-making it is clear that an implicit "order" of men exists. The conquest of strict equality for women with men in political assemblies—whether national or local—is thus also symbolic. ("De la parité" 42)

The route to passage of such a law, however, was not easy. Ironically, not because it was hard to mobilize political opinion (the *paritairistes* proved to be brilliant strategists and in less than a decade forced the hand of reluctant politicians with, among other things, poll results that showed more than 70 percent of the electorate, with no difference between women and men, in favor of passage of a fifty-fifty law) but because it proved difficult to maintain the philosophical integrity of the argument. The original *paritairistes* distinguished between anatomical dualism and sexual difference; the one was an abstraction—the assertion of the neutrality, the essential meaninglessness, the *disembodiment* of sexed bodies—the other was substantive, it designated social, cultural, and psychical attempts to establish meaning. They were two different registers of thinking. The problem was that it was hard to keep the registers apart because they were related but not identical. It was difficult to abstract bodies from the meanings attributed to them, especially since those meanings usually offered the duality evident in nature as their justification. So the invocation of "men" and "women" called up the very symbolization the *paritairistes* wanted to change—the abstraction of anatomical duality became the concrete phenomenon of sexual difference.

However precise their formulations, the proponents of parity were often misheard. Gaspard's careful statement—"Our struggle for parity should be situated in the perspective of an equality of the sexes founded not on the denial of difference, but on a difference that has been overcome, that is, recognized the better to be evacuated from the sites where it produces inequality"—was taken by some of her critics to be an endorsement of the idea that biology determined social behavior ("De la parité" 13). Some feminists charged that the *paritairistes* were betraying decades of attempts to repudiate the connection between nature and gender, and some republicans accused them of trying to substitute American multiculturalism for French universalism. Most disappointingly, some supporters of the movement themselves justified it in essentialist terms. In its conceptualization a form of humanistic egalitarianism, parity became—in the minds of its critics as well as some of its supporters—nothing other than identity politics.[6]

In my book on this topic, I track the slide between the registers of abstraction and embodiment (Scott). My point here is that the kind of philosophical distinction the *paritairistes* offered could be elusive. Although the grassroots demonstrations and petitions they so brilliantly organized effectively translated philosophical argument into practical politics by (among other things) studiously avoiding any call for a separate women's interest and insisting instead on fairness and equality of access to elective office, there were inevitably feminists who rallied to the cause in the name of the essential difference of women. This slippage does not seem to have mattered too much until 1998, when in the context of fierce debates about a domestic partnership law for homosexuals, the philosopher Sylviane Agacinski (wife of the then prime minister Lionel Jospin) published a book that collapsed the two registers into one. In her hands, duality became difference, and the heterosexual couple replaced the abstract individual as the proper unit of citizenship.

I won't rehearse here the story of the campaign for what became the PACS— the pact of civil solidarity. It is a long and fascinating tale that centered around the question of whether or not gay couples could be defined as families, that is, as kinship units having the right to establish lineages by adopting (or in the case of lesbian partnerships, bearing) children. Nor will it be surprising if I simply mention the fact that all parties to the debates made their case in terms of universalism. Everyone agreed that this was not to be a law for gay people only; the stain of "differentialism" had to be avoided at all costs. Thus, the law that eventually passed recognized gay couples as "concubines"—unmarried sexual partners committed to a life in common and sharing a bed. But everyone did *not* agree about whether these concubines could constitute families. To qualify for that status, marriage was required or, if not marriage, heterosexuality. Thus, although the law was supposed to be universal in its applicability, it made a distinction between gay and straight concubines. (Gay couples can neither adopt nor have access to reproductive technologies, although those options exist for unmarried heterosexual couples.) A higher principle was thought to be at stake here, another kind of universalism: the universal law of sexual difference. "The symbolism of gender, of masculine and feminine, exists in all human societies; it is the way culture makes sense of the sexed nature of the living species," wrote the sociologist Irène Théry, a fierce

6. See, for instance, Amar.

opponent of the PACS (178). If human-made law had to abstract people from particular social categories, Théry seemed to be saying, gay couples could be absorbed into the category of "concubines"; but this law could not override the law of sexual difference, which was prepolitical, not biological but cultural, and for that reason fundamental for human self-understanding. As such, it was a difference that could admit of no abstraction for political purposes. The anthropologist Françoise Héritier spoke of sexual difference as *the* primary difference: "It is the fundamental opposition that allows us to think at all. For thinking means, first of all, classifying, and classifying means discriminating, and the fundamental form of discrimination is based on the difference between the sexes"(*La Croix*). According to Héritier, "all our modes of thought and our social organization are founded primarily on the observation of the difference between the sexes. It is impossible to maintain reasonably that this difference can be displaced upon the homosexual couple." Despite Claude Lévi-Strauss's refusal to endorse these arguments (he suggested that the issue was not the enduring facts of culture but a political struggle about establishing natural referents for social organization), what the sociologist Eric Fassin has labeled "the anthropological illusion" persisted.[7] It became the cornerstone not only of attacks on the PACS but also of defenses of the law and its exclusions. Sexual difference, embodied by the heterosexual couple, was taken to be the symbolic mastercode of humankind. "The institution of marriage is itself that of the difference of sex" (Théry, "La fausse"). Sexual difference was an "objective" and "universal" reality (Anatrella).[8] Agacinski repeated these arguments in her book *Politique des sexes*, which was ostensibly a brief for *parité* but in fact a strong argument against homosexual families. She grounded her support for parity in what she took to be the irrefutable facts of nature: not only were there two sexes but theirs was a necessary relationship of heterosexuality, based in procreation. ("Same-sex attraction is accidental, it is a sort of exception that, however frequent, confirms the rule," 108.) This couple was necessarily interdependent—procreation and the survival of the species required it—and it was the basis for systems of kinship and lineage in all human societies. Social sexuality, she insisted, was a reflection of biological sexuality. And so children had the "right" to know that they were the product of a mother and father, a woman and a man. Changes in family law must be limited to those measures that do not deny the rules of natural procreation (even if the child is cloned or conceived in a test tube). This means, above all, that two parents of the same sex is an oxymoron, and the law must not contradict natural fact.

In the past, Agacinski continued, the relationship of the couple was constructed hierarchically; in the family and in politics, women were subordinate to men. But now there was an opportunity to change that, to fully realize the long-held dream of equality between the sexes. Women and men were different, but their roles were complementary; together they embodied the human. And so, she wrote, it was time to bring this notion of complementarity into the political

---

7. For the Lévi-Strauss comment, see Borillo, Fassin, and Iacub 110.

8. See also Borrillo and Lascoumes.

realm—because it was scandalous not to and because modern democracy required it. It was time to share power equally, to acknowledge that the sovereign people came in two sexes, to introduce complementarity into the notion of sovereignty. "Parity must stand for the mixed nature [*la mixité*] of national representation *in its totality* so as to represent the mixed nature of the nation's humanity in *its totality*" (196). This explicitly did not mean dividing the national representation by gender, for it did not assume that men represented men and women, women. Rather (and here she was in agreement with the original *paritairistes*), Agacinski argued that the nation was a fiction realized through political representation and that *parité* was concerned with the reconfiguration of that representation. "The equal representation of women and men must therefore be a pertinent figure for what a 'people' is universally, that is to say, a people made up of men and women" (202). Those who worried that figuring "le peuple" as double (man and woman) would fracture national sovereignty were wrong. *Mixité* was precisely not divisiveness or fracturing, Agacinski insisted, but a kind of unity, the unity exemplified by the reproductive couple merging to conceive a child. Parity would institute *mixité*, a notion borrowed from coeducation and denoting the equality of different, complementary types. "To think of *mixité*," Agacinski promised, "is to accept two versions of man and to represent humanity as a couple" (101).

It was in the translation of anatomical dualism into a heterosexual couple that Agacinski departed from the thinking of the founders of the parity movement. The idea of the couple served to join her two concerns: she could oppose homosexual families and support political equality for women in the name of the *mixité* of the heterosexual couple. The standard for equality became marital complementarity in families as well as in politics. Same-sex institutions—whether parliaments or marriages—were simply not acceptable because they could not realize this equality.

In the context of the PACS debates in 1998–99, and the apparently deep-rooted fear of "unnatural reproduction" that it played upon, Agacinski's vision of *parité* became the dominant one, eclipsing the finely wrought arguments that had marked the early parity campaign. If essentialist possibilities always hovered around those arguments, they did not drive or define them. It was Agacinski's book that brought them out. In her hands, parity became an endorsement of normative heterosexuality as well as of the homophobic impetus that informed the government's version of the PACS. It may well be that her book helped to convince legislators to pass both laws (it was she, and not Gaspard, Servan-Schreiber, and Le Gall, whose writing was repeatedly cited in the National Assembly and Senate debates); it is certain that her version of *parité* became the dominant one in the months and years that followed the book's publication. Intellectuals who should know better—among them, most recently, Jacques Derrida and Elisabeth Roudinesco—have taken Agacinski's views to be representative of the movement, and so they worry that the results of the parity law may be the reification of a certain "maternalism" (57). In a final irony, it may be that Agacinski accomplished exactly the opposite of what the *paritairistes* intended. While they sought a way to make anatomical duality compatible with the discourse of abstraction (gaining the equality of women and men *as individuals*), she moved the conversation to another register—to the discourse of gender or sexual difference. She replaced the abstract individual with the embodied couple. And as a result, she reinscribed sexual difference as incompatible with (antagonistic to) abstract individualism, reaffirming the conception that, since 1789, had been the basis for the exclusion of women from politics.

How are we to understand this story? Where does it fit in the great philosophical debates about universalism that have preoccupied so many of us over the course of the last decade? Is my story a confirmation of Judith Butler's claim that sexual difference cannot ever be separated from its historical and social formulations? Is it the case that no amount of abstraction can extricate it from its symbolizations? Here is Butler:

> Precisely because the transcendental does not and cannot keep its separate place as a more fundamental "level," precisely because sexual difference as a transcendental ground must not only take shape within the horizon of intelligibility but structure and limit that horizon as well, it functions actively and normatively to constrain what will and will not count as an intelligible alternative within culture. Thus, as a transcendental claim, sexual difference should be rigorously opposed by anyone who wants to guard against a theory that would prescribe in advance what kind of sexual arrangements will and will not be permitted in intelligible culture. The inevitable vacillation between the transcendental and social functioning of the term makes its prescriptive function inevitable. (148)

Or should we take Slavoj Zizek's alternative, offered in the name of Jacques Lacan? For Lacan, Zizek writes,

> sexual difference is not a firm set of "static" symbolic oppositions and inclusions/exclusions, but the name of a deadlock, of a trauma, of an open question, of something that resists every attempt at its symbolization. Every translation of sexual difference into a set of symbolic oppositions is doomed to fail, and it is this very "impossibility" that opens up the terrains of the hegemonic struggle for what "sexual difference" will mean. ("Class Struggle" 110)

Aside from the fact that these are not exactly arguments about the same thing, I think the founders of *parité* would suggest—with some deference, because they do not claim to be philosophers—that it is too soon to know what the effects will be of the law passed in June 2000. And, they would add, it is the law after all that will matter in the end. That law requires that women candidates constitute half of electoral lists in municipal and regional elections, in elections for the Corsican Assembly, for the part of the Senate that is elected proportionally, and for the European parliament. The lists for the Senate and the European parliament must alternate candidates by sex; those for municipalities (of more than 3,500 inhabitants), regional assemblies, and the Corsican Assembly must have three women and three men in each group of six. Those lists that do not comply will be disqualified. For the legislative elections, where there are single candidates, not lists, parties that do not respect parity in the designation of candidates must forfeit government financial support for their campaigns (Marques-Pereira 158–160).

The first test of the new law came in the municipal elections of March 2001. The predictions that women would not want to run, were unqualified, or simply had no time, proved wrong. Thousands of women ran for municipal council seats;

many of them had never before participated in politics. In the end, *parité* produced the desired results: women are now 47.5 percent of municipal councilors (in towns with populations over 3,500) as compared to 25.7 percent in 1995. With this change came an undeniable reinvigoration, a sense of new possibility in the political field. True, hopes for a quick revolution were dashed during the legislative elections of 2002, when, in the face of the threat posed by Jean-Marie Le Pen (who had come in second in the first round of the presidential elections), the major parties refused to comply with the law, choosing instead to lose government subsidies. (The feeling that incumbents stood a better chance than newcomers—but also that women couldn't hold off the rightist menace as well as men could—were the reasons given for this decision.) Women are now only about 12 percent of the deputies in the National Assembly, and there is some talk about whether, at this level, parity will ever be enforceable. But it is also clear that the law will not be overturned. Most politicians think it is too popular to touch.

If the law stays in place, it will provide a ready lever for feminist pressure, and it may gradually do the work of resymbolization that the *paritairistes* thought it would. They believed that although law seemed to reflect existing beliefs and practices, it in fact had the power to change them. Eventually the new order, slowly and sometimes imperceptibly brought into being by the law, would be taken to be self-evident and a reflection of the nature of things. Servan-Schreiber put it eloquently in an address to a large gathering of women in 1994.

> I will end by reminding us that the rights of women, all the rights obtained in the course of history, have arisen from struggles that ended with the inscription of these rights in the law. Today, those rights seem to us to be self-evident: we have forgotten, fifty years after the institution of universal suffrage, that for many, many generations, women's right to vote did not seem so self-evident, not at all. I am convinced that one day it will be said that parity was instituted by law precisely because it, too, was "self-evident." ("Pourquoi" 34)

Should Servan-Schreiber be right, then at least in the realm of political representation, women will someday be considered equally susceptible to abstraction, individuals fully capable of representing the nation. At that point, universalism—French universalism—will have achieved its intended end.

To project this ending, of course, requires thinking that French universalism, as mythologized in the 1990s, will remain in place indefinitely, continuing to set the rules of politics. It is not at all clear that this will be the case. The battle for parity, as for the PACS and for the rights of North African "immigrants" to be redesignated as "French," can also be seen as a set of pressures for the democratization (dare I say it, the Americanization) of French political life. And this would involve not the abstraction of difference but its recognition, and thus a more pluralistic vision of the nation. This is not the kind of outcome the founders of the parité movement had in mind. They were firmly committed to universalism and to the idea that abstraction was indeed a key to equality; the possibilities for democracy, they believed, were best realized through some version of abstract individualism. The questions now are whether the implementation of parity will affect the workings of democracy in any way beyond the increased access of women to public office and how that effect will be achieved. That is a question that awaits its answer in the years to come. I end, then, on an inconclusive note, for the story of parité awaits its conclusion not in the judgments of philosophers but in the contingencies of history.

Bibliography

Agacinski, Sylviane. 1998. *Politique des sexes*. Paris: Seuil.

Amar, Micheline, ed. 1999. *Le Piège de la parité: Arguments pour un débat*. Paris: Hachette Littératures.

Anatrella, Tony. 1998. "Une precipitation anxieuse." *Le Monde* 10 (October).

Balibar, Étienne. 1995. "Ambiguous Universality." *differences: A Journal of Feminist Cultural Studies* 7, 1: 48–74.

Birnbaum, Pierre. 2001. *The Idea of France*. New York: Hill and Wang.

Borillo, Daniel, Eric Fassin, and Marcela Iacub. 1999. *Au-delà du PACS: L'expertise familiale à l'épreuve de l'homosexualité*. Paris: PUF.

Borrillo, Daniel, and Pierre Lascoumes. 2002. *Amours égales? Le PACS, les homosexuals, et la gauche*. Paris: La Découverte.

Butler, Judith. 2000. "Competing Universalities." In Butler, Laclau, and Zizek 2000, 136–181.

Butler, Judith, Ernesto Laclau, and Slavoj Zizek. 2000. *Contingency, Hegemony, Universality: Contemporary Dialogues on the Left*. London: Verso.

Collin, Françoise. 1996. *Projets féminists* 4–5 (February): 103.

de Beauvoir, Simone. 1952. *The Second Sex*. New York: Vintage.

Derrida, Jacques, and Elisabeth Roudinesco. 2001. *De quoi demain . . . Dialogue*. Paris: Fayard.

Dialogue des femmes. 1992. Meeting of October 18. Typescript.

Fassin, Eric. 1998. "L'illusion anthropologique: Homosexualité et filiation." *Témoin*, May 12, 43–56.

Favell, Adrian. 2001. *Philosophies of Integration: Immigration and the Idea of Citizenship in France and Britain*. Basingstoke, England: Palgrave.

Gaspard, Françoise. 1990. *Une petite Ville en France*. Paris: Gallimard.

———. 1994. "De la parité: Genèse d'un concept naissance d'un mouvement." *Nouvelles Questions Feministes* 15, 4: 29–44.

———. 1997. "La Parité, pourquoi pas?" *Pouvoirs* 82: 115–125.

Gaspard, Françoise, and Claude Servan-Schreiber. 1984. *La Fin des immigrés*. Paris: Seuil.

Gaspard, Françoise, Claude Servan-Schreiber, and Anne Le Gall. 1992. *Au Pouvoir, citoyennes! Liberté, Égalité, Parité*. Paris: Seuil.

Héritier, Françoise. 1998. "Aucune société n'admet de parenté homosexuelle." Interview with Marianne Gomex. *La Croix*, November.

Jenson, Jean, and Mariette Sineau. 1995. *Mitterrand et les Françaises: Un rendez-vous manqué*. Paris: Presses de la Fondation Nationale des Sciences Politiques.

Kriegel, Blandine. 1999. "Non, la mariée n'est pas trop belle." *Le Monde*, February 17.

Levy, Darlene, Harriet Applewhite, and Mary Johnson, eds. 1980. *Women in Revolutionary Paris, 1789–1795*. Chicago: University of Chicago Press.

Marques-Pereira, Bérengère. 2003. *La citoyenneté politique des femmes*. Paris: Dalloz.

Perrot, Michelle. 1999. "Oui, tenter cette expérience nouvelle." *Le Monde*, February 25.

Rancière, Jacques. 1994. "Post-Democracy, Politics and Philosophy." *Angelaki* 1, 3: 171–178.

———. 2000. "Citoyenneté, culture, et politique." In *Mondialisation, Citoyenneté, et Multiculturalism*, ed. Mikhaël Elbaz and Denise Helly. Québec: Presses de l'Université Laval, 55–68.

Rosanvallon, Pierre. 1998. *Le peuple introuvable: Histoire de la représentation démocratique en France*. Paris: Gaillimard.

Schor, Naomi. 1995. "French Feminism is a Universalism." In *Bad Objects: Essays Popular and Unpopular*. Durham, N.C.: Duke University Press, 3–27.

Scott, Joan W. 2005. *Parité: The French Movement for Sexual Equality in Politics*. Chicago: University of Chicago Press.

Servan-Schreiber, Claude. 1996. "Pourquoi la parité est nécessaire et légitime." *Après-demain* 380–381 (January–February): 33–34.

Sineau, Mariette. 1997. "Les femmes politiques sous la Vième République—à la recherche d'une légitimité électorale." *Pouvoirs* 82: 54–55.

Théry, Irène. 1997. "Le contrat d'union sociale en question." *Esprit* 10: 159–211.

———. 1997. "La fausse bonne idée du contrat union sociale, c'est de tout mélanger." *Le Monde*, November 25.

Tixerant, Jules. 1908. *Le Féminisme à l'époque de 1848 dans l'ordre politique et dans l'ordre économique*. Paris: V. Girard et E. Brière.

Villemot, Émile. 1877. *Le Gaulois*, June 7.

Zizek, Slavoj. 2000. "Class Struggle or Postmodernism?" In Butler, Laclau, and Zizek 2000, 90–135.

———. 2000. *"Da Capo senza Fine."* In Butler, Laclau, and Zizek 2000, 213–262.

3

Battered Women, Intimidation, and the Law

Sandra Bartky

Intimidation, though it pervades our culture, has been neglected in the literature of moral psychology. My essay has two parts: in the first part I shall attempt a preliminary characterization of intimidation, only profiling some of the ways it can be embodied. In the second part, I shall offer an extended example drawn from the literature on battered women that brings out the intimidation of certain institutions and environments on which, ironically, the safety and rights of such aggrieved citizens depends.

Intimidation per se is, in the most general sense, a threat of harm by one or more persons to one or more persons, a warning of bad things to come. If I am a small shopkeeper, visited by the Mafia chieftain's lieutenants who warn of bad things to come unless I pay protection money, and if I am frightened and pay what they ask, then I have been successfully intimidated. But intimidation can go awry. If their threats fail to frighten me or I stand pat, frightened but nevertheless refusing to pay, and if my store is firebombed as a consequence, then I have been harmed without having been intimidated. Of course I may now be intimidated by the firebombing itself, taking their threats seriously in a way I may not have before, or I may be no more intimidated than I was in the beginning. I need not feel intimidated; I might feel outraged and vengeful. Thus, a Sartrian would say that it is up to me, in such a situation, whether to allow myself to feel intimidated or not. In this example, a number of factors are involved in whether the intimidation succeeds: my knowledge of the Mafia's methods, its history of success or failure in my neighborhood, what resources are available to me (do I have an uncle who is a don in another Mafia family?), my temperament. The example makes clear too that the intimidation and

I thank Bob Stone for his inestimable help in the preparation of this essay. I extend my sincerest thanks as well to the editor of this volume and to Iris Marion Young for their insightful and critical comments. As always, I am indebted to Al Vileisis for his conceptual and technical support.

the harm of which it is a warning are logically distinct. Harm and the threat of harm are not the same. Intimidation in this example is a form of harm though not of the greater harm that it threatens. During the attempt at intimidation I may suffer psychological violence, or be thrown against a wall or punched; the Mafiosi may show me a knife or a gun. So intimidation, if it succeeds, is undoubtedly a form of psychological violence, and it may or may not involve some physical violence. But intimidation per se is always a threat of greater harm to come. Hence the peculiar temporality of intimidation. Something is still outstanding: the harm beckons from out of the future. Intimidation is an unpleasant promise of unpleasant things to come.

There are a number of variations on what I have called "intimidation per se." One can be intimidating without intending to; indeed, one can be blissfully unaware that she is found intimidating by other people. The qualities that make someone intimidating to one person may leave another person totally unaffected. Hence, in some cases the feeling of intimidation may be rooted more in the psychology of the one intimidated than in anything the one regarded as intimidating may have said or done. An example may make this clearer. I was dumbfounded to discover that some of our female graduate students, especially the new students, found me intimidating. Had I gone from being intimidated for much of my life to being intimidating with nothing in between? I always try to be friendly and accessible to our graduate students, especially to the new ones, remembering how frightened and ill at ease I had been during my first year of graduate study. I tried to get to the bottom of this. What did these students have to fear from me? What harm did they think I might do them? It turned out that they had read some of my work and admired it and they knew that I was known by many in the still marginalized field of feminist philosophy. They believed that I was the sort of person who could detect their intellectual inadequacies and who would hold them in contempt if they didn't measure up to my intellectual standards. Now I had this power, and since people in our society often use what power they have for self-aggrandizement, these students, not knowing me, didn't know whether I would use my power and reputation to demean them. Of course anyone on the faculty could detect their intellectual inadequacies; they could detect one another's intellectual inadequacies and, if they had looked a bit more closely, they could have detected my own intellectual inadequacies. But being held in contempt by someone you admire is worse than being put down by someone whose opinion you do not especially value. When these students got to know me better, they saw that they had nothing to fear from me, that the harm they imagined I could do them was largely fantasized.

Intimidation, then, rests on power, real or fantasized: its paradigm cases show an asymmetry of power. There are special cases when those lacking ongoing superiority of power over us may intimidate us, but this is usually in an area where we are vulnerable, that is, an area in which the other enjoys greater power. In my second example, the power in question is the power to belittle, to demean, to hold in contempt. Here, the harm anticipated need never come about, indeed, need never have been contemplated. Of course one can intimidate without intending to, through gesture, word choice, body language, tone of voice. Here, the intimidation is more than a reflection of the insecurity of the one intimidated; it is an objective and observable feature of the situation. Of course if a person's behavior consistently has this effect on others, especially vulnerable others, we must suspect the disclaimer, "I never intended it." When our behavior consistently produces certain consequences, it is hard to avoid the suspicion that these consequences are in some way, perhaps unconsciously, intended, or, as a Sartrian might describe the situation, "in bad faith."

It is difficult to distinguish intimidation from fear. Indeed, in some cases, they are indistinguishable. Intimidation, however, has an interpersonal dimension of a sort that fear often lacks. We may say that we fear fires and floods, but it would be odd to say that we are intimidated by them, attributing some human-like agency to them. True, we can say that we are intimidated by the architecture of a place (as I was once by the imperial architecture of Washington, D.C., when I went there to lobby) or the effect on us of some institution, say, the effect of a large university on a first-year student from a small town, but these depend on human agency. And here again, it would be odd to say that I was afraid of the architecture in Washington but not that I found it intimidating. Buildings and institutions are made by human beings, and they reflect their values and intentions. They are thus carriers of communication. Of course a building that I find intimidating, someone else might find noble and uplifting.

Unlike buildings, the most prominent of which can be identified as the work of a particular person, institutions are the result of many decisions made over time by many different persons; thus, the final product is not the projection of a single mind. Nevertheless, the place will have the character it has because various persons made various decisions. Who was it who decreed that the institution be allowed to become the huge place that by its very size intimidates the hapless freshman? Who approved the high ceilings and marble facing that make the place feel to the hapless freshman like a tomb or monument? Who was it who decided that there be no greeter to meet the newcomer and offer him or her a hand of friendship and a tour? Even Wal-Mart has a greeter.

I can be intimidated by an animal—for example, by Skipper, my neighbor's dog, who runs up to me barking angrily as I jog past his house but has never actually bitten me. His behavior recalls that of a neighbor we had when I was a child who would do the equivalent of barking and snarling whenever one of our balls accidentally flew over the fence that separated our yard from hers. While I never actually thought that Mrs. Mueller would bite me, I was afraid that she would tell my mother, in which case some punishment would be visited upon me. If I suddenly encounter a grizzly bear on a back trail while hiking in Glacier National Park, I am likely to feel terror, though a bear expert who can read bear behavior in a way I cannot, might feel neither fear nor intimidation. My own reading of the bear's behavior is not so very different than my reading of Mrs. Mueller's behavior: "I have violated her turf; she is angry; she intends to drive me away or worse." I ascribe to the animal emotions and intentions that I do not ascribe to fire or flood (except by literary extension). We interpret animal behavior in much the same way we interpret the behavior of other human beings.

Summing up, then, intimidation is a threat of harm to come which, when successful, may also constitute a present psychological or physical violence; its paradigm cases involve some form of human agency, typically exercised by those who have superior power over us, real or fantasized. These features will need to be kept in mind in considering the example that follows.

To put this example in context, it will be necessary to consider the prevalence and seriousness of domestic abuse of women. Domestic violence is the leading cause of injury to women between the ages of fifteen and forty-four. According to the FBI, 40 percent of women who are murdered are murdered by a husband or lover. Domestic violence results in almost 40,000 visits to physicians, according to the American Medical Association. It is difficult to determine with precision just how widespread such violence may be, since women are often fearful or ashamed or too intimidated to report it. One well-regarded study puts the number of women battered at least three times in one year at over two million. This study, the National Violence Against Women Survey, lists the following as violent behaviors: "threw something that could hurt; pushed, grabbed, shoved, pulled hair, slapped, hit, kicked, bit, choked, tried to drown, hit with object, beat up, threatened with gun, threatened with knife, used gun, used knife."[1] This study does not count sexual violence, such as marital rape, or profound psychological abuse, which it should. Nor did this study count women in shelters, group homes, households without telephones, women who are victims of stalking, teen-age girls beaten by their boyfriends, or homeless women. It is estimated that half of all homeless women are on the street because they are fleeing the violence in their homes.[2] If these many women had been counted, the number would greatly exceed two million. Indeed, Lifetime, a TV channel for women, puts the number of women who suffer domestic violence closer to four million, a statistic endorsed by the ACLU.[3] In 1996, in Massachusetts alone, there were over 50,000 requests for restraining orders or court orders for protection. A survey of hospital emergency rooms found that over 45 percent of women's injuries were due to domestic violence. And abused women seek medical help for less obvious problems: depression; anxiety; alcoholism. Most women who file for orders of protection fear retaliation; bravely, they request them anyhow. Murders of women are increasing as well; women are most at risk of being murdered when they leave, or threaten to leave, or after they have left an abusive partner.[4] So much for the question: "Why do they stay?" Clearly a very large number of women need the protection of the state and as citizens deserve it.

My extended example presents the experience of a typical battered woman, especially, but not invariably, a woman disadvantaged by race or social class who

---

1. NVAW Survey, as reported in Patricia Tjaden and Nancy Thuennes, "Full Report of the Prevalence and Incidence of Violence Against Women," U.S. Department of Justice, available online at: Ojp.usdoj.gov, November 2000, 28.

2. American Civil Liberties Union, "Fact Sheet on Domestic Violence," available online at: aclu.org/news/2001/domviolence-factsheet, http 1 (July 23, 2002).

3. *"One Every Nine Seconds,"* aired on Lifetime, the Channel for Women, July 30, 2002.

4. The murder of women by their partners doubled in Massachusetts between 1986 and 1996. James Ptacek, *Battered Women in the Courtroom: The Power of Judicial Responses* (Boston: Northeastern University Press, 1999), 66.

applies to the criminal justice system for a restraining order. The restraining order, written initially for no more than ten days—though it can be extended—is intended to keep the batterer away from herself and, often, her children. A restraining order can also set out terms for child visitation, child support, and spousal support. These orders are typically violated by violent partners.

Ever since the women's movement brought family violence to vastly increased public attention, there have been articles on it in magazines and reports on it in newspapers. There are many books on the topic; college curricula have been developed, government-sponsored as well as privately funded academic research has been carried out, laws in regard to domestic violence have been strengthened, new legal instruments have been invented to discourage it—such as antistalking laws, the federal Violence Against Women Act (much of which has been found, unfortunately, unconstitutional), mandatory police reporting of violent incidents in some venues, whether the woman involved presses charges or not. Television "problem" plays and documentaries on mainstream cable channels, such as Lifetime and Women's Entertainment, have treated the subject many times over. In spite of this unprecedented attention, there is no evidence that the level or severity of domestic violence has receded, or that there has been a drop in the number of women murdered by their current or former intimate partners.

So what happens when battered women try to use the mighty edifice of the law to protect themselves—the law, their birthright as citizens? Battered women are of course intimidated by their batterers. But I want to look at the ways that battered women can be intimidated in gross or subtle ways by the court system itself. A battered woman knows that to seek relief is to bring upon herself the possibility of further, escalated violence; this requires courage in and of itself. I shall look at instances of spatial, cultural, and linguistic intimidation, intimidation by lawyers and by judges. Seeking relief from intimidation, the battered woman comes to that branch of the state whose business is to protect all citizens, having arrogated to itself a monopoly on violence for that express purpose.

The court building may overawe the woman who comes to end her living nightmare, especially if it is done in the ponderous style of so many of our public buildings, for example, Richardson Romanesque, with its huge hewn boulders, or neoclassical, with its soaring ceilings and white marble pillars. Even the International Style, whose inventors were trying to produce a truly democratic architecture, is often cold, faceless, and forbidding. The battered woman, who has perhaps come from a bungalow, a tenement, a shelter, or a mobile home, finds herself in a temple. If intimidation involves the anticipation of harm, the harm in question here is the feeling of alienation, of not-belonging, of insignificance, helplessness, and powerlessness.

The judge on his bench is literally elevated above everyone. His or her spatial elevation is the perfect image of the power he or she can wield against anyone in the courtroom. He (or, less often, she) wears black robes that announce his or her authority, clothing that is similar to that worn by priests and rabbis, who are supposed to interpret for us the divine law; this is parallel to the judge's interpretation and determination of human law. "Your Honor" is addressed differently from anyone else in the courtroom. All must rise when he or she enters and again when he or she leaves. The special title, the judicial robes, and the bodily signs of deference from those present are more suggestive of monarchy than democracy. There is a long tradition in political philosophy that justifies monarchical power by reference to supposedly "natural" paternal or patriarchal power. The power of the father, in this tradition, is exercised upon the mother and, of course, upon the child. The harms involved here are many: I would suggest an infantilization of the battered woman and the probably inchoate sense that she has passed from one patriarchal domain, the home, in which she is powerless, to another, the court. I will argue later that a good deal of what goes on in the courtroom recapitulates her experience of abuse.

The abused woman, especially if she is "disadvantaged," may find the culture of the courtroom unintelligible and alien; indeed, it is safe to predict that she will so find it. She may not be able to distinguish one officer of the court from another. Mindy Lazarus-Black reports that casual advice given to women by minor officers of the court is often taken too seriously; sometimes it is positively misleading.[5]

The language of the courtroom too must be alien to the ear of the woman who has come for redress: indeed, legal language is notoriously convoluted, technical, and often intelligible only to specialists. This intimidation-by-language may be interpreted by the battered woman as due to her poor education and lack of social status. Perhaps she assumes that everyone but herself understands what is going on. The harm at work here is an intensification of her shame and of the disempowerment of one who is intensely aware of her lack of education. The language and cultural style of the courtroom may be just as alienating to the abuser too, but, likely as not, he isn't there. She is the one who is trying to use this system to protect herself. If she is tongue-tied in such a situation, can anyone blame her? What if she stutters and falls all over her words? Because she appears unsure of herself, she may unknowingly disqualify herself; the judge may conclude that she is just as unsure of the charges she is bringing against a husband or partner.

Some of the battered woman's intimidation and bewilderment could be relieved by the advice and orientation of a good attorney. We hope that most lawyers are both conscientious and competent and try hard to represent their clients. Some may do their very best when substantial fees are at stake. Now a lawyer is not needed to get an order of protection. But if divorce, child custody, or criminal charges are at stake, the battered woman had better have one. Now many poor clients are represented by public defenders. Public defenders are very often idealists who have rejected the more lucrative domains of law (like corporate law) to represent the poor and downtrodden. But they have enormous caseloads; they are overworked and

5. My colleague, Mindy Lazarus-Black, spent eight months observing what goes on in courts that adjudicate domestic disputes. See especially Mindy Lazarus-Black, "The Rites of Domination: Practice, Process and Structure in Lower Courts," *American Ethnologist* 24, 3 (1997): 628–651. Lazarus-Black's article actually treats of efforts of women to get child support, but her analysis is quite suggestive for my own. Her project, however, is far more complex than mine, for she is interested in the ways courts reproduce and buttress structures of domination (which she calls "the rites of domination") that characterize the wider social contexts of which these courts are a part. She has done considerable research in the Caribbean (in societies that inherit the English common law) as well as the United States.

underpaid. It is often impossible for them to represent any one client with a sufficient degree of detail. Apart from unreasonably heavy caseloads, another important
factor is the lack of support staff. Unlike Perry Mason, they cannot hire an inves-
tigator to do the legwork necessary for the building of a strong case. Hence, there is
no one to ferret out the client's medical records and emergency room admissions,
data that may go back twenty years. If the legal system as a whole were truly interested in helping to get justice for battered women, it would insist that funds be made
available for research into the details of individual cases and that the caseloads of
public defenders be brought into manageable proportions. But as we know, this
hasn't happened. The public defender may be too burdened to properly prepare the
abused woman to testify. So the need to protect her dignity in this palace of power,
race, class, and gender privilege—the desire, deeply entrenched in the culture, "not
to air one's dirty linen in public"—may call forth from the abused woman a greatly
enfeebled testimony. Since 1980, a date I associate with the beginning of the dismantling of what was called the "welfare state" (was it ever that?), funds for legal aid
to the poor have been drastically reduced.[6]

What if an abused woman hires a private attorney? Sometimes one gets lucky,
but unfortunately it is all too true that in this society you get what you pay for, and
the abused woman cannot pay very much. Mindy Lazarus-Black tells of a situation
in which a woman's attorney, hired with money scraped together from her family,
failed to appear. He had simply forgotten. The judge became increasingly impatient, then angrily scolded the woman for not making clear to her attorney when
and where he was to appear, which of course she had done and which, in any case,
is the responsibility of the court. When the lawyer still failed to appear, the judge
continued the case for three weeks, and the woman left without the order of protection she was seeking. So she went home and endured several more weeks of
cruel physical abuse. When she returned to court, she had not been prepared to
testify by her negligent attorney. Overcome with shame, a shame her attorney
should have helped her to surmount, she minimized what had been done to her.
Perhaps she felt ashamed at not having been a good wife; or perhaps she believed
that her own behavior had "caused" the abuse. Perhaps she was afflicted with the
deeper shame of having failed to be the womanly creature who evokes respect and
gentleness from her partner. The upshot of the matter was that the judge threw the
whole case out.[7]

Now even a competent attorney, strongly supportive of his or her battered
client, may exhibit behaviors, recommend strategies, and use language that may be
unintelligible to the client. When one speaks a professional argot all the time so
that it becomes in effect a second nature, it may not occur to the speaker, no
matter how well intentioned, that he or she is not being understood. The client
may well be intimidated by the educational advantage, superior class position, and

---

6. If a battered woman kills her abuser, many judges refuse to admit any evidence, especially
medical evidence, that antedates the crime. Verbal communication from Margaret Byrne, director,
Illinois Clemency Project.

7. Lazarus-Black, "Rites of Domination."

perhaps racial privilege of her attorney, and so she may be ashamed—more so than a more advantaged woman—to admit that she doesn't understand what is being said to her. The courtroom may already have made her feel small, stupid, and powerless; here the situation is repeated in a far lower register.

The women's movement, which first brought domestic violence out of the closet, understood from the beginning that battered women need help, that many women lack self-esteem, feel beaten down and powerless, even before their encounters with police and the courts. So the movement brought battered women's shelters into existence and also established advocacy groups. Now there are trained advocates in some courts who have time, patience, understanding, and good advice to offer their clients. Some advocates are hired by the court; others are funded privately. But, as with shelters, the need for advocates greatly outstrips the supply. A battered woman may not know that such help is available or how to access it; or since advocacy groups tend to be clustered in large cities or in larger college towns, she may not live in a place where such help is available.

Intimidation can also be found in judicial demeanor. Courtroom observers have identified three general types of judicial demeanor: good-natured judges, judges with bureaucratic demeanor, and judges who are patronizing and trivializing.[8] The so-called "good-natured" judges try to put the battered woman at ease. They make eye contact and pay attention, sometimes offer sympathy; they also may inform her of options in her community such as shelters, advocates, counseling, and so on. They easily offer orders of protection. By contrast, judges with bureaucratic demeanor are described as impersonal, passive, and detached. While they are minimally courteous, they frequently seem rushed, bored, or impatient. Indeed, unless attorneys are present, the hearing will only last a few minutes. They ask fewer questions than the good-natured judges, do not routinely explain the restraining orders, and seem less concerned with the enforceability of the orders. They are also less likely to inform the woman of her option to bring criminal charges. Some "bureaucratic" judges neither greet the woman nor indicate that the hearing is over. Some, after very briefly listening to the woman, sign the order and hand it to the clerk without looking at the woman again. This dismissive behavior occurs while the woman, the petitioner, may be feeling fear (of the consequences of her action), even terror, and certainly anxiety, depression, shame, betrayal, and even rage. Nevertheless, one researcher found that 78 percent of the judges she observed fit the bureaucratic description.[9]

Patronizing and trivializing judges often use their power quite arbitrarily. Judges frequently take it upon themselves to lecture parties to a dispute from an assumption of superior morality, often with little grasp of the facts of the case. This may turn the embarrassment the woman has felt throughout to humiliation. He may define the situation as a moral or therapeutic problem, requiring mediation or therapy, not legal action.

8. Ptacek, *Battered Women*, 100.

9. Maureen Mileski, "Courtroom Encounters: An Observational Study of a Lower Criminal Court," *Law and Society Review* 5, 4 (1971): 473–537, as cited in Ptacek, *Battered Women*, 102.

The following story, which concerns the triple intimidation of a battered woman, was told to me by Morgen Alexander-Young, an advocate and counselor for the Chicago Abused Women's Coalition, who saw it happen. The judge, fancying himself a marriage counselor, ordered a very reluctant woman to go into the corridor, "talk it over" with her battering husband, and "make it up." The woman went, but very unwillingly. However, a judge's order is not to be disobeyed. In the corridor, she faced a husband who was enraged because she had pressed charges against him. He shook her (but not hard enough to attract the attention of a bailiff) and (softly) threatened her with severe bodily harm if she did not drop the charges. Thoroughly demoralized, the woman went back in the courtroom to tell the prosecutor that she was thinking of dropping the charges. Now it was the prosecutor's anger (expressed of course sotto voce) that she had to confront. He first tried guilt, telling her how hard he had labored over her case, spending long hours in preparation (dubious). When this didn't work, he turned to threats. He told her that if she dropped the charges, neither he nor anyone in his office would ever take her case again. This was her one chance: if she "blew it," she would never have another. (I suspect that this kind of talk is illegal, but no matter, only Alexander-Young heard it, and there was little she could do. Battered women's advocates need the good will of prosecutors.) In the end, the hapless woman obeyed the man who had intimidated her the most and whose threats were the most real: she went home with her batterer.[10]

A more terrible story involves a Boston woman named Pamela Nigro Dunn, who went to court four times—before the same judge—to seek protection from her violent husband. One of the affidavits she submitted in support of her request for an order of protection tells part of her story: "I'm a prisoner in my own apartment. He locks me in and takes the phone cord out. He choked me and threatened to kill me if I try to leave. He made me work only where he works . . . my life is in danger so long as he is around . . ."[11]

Now all court hearings in Massachusetts are tape-recorded. A *Boston Globe* reporter who later listened to the tapes cites the judge in the case: "You want to gnaw on her and she on you, fine, but let's not do it at taxpayers' expense." The court recordings of Pamela Dunn's appearances reveal the judge's dismissal of her

10. Where else might she have gone? There are battered women's shelters, but not enough places for all who need them. Besides, the amount of time one can spend in a shelter is limited. The relatives of poor women are themselves often living in such cramped quarters that they cannot house a battered woman and her children, at least not for any length of time. If the woman has no very marketable skills and no money, taking her in means feeding her too. Welfare "reform" means that a woman who has exhausted her two years must take a job, most likely a minimum wage job. It is well known that minimum wage will not bring an individual, much less a family, above the poverty line. Hence she may have to take a second job. What will the effect of this be on the quality and quantity of her mothering and on her children? The rock-bottom rents in a city like Chicago for apartments big enough to house a family of three would come to (at least) $600 a month. In order to rent, one must put down the first month's rent plus a security deposit equal to a month's rent. What poor woman with poor relatives will have $1,200 to rent an apartment?

11. Cited in "Battered Justice," *Washington Monthly*, May 1987, 83. See Ptacek, *Battered Women*, 193.

fears, his insistence that she did not need the police protection for which she had asked, and his chastisement of her for "doing a terrible disservice to the taxpayers" by taking up the court's time when it "has a lot more serious matters to contend with."[12] In August 1986, Pamela Dunn was strangled, stabbed, and shot dead by her husband. She was found face down in a pool of water at the town dump. Pamela Dunn was twenty-two years old and five months pregnant. Even though there was a great outcry in Boston about this incident and a good deal of feminist organizing to put battered women's advocates in the courts, the Massachusetts Supreme Judicial Court offered only a "private" reprimand to the judge in question, whose behavior, in effect, put Pamela Dunn directly in the path of her murderous partner.

The Pamela Dunn case is certainly an extreme one; nevertheless, the afore-mentioned statistical information indicates that the level of domestic violence is not decreasing. The historian Linda Gordon has characterized battering as a social dynamic in which institutions are directly implicated. Individual women are assaulted by individual men, but the ability of so many men to repeatedly assault, terrorize, and control so many women draws on institutional collusion.[13] I have in this essay examined the institutional collusion of the courts with some special attention to the frequent (but not inevitable) ways women can be intimidated in court. What we so often see is a somewhat uncanny resemblance between the violent home, the larger community that ignores this violence, and the courtroom. The invisibility of domestic violence is echoed in the bureaucratic demeanor of judges who never make eye contact with the women who have come to them for help. The decision to "go public" with a private shame, a decision that may escalate the violence she has suffered, ought to earn the battered woman at least some recognition from the judiciary. But unfortunately, "good-natured" judges are in the minority. Lazarus-Black tells us that women are very often spoken about as if they were inanimate objects or children. They are made invisible as adult individuals to those who are determining their fate. This refusal of recognition, together with the architectural, cultural, and linguistic intimidation I have described, may create a sense of alienation and isolation that recapitulates the isolation suffered by the battered woman. Indeed, isolation is a central tactic of control by abusive partners ("He locks me in and takes the phone cord out"), who often isolate a woman from her family and friends and forbid her to work outside the home or to go to school. And the improper moral or therapeutic stance taken by some judges may only confirm the woman's suspicion that she has brought all this on herself, that she has somehow failed to be a good wife, something the batterer too would have her believe. (Judge: "She [wants to gnaw] on you.")

To seek an order of protection requires courage and may well involve risk to the woman. It is still only a piece of paper that may be no more effective in

---

12. Eileen McNamara, "Judge Criticized After Woman's Death," *Boston Globe*, September 21, 1986.

13. Linda Gordon, *Heroes of Their Own Lives: The Politics and History of Family Violence* (New York: Viking, 1988), 285.

stopping the battering than the batterer's oft-repeated repentance and promises to reform.

What is the situation in regard to the enforcement of orders of protection such that many women have suffered embarrassment, intimidation, and perhaps fear in order to obtain them? The most egregious absence in the legal system is the lack of enforcement of its own rulings. It is relatively easy to obtain an order of protection. These orders can be issued in civil or criminal courts. If an order of protection is issued in a criminal court, the man who violates it can be arrested. But how often does this happen? What is the ratio of men in jail for violating an order of protection, indeed, for domestic battery, to those serving time for minor drug offenses? The number of police calls in Chicago for domestic abuse far exceeds calls for all other crimes. Anecdotal evidence suggests that the commitment to enforcement on the part of many police officers is lackadaisical at best. Where police are called routinely to the same address and nothing in the battering relationship seems to change, they ignore such calls. (Illinois does not have legislation that requires an arrest when the officer believes that violence has been done, whether the victim presses charges or not. One senses the frustration of police when battered women refuse to press charges; nevertheless, the murder of wives and partners is typically the climax of a long series of violent episodes that was not substantially interrupted and that led to no effective sanctions against the batterer. If one agrees with the civil verdict in the trial for damages against O. J. Simpson, the relationship of Nicole Brown Simpson and O. J. Simpson was typical of such a pattern. The woman is most at risk of murderous violence when she attempts to terminate the relationship or when she has succeeded, through divorce or legal separation, in actually leaving it.

More study is needed of the links between intimidation by the legal system and its ineffectiveness. It may be the case that what a battered woman has heard from others about such intimidation keeps her out of court entirely. It may be the case that a single encounter with the court system has been so painful that she doesn't go back, even though orders of protection typically need to be reissued.[14] Or perhaps the lack of recognition she receives from bureaucratic or demeaning judges lowers her already low morale, or finally exhausts her virtually depleted stock of self-esteem. In these ways, judicial intimidation may well collude in her victimization.

Afterword

The phenomenon of judicial intimidation also raises fundamental questions for political and moral philosophy, which we cannot pursue here, regarding the status of women who, suffering domestic intimidation, go on to suffer it again in courts,

---

14. I do not mean to suggest that no woman has ever used the court system to end her abuse. As Lazarus-Black has noted, courts are sites of contestation even while they reproduce the social hierarchies of the larger society. Lazarus-Black, "Rites of Domination," 629.

often to the peril of their very lives. I raise these issues in a subjunctive mode, without endorsing the legitimacy either of what I take to be the dominant social contract model of the state or the behavior of those who feel excluded from and by it. However, I consider these issues to be a stark challenge to our social order.

Every social contract theory of the state makes plain that one of the things bona fide citizens may expect from their state is protection from unwarranted physical injury at the hands of strangers or other citizens. Citizens are those who have given up their prerogative of personal violence in the "state of nature" in order to enjoy such protection within the state. Perhaps we ought to question whether women in sustained situations of battery are bona fide citizens of the state at all. Unprotected, have they, in effect, been returned to the state of nature? After exhausting all remedies, if a battered woman decides to kill her batterer—a woman who fears for her life and safety, a woman who may be suffering from serious internal injuries as a result of prolonged beatings, a woman whose children may have suffered physical violence, certainly grave psychological violence, in short, a woman whose life has been made a living hell—if such a woman kills her abuser, it seems reasonable to ask whether it is fair to subject her to the same legal system that has so grievously failed her.

II

Practices of Citizenship in Culture and Civil Society

4

Women's Community Activism and the Rejection of "Politics"

Some Dilemmas of Popular Democratic Movements

Martha Ackelsberg

Recent studies of gender and citizenship have raised two sets of questions—one practical, one theoretical—that I explore in this essay. The practical concerns the claim, common among grassroots activists both in the United States and elsewhere, that their activities are "not political." In some ways, of course, we might find this perfectly understandable: after a brief respite in the 1950s–1960s from a rather longstanding bad "rep," politics in the United States has again become identified with (often even treated as a synonym for) corruption and sleaze, a set of activities in which supposedly decent people should not want to be engaged. This is a perspective that was certainly common in the United States toward the end of the nineteenth century, and has long been familiar in much of Latin America, Africa, and eastern Europe. Nevertheless, while this tendency to distance oneself from politics may be all too understandable, it is particularly problematic and disturbing at a time when so much of our national (and international) politics seems aimed at a depoliticization of the populace: increasingly, for example, whether with respect to welfare policy, corporate oversight, or national security, we are told that matters are best left to experts. So one of my concerns here has to do with the implications of this "rejection of the political" for democratic politics.

I am grateful to Rachel Roth and Joan Tronto for helpful comments and suggestions in response to an earlier draft, comments that I particularly appreciated since I was unable to attend the conference for which this essay was originally written. I also want to thank Amrita Basu, Mary Katzenstein, Eileen McDonagh, Wendy Mink, and Molly Shanley for careful readings and a wonderful conversation; and the participants in the feminist theory workshop at the March 2004 meetings of the Western Political Science Association for helping me think through both this essay and the larger project of which it forms a part, tentatively entitled *Making Democracy Work: (Re)Conceiving Politics Through the Lens of Women's Activism*.

The second, theoretical, starting point is the recent growth of feminist writing about citizenship—much of it in response to Jurgen Habermas's call for the reclaiming of a "public sphere." Habermas's notions have proved particularly fertile, and generated a burgeoning literature—some of the main participants in which are contributors to this volume—including extensive feminist discussions about what Nancy Fraser has referred to as "subaltern counterpublics." While Habermas's (and his critical followers') calls for a reinvigorated, gender- and class-neutral, public sphere are certainly compelling, I often find myself wondering just how such ideals might be put into practice. How do we assure that some newly formulated public sphere will not simply recreate relationships of exclusion, power, and domination in new guise? Further, what would it take to *sustain* subaltern counterpublics?

These two sets of questions came together for me in thinking about an essay by the Brazilian feminist scholar Evelina Dagnino, who, in her introduction to a recent anthology on new social movements in Latin America, noted that most of those movements focused on broadening (or creating) a more democratic political arena and treated "the politico-cultural understanding of differences" as a necessary prerequisite to the creation of democracy—that is, to the building of a political community that can incorporate those (social, cultural, economic) differences in a more egalitarian fashion.[1] Feminist theoretical conversations in the United States, of course, have focused on "difference" for some years now; but it has all too rarely been the case that our theoretical conversations have had much to do with practical political activism. I have long believed, however, that the practical knowledge activists have gained through working in their communities might be fruitfully brought into more direct engagement with feminist/democratic theorists and theories.

This essay represents an effort at such a confrontation of practice with theory. I want to set out some questions about the meanings of democracy, politics, and participation in our current context, and then hold them up against the activities of the National Congress of Neighborhood Women, an organization founded in Brooklyn, N.Y., in 1974.[2] I want, that is, to begin the process of exploring what the NCNW might be able to teach us about some of the perquisites of democratic civic engagement.

---

1. "Culture, Citizenship, and Democracy: Changing Discourses and Practices of the Latin American Left," in *Cultures of Politics, Politics of Cultures: Re-Visioning Latin American Social Movements*, ed. Sonia E. Alvarez, Evelina Dagnino, and Arturo Escobar (Boulder, Colo.: Westview Press, 1998), p. 45. Catherine Holland issues a similar call for attention to these issues and makes a fascinating case for the linkages between citizenship and difference in U.S. political theory and practice in *The Body Politic: Foundings, Citizenship, and Difference in the American Political Imagination* (New York: Routledge, 2001). Arlene Saxonhouse locates the problem in the Greek origins of political science in *Fear of Diversity: The Birth of Political Science in Ancient Greek Thought* (Chicago: University of Chicago Press, 1992).

2. The NCNW has since become not only a national, but an international, organization, forming part of Grassroots Organizations Operating Together in Sisterhood (GROOTS), which was founded with NCNW help after the Nairobi conference in 1985.

Citizenship as a Site of Exclusion or of Inclusion?
Habermas and His Feminist Critics

Increasing numbers of critics in recent years have pointed to the fact that exclusions and divisions are central to the logic of liberal democratic theory and practice. Scholars ranging from Carole Pateman to Judith Shklar, and from Gwendolyn Mink to Charles Mills, have noted that citizenship, as it exists in many Western democracies, has been constructed through a variety of exclusions, based on gender, race, class, sexuality, migration status, and so on.[3] A great deal of feminist scholarship, of course, has focused on addressing one important context of exclusion: the so-called public-private split. Critics have pointed out that, while the public realm is presented as one where free and equal citizens engage together in striving for some common good, that arena depends on a private/domestic realm that is characterized by relationships of *in*equality and dependence, and is focused on meeting life's necessities. Furthermore, that so-called private realm tends to be defined in profoundly gendered, classed, and racialized ways: peopled by women, slaves, laborers, "barbarians," and others who fail to meet the criteria of rationality deemed necessary for citizenship. In the United States during the nineteenth century and well into the twentieth, such a formulation resulted in an ambiguous citizenship status for all those who were not self-supporting males: including poor free white men, slaves, free blacks in the post-Emancipation/pre–Civil Rights era, and women.[4] And, further, the split meant that the domain of politics (in the sense of public business) was limited to activities that took place only in that public arena. Consequently, inequalities, injustices, and various forms of domination that characterized the household and (for many years) workplaces were deemed private matters, beyond the appropriate domain of politics—or legal regulation. Equally significantly, activities undertaken to *challenge* those categories (or to broaden the domain of politics) could be ignored, or dismissed as disorderly, unruly, or otherwise inappropriate.

A central focus of feminist scholarly work in political theory has been to call into question this dichotomy and to highlight its relationship to notions of independence and dependence. Feminists have pointed out the gendered nature of both public and private domains, and the interdependence of each on the other. In

3. Gwendolyn Mink, *The Wages of Motherhood* (Ithaca, N.Y.: Cornell University Press, 1995); Judith Shklar, *American Citizenship: The Quest for Inclusion* (Cambridge: Harvard University Press, 1991); Shane Phelan, *Sexual Strangers* (Philadelphia: Temple University Press, 2001); Charles Mills, *The Racial Contract* (Ithaca, N.Y.: Cornell University Press, 1997); Ruth Lister, *Citizenship: Feminist Perspectives*, 2nd ed. (New York: New York University Press, 2003), especially chap. 2. I have explored these issues in "Embracing Ambiguities: Exclusivity, Inclusivity, Activism and Citizenship," paper prepared for delivery at the annual meeting of the American Political Science Association, Boston, September 1–4, 1998.

4. Barbara Nelson, "Women's Poverty and Women's Citizenship," *Signs* 10 (1984): 209–231; Martha Ackelsberg, "Citizenship," in *Reader's Companion to U.S. Women's History*, ed. Wilma Mankiller, Gwendolyn Mink, Marysa Navarro, Barbara Smith, and Gloria Steinem (Boston: Houghton Mifflin, 1998): 99–100; and Martha Ackelsberg, "Dependency or Mutuality: A Feminist Perspective on Dilemmas of Welfare Policy," *Rethinking Marxism* 7, 2 (1994): 73–86.

addition, they have noted the mystifications inherent in any concept of "independence," which had been taken to be the prime characteristic of actors in that "public" domain.[5] The focus on supposedly independent actors in a public/political arena, however, obscures the fact that no one is truly independent; what appears as the independence of some is premised on the dependence of others (and vice versa). Further, as Carole Pateman has argued, the mythical social contract that grounds U.S. political self-understanding obscures its *sexual* dimensions: the "independent" role is a male one, defined, at least in part, by contrast to the situation of the women and children dependent on the male.[6] These perspectives on what defines the domain of the political have far-ranging consequences. They can affect what problems are thought to merit public/political attention, what actions are considered relevant—even legitimate—political behavior, and who will participate with what effects in the larger arena of politics. Conversely, they can result in a tendency to ignore, devalue, or define as outside the appropriate domain of politics those activities that challenge the boundaries of public and private. Finally, to the degree that such frameworks successfully exclude people or issues from the agenda of politics, they can act powerfully to limit effective participation in the formal political realm.

In response to some of the problematic ways citizenship has been defined and regulated, many scholars have turned to the work of Jurgen Habermas—in particular to his notion of a discursive "public sphere"—in the hope that it could offer a framework for constructing a more egalitarian, democratic, inclusive, public space. Building on the claim that citizenship offers a powerful language for inclusionary political movements,[7] these scholars argue that the public sphere can be reclaimed

5. In addition to the works cited earlier, see Nancy Hirschmann, "Revisioning Freedom: Relationship, Context, and the Politics of Empowerment," pp. 51–74, Zillah Eisenstein, "Equalizing Privacy and Specifying Equality," pp. 181–192, and Martha Ackelsberg and Mary Lyndon Shanley, "Privacy, Publicity, and Power: A Feminist Rethinking of the Public/Private Split," pp. 213–233, all in *Revisioning the Political: Feminist Reconstructions of Traditional Concepts in Western Political Theory*, ed. Nancy Hirschmann and Christine DiStefano (Boulder, Colo.: Westview Press, 1996); Carole Pateman, "Feminist Critiques of the Public/Private Dichotomy," in *The Disorder of Women* (Stanford: Stanford University Press, 1989); Anne Phillips, *Engendering Democracy* (University Park: Pennsylvania State University Press, 1991); and Patricia Boland, *Privacy and the Politics of Intimate Life* (Ithaca, N.Y.: Cornell University Press, 1996). For a consideration of some of these issues in the context of debates about care and justice, see Julie White, *Democracy, Justice, and the Welfare State* (University Park: Pennsylvania State University Press, 2000); Joan Tronto, *Moral Boundaries: A Political Argument for an Ethic of Care* (New York: Routledge, 1993); and Selma Sevenhuijsen, *Citizenship and the Ethics of Care: Feminist Considerations on Justice, Morality, and Politics* (New York: Routledge, 1998).

6. Carole Pateman, *The Sexual Contract* (Stanford: Stanford University Press, 1988), p. 135.

7. The classic argument here is, of course, that by T. H. Marshall, "Citizenship and Social Class," in *Citizenship and Social Class and Other Essays* (Cambridge, England: Cambridge University Press, 1950). For contemporary arguments that draw on his initial insight see, for example, Sylvia Walby, "Is Citizenship Gendered?" *Sociology* 28, 2 (May 1994): 379–395; Ruth Lister, "Dialectics of Feminist Citizenship," *Hypatia* 12, 4 (fall 1997): 6–26; Lister, *Citizenship*; Nancy Fraser, "Rethinking the Public Sphere: A Contribution to the Critique of Actually Existing Democracy," in *Habermas and the Public Sphere*, ed. Craig Calhoun (Cambridge: MIT Press, 1992); Anne Phillips, "Dealing with Difference: A Politics of Ideas, or a Politics of Presence?" in *Democracy and Difference: Contesting the Boundaries of the Political*, ed. Seyla Benhabib (Princeton: Princeton University Press, 1996), pp. 139–152.

from its exclusivist uses, and reconstructed as a site for enacting broad understandings of politics and citizenship, which incorporate a full range of our diverse population.[8] Although the promises of democracy have not been fulfilled even in many supposedly democratic societies, the vision is still a compelling one. As Anne Phillips suggests, "rejecting both the false harmony that stamps out difference and the equally false essentialism that defines people through some single, authentic, identity, many look to a democracy that maximizes citizen participation and requires us to engage and contest with one another."[9]

Rethinking Democracy and the Public Sphere from a Feminist Perspective

Neither this scholarly literature nor contemporary public policy debates about the decline of civil society, however, provide us with very good models for *how* to reconceive citizenship along these lines. Indeed, there often seems to be very little relationship between public policy debates about how to increase public interest in, and/or engagement with, political institutions and the scholarly literature that highlights the ambiguities and complexities of both the theory and the practice of citizenship in the United States.[10]

8. Seyla Benhabib, "Models of Public Space: Hannah Arendt, the Liberal Tradition, and Juergen Habermas," in Calhoun, *Habermas and the Public Sphere*. See also Benjamin R. Barber, *Strong Democracy: Participatory Politics for a New Age* (Berkeley: University of California Press, 1984), and *A Place for Us: How to Make Society Civil and Democracy Strong* (New York: Hill and Wang, 1998); Harry C. Boyte, "Beyond Deliberation: Citizenship as Public Work," *Good Society* 5, 2 (1995): 15–19; Boyte and Nancy N. Kari, *Building America: The Democratic Promise of Public Work* (Philadelphia: Temple University Press, 1996); Philip Green, *Equality and Democracy* (New York: New Press, 1998); and Iris Young, *Justice and the Politics of Difference* (Princeton: Princeton University Press, 1990), and *Inclusion and Democracy* (New York: Oxford University Press, 2000). Joe Soss explores the ways public policies construct both clients and citizens and the implications of that dichotomization for our democracy in "Making Clients and Citizens: Welfare Policy as a Source of Status, Belief, and Action," in *Deserving and Entitled: Social Constructions and Public Policy*, ed. Anne Schneider and Helen Ingram (Albany: State University of New York Press, 2005). See also Soss, *Unwanted Claims: Politics, Participation and the U.S. Welfare System* (Ann Arbor: University of Michigan Press, 2000); Nelson, "Women's Poverty and Women's Citizenship"; Theda Skocpol, *Diminished Democracy: From Membership to Management in American Civic Life* (Norman: University of Oklahoma Press, 2003); and Matthew Crenson and Benjamin Ginsburg, *Downsizing Democracy: How America Sidelined Its Citizens and Privatized Its Public* (Baltimore: Johns Hopkins University Press, 2004).

9. Phillips, "Dealing with Difference: A Politics of Ideas, or a Politics of Presence?" in Benhabib, *Democracy and Difference*, p. 142. See also Young, *Inclusion and Democracy*; Catherine Holland, *Body Politic*; and Marla Brettschneider, *Democratic Theorizing from the Margins* (Philadelphia: Temple University Press, 2002).

10. Philip Green's *Equality and Democracy* (New York: New Press, 1998), Young, *Inclusion and Democracy*, and Crenson and Ginsberg, *Downsizing Democracy* are among the important exceptions. For a recent study exploring specific factors affecting participation at the community level, especially that of women, see Amy Caiazza, "Women's Community Involvement: The Effects of Money, Safety, Parenthood, and Friends," publication no. C346 (Washington, D.C.: Institute for Women's Policy Research, September 2001).

Nevertheless, some such work is being done, particularly by feminist theorists. Seyla Benhabib, for example, while recognizing that the notion of a public sphere presupposes a distinction between the public and the private that is certainly problematic, nevertheless argues that we need a "critical model of public space and public discourse" that can enable us to imagine (and people to strive for) "collective democratic empowerment over" needs, as opposed to a more distant "bureaucratic administration of" them.[11] Julie White offers a "democratic practice of care" as a way to begin constructing an inclusive arena of public deliberation—particularly over needs. Thus, she proposes *politicizing* what is often treated as *outside* politics (i.e. needs) at the same time that she argues for meaningful incorporation of diverse groups into deliberations about policies.[12] Mary Ryan suggests that "from the first the American public sphere was constructed in the shadow of both gender restrictions and an emerging private sector of social life." Nevertheless, she argues, politics in the United States has been democratized—precisely by groups fighting their way in from the margins. Recognition of this paradox points to the need to modify the idea of *a* public sphere, and to move toward a more plural and decentered vision of *multiple* arenas for participation. Further, dissidents need to be aware that actions calling for incorporation and inclusion are often labeled unruly, outrageous, or disorderly.[13]

Nancy Fraser notes that, even in highly stratified societies—where talk of a "discursive arena" can easily mask relations of domination and subordination—discussions of politics that focus on the public sphere can be valuable in pointing to the need for "subaltern counterpublics," "parallel discursive arenas where members of subordinated social groups invent and circulate counterdiscourses to formulate oppositional interpretations of their identities, interests, and needs."[14] Iris Young argues that civil society "enables the emergence of public spheres in which *differentiated social sectors* express their experience and formulate their opinions . . . the public sphere enables citizens to expose injustice in state and economic power and make the exercise of power more accountable."[15] Significantly, such visions tend to

11. "Models of Public Space," pp. 93–94. There are significant similarities here with the work of James Morone, *The Democratic Wish: Popular Participation and the Limits of American Government* (New York: Basic Books, 1990).

12. See White, *Democracy, Justice, and the Welfare State*, especially chaps. 6 and 7. I return to this constellation of factors in greater detail hereafter.

13. Ryan, "Gender and Public Access," in Calhoun, *Habermas and the Public Sphere*, pp. 267, 283–284; see also Holloway Sparks, "Dissident Citizenship," *Hypatia* 12, 4 (1997): 74–110; Ruth Lister, "Dialectics of Citizenship," *Hypatia* 12, 4 (1997): 6–26, especially pp. 8–9; Jacquelyn Dowd Hall, "Disorderly Women: Gender and Labor Militancy in the Appalachian South," *Journal of American History* 73 (1986): 354–382; Michael Lipsky, "Protest as a Political Resource," *American Political Science Review* 62, 4(1968): 1144–1158; and Frances Fox Piven and Richard A. Cloward, *Poor People's Movements: How They Succeed, Why They Fail* (New York: Pantheon, 1977).

14. Fraser, "Rethinking the Public Sphere: A Contribution to the Critique of Actually Existing Democracy," in Calhoun, *Habermas and the Public Sphere*, pp. 119, 124.

15. Young, *Inclusion and Democracy*, p. 155 (emphasis mine). See also Barber, *A Place for Us*; Harry Boyte, "Beyond Deliberation"; Boyte and Kari, *Building America*; and Boyte, *The Backyard Revolution* (Philadelphia: Temple University Press, 1980).

emphasize the importance of bringing people together in a *reconstructed* public sphere that will incorporate existing differences that, while currently marking lines of differential power and privilege, might still allow people to engage more or less equally both in determining its agenda and participating in its deliberations. Indeed, as Julie White notes, it may be that *only* in a context where differences are acknowledged and named rather than ignored is there a possibility of meaningful democratic political engagement.[16] Or, as Shane Phelan has put it, "we can only come to community by negotiating about what we will have in common, what we will share, and how we will share it."[17]

Of course, these formulations raise further questions: What is necessary to sustain "subaltern counterpublics"? What would it mean to welcome new groups into the public arena in significant ways? What are the criteria for assuring that discussions in which we "negotiate about what we will have in common, what we will share, and how we will share it" do not, themselves, perpetuate the relationships of exclusion, of power and domination, that feminists and other social critics have worked so hard to uncover and contest? What would it mean to have a truly *diverse* participating citizenry? How would we learn to engage *with* our differences, rather than trying to deny them or insist that they do—or ought—not make any difference? These remain the critical questions for a contemporary politics of inclusion and resistance. Processes of imagining a democratic public space and of engaging people in popular actions to broaden understandings both of citizenship and of the appropriate "reach" of political life are, in fact, the "stuff" of politics. The discourses of citizenship, and of a public sphere, while on the one hand constituted by exclusions, have on the other provided a space to *contest* those same exclusions. Both "citizenship" and "democracy" are powerfully evocative terms. Nevertheless, they remain deeply problematic. How do we reclaim and revive them without reinscribing the exclusions on which they have been based? Or, to phrase it somewhat melodramatically, how do we achieve broad-based participation by a truly diverse citizen body—and survive it?

The Rejection of "Politics" and the Politics of Depoliticization

The insistence on the part of many grassroots activists that their activities are "not political" is, as I suggested earlier, hardly unique to the current (post-Watergate, post-Enron, post 9/11) U.S. context. A variety of studies of such activists—focusing

16. See White, *Democracy, Justice, and the Welfare State*, pp. 152, 169; also Holland, *Body Politic*; Crenson and Ginsberg, *Downsizing Democracy*. Sheldon Wolin explored some of the earliest stages in the constriction of "the public" in the United States in "The People's Two Bodies," *democracy* 1,1 (January 1981): 9–24.

17. Phelan, "All the Comforts of Home: The Genealogy of Community," in *Revisioning the Political: Feminist Reconstructions of Traditional Concepts in Western Political Theory*, ed. Nancy Hirschmann and Christine DiStefano (Boulder, Colo.: Westview Press, 1996), p. 248. See also Susan Bickford, "Anti-Anti-Identity Politics: Feminism, Democracy, and the Complexities of Citizenship," *Hypatia* 12, 4 (fall 1997): 124.

on groups as diverse as anti–toxic waste protestors in rural North Carolina, ethnic-cultural identity movements in Latin America, antipoverty activists in New York and Philadelphia, and even some antiapartheid activists in South Africa—have pointed out that participants were hesitant to identify themselves as "political." As Nancy Naples noted in her work on community-based "activist mothers" during the War on Poverty, most of them made a separation between what they described as their "community work" and what they identified as "politics."[18] The women saw community work as simply an expression of their roles as wives and mothers, "a logical extension of their desire to improve the lives of their families and neighbors," what Temma Kaplan had earlier termed "female consciousness."[19]

In Temma Kaplan's recent work on women in a variety of grassroots movements, as well as in numerous case studies of United States–based local community activism, and in studies of new social movements in Latin America, we find similar rejections of "politics."[20] Furthermore, we see patterns of mobilization and consciousness that seem to link this "refusal of politics" to a distinction similar to that Nancy Fraser describes as a "politics of needs" as opposed to a "politics of rights."[21] In his study of women's participation in urban movements in Mexico City, for example, Miguel Díaz-Barriga notes that many of the activists deny that they are engaging in politics, which they seem to identify with "the violent and corrupt public sphere of male politics." Rather, their activism seems to depend on their understanding of it as separate from more traditional forms of political activity, and as rooted in "necesidad." In doing so, he argues, they believe themselves to be creating a "borderland region between the domestic and public spheres."[22]

This splitting between an activism based on needs and what participants understand to be "politics" represents a theme common to many of these movements. Yet Naples, Kaplan, Molyneux, Díaz Barriga, and others have all argued that, although many activists may initially be drawn out of their households by relatively conventional understandings of their roles as women, these activities often bring

18. See Naples, *Grassroots Warriors: Activist Mothering, Community Work, and the War on Poverty* (New York: Routledge, 1998). I am drawing here on my summary of Naples's discussion in "(Re)-Conceiving Politics? Women's Activism and Democracy in a Time of Retrenchment," *Feminist Studies* 27, 1 (spring 2001): 395–397.

19. Kaplan, "Female Consciousness and Collective Action: The Case of Barcelona, 1910–1918," *Signs* 7 (spring 1982): 545–566. Kaplan takes up the idea again in *Crazy for Democracy: Women in Grassroots Movements* (New York: Routledge, 1997); and in *Taking Back the Streets: Women, Youth, and Direct Democracy* (Berkeley: University of California Press, 2004); see also Maxine Molyneux, "Mobilization Without Emancipation? Women's Interests, the State, and Revolution in Nicaragua," *Feminist Studies* 11 (summer 1985): 227254.

20. Sometimes, of course, that rejection is a self-consciously strategic move, as Temma Kaplan makes clear in her treatment of El Poder Femenino and other right-wing groups that mobilized women against the government of Salvador Allende. She notes that "these groups insist that they are not challenging the prevailing gender system" and are not "political" but simply trying to meet the needs of their families. Nevertheless, through their actions they undermined the legitimacy of the regime and paved the road for the military coup. On the complexities of the women's activities see especially pp. 46–47, 58, 60, 65–68.

21. I am drawing here on my review essay "(Re)Conceiving Politics," especially p. 413.

22. Miguel Díaz Barriga, "Beyond the Domestic and the Public: *Colonas* Participation in Urban Movements in Mexico City," in Alvarez, Dagnino, and Escobar, *Cultures of Politics*, p. 260.

them into confrontation with political authorities, or with men and women of other communities, awakening them to a consciousness of inequality, motivating them to further struggles, and, ultimately, politicizing them.[23] Nevertheless, if the protestors, themselves, reject a construction of their actions as "political," then to what extent *are* they being politicized? How likely are they to translate (or transfer) the knowledge they have gained in their struggles around necessities in their communities to any broader political context? How likely are they to change their understandings of themselves in relation to the larger community? How effective is such activism in creating the building blocks of more inclusive democratic practices? More to the point: under what circumstances do people shift from an *essentialized* understanding of needs as *outside* the realm of politics to a *politicized* view of them as the "stuff" of politics?[24]

It is in such a context that we can see the potentially critical role of the language of democracy. What is needed, here, is a reshaping not just of the ways the *academy* defines politics and activism[25] but also of what constitutes the *public's* understanding of these terms. So, for example, Iris Young defines "civil society" as a kind of activity identified with the "associational life world" rather than with *either* the state *or* the economy.[26] She goes on to describe three levels of associative activity within civil society: private association, civic association, and political association. Political associations are those that "self-consciously focus ... on claims about what the social collective ought to do.... Political activity is any activity whose aim is to *politicize* social or economic life ... to raise questions about how society should be organized.[27] Thus, she argues, contrary to much commonly held belief, to be "political" is not necessarily to engage in the formal electoral/political system, that is, to engage with the state; but it *is* to struggle, together with others, to influence what will be on the *agenda* of the community. The question remains, however: how to enable/encourage those who see themselves as engaging with

23. Myrna Breitbart and I made a similar argument about the political significance of being drawn out of familiar spaces in "Terrains of Protest: Striking City Women," *Our Generation* 19, 1 (fall 1987): 151–175. Note, as well, Julie White's related argument about the move from "essentializing" to "politicizing" needs, *Democracy, Justice, and the Welfare State*, p. 154.

24. I owe this particular framing to Julie White's discussion of needs and care, especially in *Democracy, Justice, and the Welfare State*, p. 154.

25. I have argued for a broader understanding of what constitutes politics in "Women's Collaborative Activities and City Life: Politics and Policy," in *Political Women: Current Roles in State and Local Politics*, ed. Janet Flammang, Sage Yearbooks in Women's Policy Studies, vol. 8 (Beverly Hills, Calif.: Sage, 1984), pp. 242–259; in "Communities, Resistance, and Women's Activism," in *Women and the Politics of Empowerment: Perspectives from the Community and the Workplace*, ed. Ann Bookman and Sandra Morgen (Philadelphia: Temple University Press, 1988), pp. 297–313; and in "Broadening the Study of Women's Participation," in *Women and American Politics: New Questions, New Directions*, ed. Susan J. Carroll (New York: Oxford University Press, 2003), pp. 214–235. See also Marla Brettschneider, *Democratic Theorizing from the Margins*, especially chap. 6.

26. Young, *Inclusion and Democracy*, p. 160. She draws, there, on Jurgen Habermas, *The Theory of Communicative Action* (Boston: Beacon Press, 1984); Jean Cohen and Andrew Arato, *Civil Society and Political Theory* (Cambridge: MIT Press, 1992); and Michael Walzer, "The Idea of Civil Society," in *Toward a Global Civil Society*, ed. Michael Walzer (Providence: Berghahn Books, 1997).

27. Young, *Inclusion and Democracy*, pp. 162–163.

others "simply to meet their needs" to recognize that such engagement *is* a form of politics? Does the language of needs contribute to, or inhibit, that recognition? Do people see themselves as citizens or as clients? And how do changes in the realm of public policy affect those understandings?[28]

But the problem with a language of "meeting needs," rather than of "engaging in politics," goes even deeper; for basing claims on needs can sometimes be more *dis*empowering than empowering. In the U.S. context, for example, Patricia Williams has questioned the value of a needs-based strategy for achieving greater equity for African Americans. If we look historically, she argues, blacks have *not* been well served by a language of needs; on the contrary, their needs have been consistently denied. For African Americans in the United States, the critical issue is not to assert needs but "to find a political mechanism that can confront the *denial* of need."[29] Although a language of rights does not guarantee anything— slaves, for example, were not protected by a rights discourse because they were not granted the basic status of "rights-bearing individuals"—at least it provides an *opening*. Williams's argument is parallel to the claim that the discourse of citizenship can open a space for inclusionary movements, even if it has often been applied in exclusionary ways. What if Williams's claim holds more broadly, however, and those who say they are not engaging in politics but, instead, are organizing to meet their community's needs are, in effect, *undermining* their long-term prospects for effecting meaningful change? (Another prime example of the way a language of needs can be *de*politicizing is, of course, in the discourse of welfare, where those with "needs" for public assistance are increasingly defined *in terms of those needs* and treated as less than full citizens.)[30]

Finally, many of the same studies also highlight the ambiguous role of the state in providing a context for community-based activism. Naples's study of women antipoverty activists during the War on Poverty notes that activism was both facilitated and inhibited by state policy.[31] The state often plays a contradictory role as

28. Joe Soss makes an interesting argument about the ways different social welfare schemes construct people as citizens or as clients in "Making Clients and Citizens." I am grateful to Peregrine Schwartz-Shea for calling this analysis to my attention. See also Nelson, "Women's Poverty and Women's Citizenship." A number of recent works discuss the increasing construction of *all* of us more as consumers/clients than as active citizens. See especially Crenson and Ginsberg, *Downsizing Democracy*, and Skocpol, *Diminished Democracy*.

29. Patricia Williams, "The Pain of Word Bondage," in *The Alchemy of Race and Rights* (Cambridge: Harvard University Press, 1991), p. 152.

30. See, on this point, Ackelsberg, "Dependency or Mutuality"; White, *Democracy, Justice, and the Welfare State*; Soss, "Making Clients and Citizens"; and Nelson, "Women's Poverty and Women's Citizenship."

31. Naples, *Grassroots Warriors*, p. 199. See, in addition, Frances Fox Piven and Richard A. Cloward, *Regulating the Poor* (New York: Pantheon, 1970), and Piven and Cloward, *Poor People's Movements*. Irene Diamond and I explored the complicated and ambiguous relationship between state policies and women's participation in "Gender and Political Life: New Directions in Political Science," in *Analyzing Gender: A Handbook of Social Science Research*, ed. Beth B. Hess and Myra Marx Ferree (Beverly Hills, Calif.: Sage, 1987), pp. 504–525. See also my "Review Article: Feminist Analyses of Public Policy," *Comparative Politics* (July 1992): 477–493.

both a "catalyst for, and site of, women's politicization." It "not only supports the reproduction of gender, racial-ethnic, and class inequality, but also provides avenues through which these patterns can be challenged."[32] LaDoris Payne, now director of WomanSpirit—an NCNW-affiliated organization in St. Louis—got her start as an organizer through the War on Poverty, when she was hired as a Community Outreach worker.[33] In Brooklyn, the NCNW used money from Comprehensive Employment and Training Act (CETA) to employ low-income women from the neighborhood and to pay them for (among other things) community organizing. Those funds—together with NCNW's neighborhood college program—helped to support and politicize significant numbers of neighborhood women. Conversely, however, when federal funds ran dry, many of the organization's programs had to be discontinued or dramatically scaled back. Ultimately, as Iris Young also argues, effective social change will require not only an active (politicized) civil society but also engagement in more traditional domains of politics, such as elections, lobbying, and so on.[34] Further, the former may well lead (or contribute) to the latter.

Incorporating Difference: NCNW

A focus on the programs of the NCNW allows us to explore the ways these questions of politics, needs, empowerment, and public space have played out in practice. The NCNW was established in 1974–75, with the aim of "meeting the needs and strengthening the abilities and power base of poor and working class women."[35] Its goal was "to provide a voice for working class and poor women working on issues to improve their communities, families, and their own status,"[36] by (1) working with them to recognize and develop the strengths they already had, and (2) teaching skills to enable them to take more active roles in the revitalization of their neighborhoods and communities. The organization saw itself explicitly as "encouraging political involvement" in broad terms:

> We favor self-determination and self-help for ourselves and our communities, but we believe that government has a responsibility to assist people to help themselves.

32. Nancy Naples, "Women's Community Activism: Exploring the Dynamics of Politicization and Diversity," in *Community Activism and Feminist Politics: Organizing Across Race, Class, and Gender*, ed. Naples (New York: Routledge, 1998), p. 343.

33. LeDoris Payne, interview with the author, Northampton, Mass., February 21, 2004.

34. *Inclusion and Democracy*, p. 156. See also Ann Shola Orloff, "Gender and the Social Rights of Citizenship: The Comparative Analysis of Gender Relations and Welfare States," *American Sociological Review* 58, 3 (June 1993): 303–328; and White, *Democracy, Justice, and the Welfare State*, especially pp. 156–165.

35. From "National Congress of Neighborhood Women," n.d. [1982?], 2 pp., typescript, Papers of the National Congress of Neighborhood Women (hereafter cited as NCNW Papers), box 3, folder 14, Sophia Smith Collection, Smith College.

36. From National Congress of Neighborhood Women, "Report of Activities for 1980–1981," prepared by Wanda Wooten, July 8, 1981, NCNW Papers, box 1, folder 23, p. 1.

>   While we are non-partisan and non-ideological, we encourage political involve-
>   ment and the use of political activity to accomplish our goals.[37]

This phrasing articulates a rather sophisticated understanding of "political involvement," one not limited to conventional forms of political participation. But it is not
always clear that this politicized perspective on community activism was fully shared
by all those involved. Equally significant, I want to explore the relationship between
these overtly political goals of the NCNW and its policies and programs on diversity.

Naming Women's Leadership

Why an organization specifically for working-class women? Because, as NCNW
literature and spokespersons made clear, the first step toward effective activism is
awareness—coming to recognize *oneself* and one's friends/colleagues as capable
participants.[38] Further, as Jan Peterson, the founder of the organization, noted, both
mainstream (largely middle-class-oriented) women's organizations and the overwhelmingly male leadership of the local community were ignoring the needs and
concerns of working-class, community-based women. When she moved to Brooklyn
in the early 1970s to direct a CETA antipoverty program in the Williamsburg-
Greenpoint neighborhood, in Brooklyn, Peterson discovered that the traditional
leaders of the community were not listening to her, or to other women:

>   She could see that the "overseers" and many local leaders were in agreement on
>   one thing: a woman's place was in the home. Even so, many ordinary "house-
>   wives" were actually working very hard to sustain and enhance the life of the
>   community through PTAs, block associations, tenants' groups in the projects,
>   political clubs, and churches.[39]

Eventually, Jan was able to use the framework of CETA to hire some of these
women to work on community improvement—in the course of which they began
to recognize their own and one another's skills.

Jan Peterson's background in both the civil rights movement and the women's
movement seems to have been quite important to her understandings of "politics"
and of activism, and in the consequent formulation of many of NCNW's approaches. In both of those movements, politics was understood to mean connecting

37. "National Congress of Neighborhood Women: Principles," 2 pp., typescript, undated [fall/
winter 1974?], NCNW Papers, box 1, folder 8. This understanding of "political involvement" would
seem to provide an example of what Iris Young describes as a civil society association of the political sort.

38. Note the similarity with the perspective of the Spanish anarchist women's organization Mujeres Libres, which I explored in *Free Women of Spain: Mujeres Libres and the Struggle for the Emancipation of Women* (Bloomington: Indiana University Press, 1991), especially. chaps. 4–5; and, of course,
the consciousness-raising feature of the early women's movement. The issue of recognizing women—
and their leadership—came up repeatedly in virtually all the interviews I conducted with women active
in NCNW—both those involved in the early years and those still affiliated.

39. Mary Field Belenky, Lynne A. Bond, and Jacqueline S. Weinstock, "The National Congress
of Neighborhood Women," in *A Tradition That Has No Name: Nurturing the Development of People,
Families, and Communities* (New York: Basic Books, 1997), p. 206.

the personal and the political through programs of education and consciousness-raising, with the aim of enabling those who had been subordinated to develop, in the words of Martin Luther King, Jr., a sense of being "somebody." Further, her experiences in the civil rights movement made her particularly sensitive to issues of incorporating women of diverse ethnic and racial groups within the organization. As she put it: "the civil rights movement saved my life." In addition, having the CETA money "allowed us to try experiments like that. . . . We had CETA; we could sit in rooms and argue it out with one another. . . . It was an incredible luxury; but it also made possible some tremendously important learning."[40]

Both my own interviews with members of the NCNW and others recorded at various points in the history of the organization indicate that many had an ambiguous relationship to the feminist movement. On the one hand, Jan Peterson, in particular, was a committed feminist, and had ties to feminist organizations in Manhattan (where she had lived before moving to Brooklyn). On the other hand, many of the local women participants in the group—in Williamsburg, initially, mostly Italian American working-class women; later, and elsewhere, including many African American and Latina working-class and poor women—reported considerable alienation from mainstream feminism. One major source of their suspicions had to do with the place of family and community in their lives. Jan Peterson noted that

> the original feminist analysis was that in order to gain power over our own lives, we had to leave our families and neighborhoods. That's how I got from a small town in the Midwest to New York. The National Congress of Neighborhood Women grew out of the attempt to support women who have a commitment to family and neighborhood. . . . There are two different women's movements. Our women's movement deals with poor and working class women who see their families and neighborhoods as fundamentally part of who they are.[41]

One local woman who was active in NCNW had actually attended a meeting of the National Organization of Women (NOW) in Manhattan but "couldn't relate to the women there: "We were family people and we lived for our families. . . . We were largely Italian and that means a strong sense of family. In our eyes, they were telling us to leave our families and homes."[42]

40. Jan Peterson, interview with the author, Williamsburg, Brooklyn, August 21, 2002. Belenky, Bond, and Weinstock also give some hints in this direction in "National Congress of Neighborhood Women."

41. Cited by María Giordano, in untitled paper on class and feminism, NCNW Papers, box 118, folder 5. Similar sentiments were expressed by many of the participants in the NCNW's "Sharing Strategies" conference that took place at Smith College, Northampton, Mass., February 19–22, 2004.

42. "Consciousness Interview with Ann Giordano, National Congress of Neighborhood Women," July 15, 1981, lkg [Linda Grey?], interviewer, 14 pp., typescript, with hand-written corrections. NCNW Papers, box 109, folder 2. She made similar comments in a joint interview conducted by Mary Belenky with Maria Fava, Ann Giordano, Elaine Carpinelli, Sandy [Schiaparelli?], and Jan [Peterson], March 26, 1992, transcript in NCNW Papers, box 8, folder 4. See also Terry Haywoode's comments in "Women Against Women: Middle-Class Bias in Feminist Literature," paper presented at the annual meeting of the Society for the Study of Social Problems, San Francisco, September 2, 1978, NCNW Papers, box 118, folder 4; and "Working-Class Women and Local Politics: Styles of Community Organizing," *Research in Politics and Society*, 7 (1999): 111–134.

Nevertheless, even though the women saw themselves as rooted firmly in their families and community, the place where they faced the most blatant sexism was within community organizations. As one participant wrote, describing their experiences:

> They live in a world where "Father knows best," and if mother knows best, she keeps it to herself. The men in the community weren't threatened by the women's activities until they began to enter the male "sphere." Women worked hard fighting for community issues as "auxiliary divisions" of male-based organizations. However, once federal funds became available or bows were to be taken, it was suddenly the men who did it all.[43]

She went on to cite the depiction by another woman (Ann Giordano) of her first foray into the official public arena:

> The first time I spoke in public, I was so scared I almost dropped dead. The only reason that I could do it was that I was so hopping mad at the men in the meeting. They either refused to recognize the women who'd had a lot of experience on the issue, or kept shutting them up. I sat there for over two hours, just seething and burning. Then I spoke over the men's voices: They were all screaming for me to sit down. I kept screaming too. That was my first speech.
> Hysterical . . .[44]

NCNW's programs and training materials addressed both these issues — "feminism" and the empowerment of women *as* women on the one hand and the need to recognize and highlight women's contributions to the community on the other. As early as its founding in 1974, NCNW's principles included the following:

> *Empowerment*: We are committed to building women's consciousness of their power and potential, of their right to self-realization, of their right and capacity to define and solve their own problems, and to doing this by stressing recognition of their strengths and by offering education and skill-building in a manner that does not alienate them from themselves and their roots.
> *Families*: We recognize that families come in ever-changing forms; but what-ever the form, we affirm the importance of families to the healthy development of both adults and children. And, we are committed to strengthening family life and to helping families function well for all their members.[45]

---

43. María Giordano, untitled paper. The pattern is an all-too-common one in many commu-nity organizations. See, for example, Ronald Lawson and Stephen E. Barton, "Sex Roles in Social Movements: A Case Study of the Tenant Movement in New York City," *Signs* 5 (winter 1980): 230–247.

44. María Giordano, untitled paper.

45. "National Congress of Neighborhood Women: Principles." The wording here is significant. They were *not* saying that women had to *learn* to be leaders; rather, that they needed to become more aware of the significance of what they were *already* doing, and to develop their skills to improve their ability to function effectively.

The framing of issues is also significant here: as early as 1974, and continuing until today, what we find is less a language of women's rights than of a community's needs; as Jan Peterson describes it, "We are *not* rights-based; we're about development. About implementation on the ground, and improving the situation of *communities*, and of women *in* them."[46] Or, in the words of LaDoris Payne, discussing her work in St. Louis:

> The part of St. Louis that we live in is an underdeveloped nation within a developed nation...The community that I live in doesn't have a public library, it doesn't have a restaurant that you can sit down in, it doesn't have a movie theater...It doesn't have many of the things that you would expect to see in a community...no hospitals...The community I live in is underresourced and underdeveloped. It is gentrifying, and slated for industrial development. Unemployment and health care are our big issues....I got involved about 30 years ago through War on Poverty Programs as a community outreach worker...it was as much self-help as anything. I never was working on behalf of other people. I'm not a social worker by training or inclination; I'm a freedom fighter![47]

Virtually none of the many women with whom I spoke used a language of rights; they described their concerns and activities in terms of meeting needs and, most directly, improving the community: establishing a senior center, a day-care center, struggling for traffic lights, and so on.

Initially, many community women were wary of the organization. Ann Giordano acknowledged that, when she first met women who identified as feminists, she wasn't particularly interested in what they had to say: "We didn't want to philosophize and ideologize about how women are discriminated against." But when Jan sent around a survey asking what the women might want, "people got interested because it was *doing*, not sitting around and talking....And they were taking these classes to better their families and the community.[48] Similarly, Habiba Soudan, who has been active in organizing in the African American community in Camden, N.J., for many years, and became involved in NCNW in the late 1980s, noted that NCNW enabled women not just to *find* their voices but to *use* them—for the betterment of themselves, to be sure, but also for their communities and families.[49]

The language of "needs" is not insignificant here, in two respects. First, the early organizers approached community women not in terms of what their (political) *demands* were but what their self-defined *needs* were. This made the process less threatening. But, second, that approach allowed/enabled the women to *participate in the definition and interpretation of their needs*, a process that Julie

---

46. Interview with the author, August 21, 2002, Brooklyn.

47. Interview with the author and Tamar Carroll, February 21, 2004, Northampton, Mass.

48. "Consciousness Interview with Ann Giordano," July 15, 1981.

49. Interview with the author, Camden, N.J., May 7, 2004. Along similar lines, Carol Judy (who has been involved with an NCNW-affiliated organization in East Tennessee for many years) spoke often about the importance of finding, and using, her voice. Interview with the author, February 21, 2004, Northampton, Mass., and during NCNW's "Sharing Strategies" conference, Smith College, February 19–22, 2004.

White, for example, names as critical to what she terms a nonpaternalist "democratic politics of care."[50] On a related note, a number of the women pointed out that, when they first got involved with the Congress, they did so out of their concerns as mothers. In the words of one: "I was always a fighter. In my own little way, . . . I always fought for the issues—if I knew it would affect my kids, I would fight for that, no matter what.[51] NCNW's programs helped her both to recognize herself *as* a leader and to see that her activities had political significance beyond the needs of her family.

The organization developed materials that would translate these concepts into simple language—making clear to women who had long been involved in their communities that they *were* leaders and could—and should—take themselves seriously as such. Thus, a training manual prepared for the James Weldon Johnson Tenant Association in East Harlem, N.Y. (which developed in collaboration with the NCNW) offered a brief quiz, "Am I a leader?" in which it asked readers whether they had been involved with tenant association meetings, PTAs, church suppers, talking with neighbors about community issues, and then went on to insist: "These are all LEADERSHIP ACTIVITIES. . . . And *you* do some of them! . . . YOU ARE A LEADER!!"[52]

In addition to working with the women to help them recognize their own leadership capacities and to develop new ones, the organization reached out to other groups in the community to encourage them to overcome their sexism and incorporate women more fully—insisting that such practices would benefit everyone. So, for example, in February 1981, Jan Peterson sent out a two-page memo to "Neighborhood Leaders" with suggestions about "how to include women effectively in your efforts to revitalize neighborhoods." Its opening paragraph read:

> Women have long supplied the raw labor power in grassroots organizations, yet their needs and issues have not been addressed. Volunteer women may organize the church supper to raise money, but they are excluded from the decision-making body that plans how the money is spent. Often grassroots organizing begins with the women, only to have leadership become male as the group mushrooms into coalition with broader recognition or obtains sizeable funding such as the neighborhood community corporations around the country. . . . Finally, since men and women have been conditioned to different priorities, issues at the local level such as women's health care services and daytime street safety, are not as readily attended to. In fact, most grassroots women's programs like those dealing with wife

50. See White, *Democracy, Justice, and the Welfare State*, especially pp. 132, 135–136. I discuss hereafter the connections between this notion of a democratic politics of care and the ambiguous status of "leadership training" or "leadership development" in a democracy.

51. Interview by Mary Belenky with María Fava, Ann Giordano, Elaine Carpinelli, Sandy [Schiaparelli?], and Jan [Peterson], March 26, 1992. Note, too, in this context, the recent study by Amy Caiazza and Heidi Hartmann, indicating that parenthood (particularly having children aged between five and seventeen) tends to *increase* participation rates for both men and women, but especially for women, in community-based/civic organizations. Caiazza, "Women's Community Involvement."

52. James Weldon Johnson/Neighborhood Women, "Organizing Your Group: Finding, Keeping and Supporting Neighborhood Leaders," Manual no.1, pp. 12–13, NCNW Papers, box 109, folder 13.

abuse, rape, etc. are not even perceived as part of the organized neighborhood effort.

We believe that all of these problems occur because people are not aware of how to incorporate women effectively in the effort to revitalize neighborhoods.

This introduction was followed by a list of questions that the organizations could ask themselves about their programs, such as "Are women involved in initiation?" "Do women participate in the direction of the project?" "What are the benefits of this project to women? Directly? Indirectly? Do the participants perceive them as benefits in key areas in their lives.... Does the project contribute to increasing women's access to knowledge, resources, the power structure?" Finally, "Does this project increase women's options, raise their status?"[53]

The first step, then, is awareness of—consciousness-raising about—the *need* for empowerment, for women to take significant roles in their communities. NCNW took—and continues to take—the issue of empowerment very seriously. At the core of its activities were programs of education and leadership training.

Leadership Training as Recognizing the Strength in Diversity

> "We needed to *talk* about our different experiences so that people could understand each other. We *were* different; we couldn't pretend that different things didn't bother us."
>
> —María Rivera Brown

An early NCNW report on its activities made clear that the development of an awareness of women's leadership potential was a primary focus of its programs. I want to focus, here, on what seems to me a particularly unusual aspect of those programs: the NCNW's insistence—in the context of an otherwise relatively fractured women's movement—that critical to the development of that potential was an ability to work with, and to value, diversity. In particular, its leadership training program aimed to "help women to see why they need the support of other women leaders, how to build and maintain a support system, how to network and share skills with other women, and how to build alliances across lines that have often divided people and prevented poor and working class communities from obtaining power."[54] As Jan Peterson noted, when asked about the goals of the NCNW:

> the role of NCNW is to strip women of all those kinds of things—the indifferences, and divisions of color, culture, religion and all the other kinds of things that prevent women ... from working together—and *make them deal with them* so that we can work towards the real goal ... [which] is providing a country that we all feel

53. Jan Peterson, "How to Include Women Effectively in Your Efforts to Revitalize Neighborhoods," Memorandum for Neighborhood Leaders from National Congress of Neighborhood Women, 2-81 [February 1981], 2 pp., NCNW Papers, box 109.

54. "National Congress of Neighborhood Women."

good about as women. Where there are decent jobs for all people, decent salaries for all our people; decent housing for all people.[55]

Before turning to a more in-depth exploration of those programs, however, I want to acknowledge the complicated place of leadership, and especially of leadership development, in a participatory-democratic organization. On the one hand, such programs might seem like contradictions in terms: if one insists that women are equally capable, along with men, of taking leadership in their communities; if one insists, in fact, that women *are already* leaders in their communities, whence a need for leadership training? What is the relationship between leadership *training* and leadership *support*? Is not any concept of leadership training self-contradictory?

The short answer to this last question is: yes and no. Many democrats have acknowledged that democratic skills need to be nurtured and developed. People are capable of participation; but they will participate more effectively if they are "prepared" to do so.[56] What is critical is the level of respect accorded to the perspectives of community people themselves. Julie White's framing of a distinction between "paternalism" and a "democratic politics of care" is helpful here. White calls for a "participatory politics of need interpretation" that stands in opposition to paternalism, understood "not as the problem of intervention in the lives of (self-regarding) others, but as speaking for others in the process of defining their needs." An alternative process would privilege "the voice of those presently 'in need' in the course of defining 'need' and determining arrangements of resources to meet those needs."[57] The leadership training programs of NCNW should be considered within such a context: they were developed in response to a survey of neighborhood women in which those women expressed a desire to improve their organizational leadership skills.

To return, then, to the place of diversity work within these leadership programs: virtually every member spoke of the importance of that work as a central feature of NCNW's activities. Ann Giordano credits the work with a broad impact on the community of Williamsburg-Greenpoint:

> I've always taken pride that we, as diverse as we are, have not had the kind of problems that Crown Heights has had, that Bensonhurst has had.... Because the National Congress did so much diversity work and had so many people out there that even if you don't agree with it all, you can't sell it out.... You can't buy

---

55. Interview with Jan Peterson and Bertha Gilkey, March 17, 1983, 8 pp., typescript, NCNW Papers, box 108, folder 2 (emphasis mine).

56. On the meaning and importance of preparation (and *capacitación*) within the Spanish anarchist movement, see my *Free Women of Spain*, especially chap. 5. In the U.S. context, the Highlander Center in Tennessee has long been involved in mounting programs of education and training for would-be organizers and activists in a variety of popular movements. And, of course, the civil rights movement had an important educational component, as well. For a discussion of the role of education in support of organizing among General Electric workers in East Tennessee see Eve Weinbaum, "Transforming Democracy: Rural Women and Labor Resistance," in Cohen, Jones, and Tronto, *Women Transforming Politics*, pp. 324–339, especially pp. 331–333. I am grateful to both Rachel Roth and Joan Tronto for pressing me to address this issue and for suggesting useful resources.

57. White, *Democracy, Justice, and the Welfare State*, p. 136.

into racism totally, even if you are a racist, because there's a part of you that knew a nice Black person or a nice Hispanic person. So you can't sell that person out.[58]

Training programs that specifically addressed issues of diversity were a key part of NCNW's goals from the beginning. For example, its 1974 statement of principles included:

> *Support Groups and Networks*: Because of multiple and conflicting demands made upon women which often lead to feelings of inadequacy, isolation, illegitimacy and self-denial, we believe in the importance of women's support groups and supportive networks . . . support groups should promote the honest sharing of feelings, information and aspirations in an atmosphere of caring and confidentiality where difference is both recognized and respected.
> *Diversity*: We are committed to fostering understanding and respect for personal and group diversity, especially class, race and cultural differences, and to the use of consciously adopted methods to accomplish this. We are convinced that these and other differences must be made visible and celebrated for true tolerance and community to exist.[59]

Early in its existence, NCNW surveyed women in the community who *had* taken some leadership, and asked them what they felt they needed to move to a "next step." Their responses indicated that "they felt they had to develop certain skills to build self-confidence." In addition to developing basic skills necessary for leadership, they needed work on issues of diversity: "women in these communities haven't had the experience of working together because things are basically structured around the family unit. A lot of these women had never worked with different ethnic or racial groups. In order to make the community survive, they have to have the experience of understanding their common needs."[60] The overall goal of the organization, then, was "not only to empower [low-income and working-class] women, but [to] build coalitions among different ethnic groups . . . that are concerned with the same kind of issues."[61] Critical to the achievement of that goal was making face-to-face contact with women, encouraging them, and urging them to be in touch with women in other communities who were similarly situated.

58. Interview by Mary Belenky with María Fava, Ann Giordano, Elaine Carpinelli, Sandy [Schiaparelli?], and Jan [Peterson], March 26, 1992, NCNW Papers, box 8. Interestingly, many theorists of discursive democracy—including White, Bickford, Phillips, Mansbridge, and Young—argue for the importance of *inclusion* (or, in Phillips's framing, the "politics of presence") to make that democracy more possible. Jan Peterson, Lisel Burns, and others involved in the creation of the leadership training program seemed to have a clear sense of that need *in practice*: perhaps this stemmed from their earlier experiences with the civil rights movement?

59. "National Congress of Neighborhood Women: Principles." See also report of a task-force on developing a statement of goals, November 27, 1979, NCNW Papers, box 1, folder 11.

60. "A Dialogue on the Organization, Goals, and Needs of the National Congress of Neighborhood Women," transcript of taped discussion, June 1978, between two NCNW board members (Michaela Hickey and Inez Padilla) and Christine Noschese, the NCNW executive director, 35 pp., typescript. NCNW Papers, box 1, folder 8, pp. 1–2.

61. "A Dialogue on the Organization, Goals, and Needs," p. 7.

The centerpiece of NCNW's programs to develop women's leadership is the Leadership Support Group, designed to enable "women to get together with their peers to share experiences, feelings, ideas, strategies, skills and other resources in a supportive environment."[62] The basic idea is to provide a confidential and nonjudgmental context for women leaders to think through, together with others, the issues they are confronting in their neighborhoods and communities. Groups consist of ten to fifteen women, who commit to meet once a week for a minimum of three months, in two- to four-hour sessions. Suggested plans for sessions include a general discussion topic (e.g., availability of child-care in the community, growing up, relationships with people in other groups) and then time for an "individual problem discussion," in which one of the members has an opportunity to present a problem she is dealing with and to get feedback from the group.

It is in the guidelines for general discussions that we see the explicit addressing of issues of diversity. Many of the suggested topics deal with personal issues, and are designed to give participants a chance to get to know one another, as well as to explore dimensions of their own lives that they might not have thought about in this way. Participants are to think about the question at hand (e.g., "growing up as girls") in terms of a variety of factors that might have affected their experience, including gender, race, class, ethnicity, age, sexual orientation, and others. After addressing personal issues, groups are encouraged to move on to look at institutions (family, financial, churches, educational, media, various movements), thinking about how they (and members of their group) have been affected by them, or might (have) organize(d) to effect change in them. Making attention to issues of difference among the women an explicit focus of every session represented an effort to break down the barriers that often divide women from one another and that may prevent their building the sorts of alliances and coalitions that would be necessary for any change to occur. The "personal was political," but not in some narrow sense. More accurately, perhaps, "the personal/political is diverse."[63] Participants who reflected back on their experiences noted, repeatedly, that this process of learning about themselves and one another was one of the most valuable aspects of their participation in the organization. Finally, it's important to note that the organization seems regularly to have undertaken these sorts of workshops with its own staff, enabling them to address issues of difference among themselves—including between professional and clerical staff.[64]

Finally, the groups were meant to address women's fears related to taking power, and the tensions that can arise from competition.

> The final issue regarding support is to learn that providing support to another's leadership growth doesn't take away from ours. . . . Enjoying watching another woman grow and seeing that every woman taking a step means that more of us can do it is essential. . . . We must get over past hurts and internalized ideas that say

---

62. "Guidelines for Women's Leadership Support Groups," undated, 26 pp., typescript, NCNW Papers, box 109, folder 12.

63. I am grateful to Amrita Basu and Eileen McDonagh for this framing of the issue.

64. See reports of such workshops in NCNW Papers, box 11, folder 6.

that women can't stick together or must claw each other. In our support groups we will learn how to deal with how we have personally hurt each other; learn how women have been historically pitted against each other, and develop ways to change all this and develop relationships built on mutual trust.[65]

By 1982, NCNW was able to report, in a description of its Leadership Development Project, that:

over the past 18 months, with government and foundation support, NW [Neighborhood Women] has involved over 400 women leaders in its first National Leadership Development Project. With the assistance and commitment of a diverse group of ten neighborhood women leaders from around the country, NW has developed a leadership support training model that draws on the experience of poor and working class women's work in their communities. The training helps women to see why they need the support of other women leaders, how to build and maintain a support system, how to network and share skills with other women, and how to build alliances across lines that have often divided people and prevented poor and working class communities from obtaining power.[66]

One of the most important lessons learned from this process has been the overcoming of the resignation that characterized the lives of so many women in the community:

A lot of what I do in my work today is . . . understanding yes, you're in poverty, but you don't have to stay there . . . it's helped me tremendously to . . . try and pass on to other women that you never have to accept where you are in life. . . . The feeling of powerlessness and the acceptance is so strong in people, and how do you break it? It's like a constant struggle . . . to show people that you don't have to do it.[67]

Empowered by their participation in these groups, women from NCNW established a college program in the community, organized to "save" a firehouse, worked with others to preserve bus routes in the community (and institute new ones), called local politicians to account, helped rehabilitate an abandoned hospital into housing for low-income families, and engaged in numerous other activities that eventually drew together women from both Italian American and African American neighborhoods in the community.

Beginnings of Conclusions

For the women of the NCNW, the need for civic participation—for women to take a role in improving their communities and in developing plans for the future—was

---

65. Lisel Burns and Jan Peterson, "Policies on Support Groups and Political Issues," edited by Ann Giordano, NCNW National Office, 3pp., typescript, undated, NCNW Papers, box 109, file 15.

66. "National Congress of Neighborhood Women," undated [1982], typescript, 2 pp., NCNW Papers, Box 3, Folder 14.

67. Interview by Mary Belenky with María Fava, Ann Giordano, Elaine Carpinelli, Sandy [Schiaparelli?], and Jan [Peterson], March 26, 1992.

a given. But they recognized that, in a context of inequality and massive structural oppression, such activities would not necessarily come easily or "naturally." Women needed concrete and ongoing support if they were to break free of dominant communal stereotypes (like: women belong in the kitchen) and claim recognition for the roles they were, in fact, already filling in their communities. Activism by isolated, individual women, or activism that was limited to one specific issue, was not their goal. Rather, if women were to become more fully engaged citizens on an ongoing basis, and see themselves as such, those taking part in activities needed to name what they were doing *as* political engagement and to recognize themselves as leaders. Only that combination of acknowledgments—of themselves, from others, and from the larger community—would enable them to continue to engage, and to move into larger, and potentially more conflictual, arenas.

But the organization went beyond empowerment at the level of the individual or even the neighborhood or community. Recognizing that a significant part of the experience of women, in particular, in working-class communities in the United States is to be alienated from ongoing structures and institutions of power and influence, to be subject to economic and social forces over which those communities have little control, NCNW insisted that working-class women learn how to build bridges to others who might seem unlike them, to overcome precisely those divisions based on race and ethnicity that have traditionally kept such communities apart from one another, and vying for limited resources. Thus, almost from the beginning, *diversity* work was seen as critical *both* to leadership development *and* to encouraging/facilitating broader participation. It is almost as though the confrontation with diverse women's stories is, itself, politicizing.

What does this experience have to contribute to addressing the questions I raised earlier, about the rejection of "politics" and the construction of alternative public spaces? What can we learn from NCNW's activities that is relevant to some of the theoretical puzzles with which scholars of gender and citizenship have been engaged?

First, with respect to constructions of "politics." They began with programs rooted in family and community, rather than with abstract critiques, or even with explicit calls for political engagement. But their programs focused on making connections between the women's concerns as wives and mothers, the skills they had developed in those capacities, and the contributions they had already made and would continue to make to the broader community. They started, that is, with needs, but they helped the women to see connections between those needs and their rights as citizens, *and* to perceive commonalities between their needs and those of others. This two-pronged focus on needs became an important part of a process of politicization: overcoming both their suspicion of "politics" *and* their suspicions and wariness of others. Participants came to believe that only *through* collective action—and, at least on occasion, by making demands of formal political institutions—did those needs stand a chance of being met.

But what would make collective action possible? Skills training (including the development of analytical tools) and diversity work. NCNW's skills-focused programs (especially the college program)[68] helped the women to locate themselves and their community within a broader political-economic context. Many came to see that action to address the needs of their families required them to think *structurally* about their situation and to engage with similarly situated women in other neighborhoods. They developed an *analysis* of their situation, that is, that brought them to a broader understanding of politics and an awareness of the political character of their concerns and that may well have helped them to overcome their earlier rejection of "politics."

This analysis alone, however, would not have been sufficient to build and sustain what Fraser referred to as a "subaltern counterpublic." The NCNW coupled programming that educated its members politically (or politicized them) with programming that helped them address issues of diversity and difference—notably the leadership training program. I think we can understand this dimension of its activities as a partial, but critical, component of an answer to the question: What is necessary to sustain a "subaltern counterpublic"? From NCNW's vantage point, a counterpublic must be inclusive; it must have at its core a commitment to dialogue and support across differences of race, ethnicity, religious background, and sexuality. The NCNW insisted that the achievement of such inclusion was not automatic or easy: in a society divided by differences of race and ethnicity, in particular, it would have to be deliberately created, at the grassroots, and in small-group settings, to build the trust and the knowledge of one another that alone would make possible the perception of a shared fate critical to sustained joint action.[69] And what facilitated the building of that trust was, precisely, the ways they developed of *connecting* diverse personal stories in a consciousness-raising context: making manifest, that is, not only that the "personal is political" but that "the personal that is political is diverse."

That the NCNW has been extraordinarily successful in many of its efforts has been documented elsewhere.[70] What this exploration of the leadership training program suggests is that at least one key to the successful politicization of working-class women in their communities—enabling them to see that their actions *are*

---

68. On the college program, see Belenky, Bond, and Weinstock, "The National Congress of Neighborhood Women," especially pp. 215–218; also Terry Haywoode, "College for Neighborhood Women: Innovation and Growth," in *Learning Our Way: Essays in Feminist Education*, ed. Charlotte Bunch and Sandra Pollack, (Trumansburg, N.Y.: Crossing Press, 1983); Terry Haywoode, "Neighborhood Women Keeping It Together," *City Limits* (April 1985): 20–21; and Terry Haywoode and Laura Polla Scanlon, "World of Our Mothers: College for Neighborhood Women," *Women's Studies Quarterly* 21, 3 and 4 (1993): 133–141. On the importance of *education* in the process of conscientization and politicization, see Ackelsberg, *Free Women of Spain*, chap. 5, and Rina Benmayor and Rosa M. Torruellas, "Education, Cultural Rights, and Citizenship," in *Women Transforming Politics*, ed. Cohen, Jones, and Tronto, especially pp. 197–201.

69. I am reminded, here, of the song from *South Pacific* about hatred and prejudice: "You've Got to Be Carefully Taught." NCNW's programs recognized that, in the context of a society characterized by inequalities and prejudice, tolerance and a sense of commonality also has "got to be carefully taught."

70. See, for example, Ida Susser, *Norman Street: Poverty and Politics in an Urban Neighborhood* (New York: Oxford University Press, 1982); *Metropolitan Avenue* (video); and the sources cited heretofore in notes 39 and 68.

"political"—is the combination of an explicit focus on difference and diversity and a recognition that effective activism, like any other skill, can be taught, and learned. In such a context, those committed to improving their lives and those of their families by working in their communities need not deny that they are engaged in politics; rather, they can come to take pride in discovering that they, too, are political beings.

5

Arenas of Citizenship

Civil Society, the State, and the Global Order

ALISON M. JAGGAR

Citizenship has always been a cluster of privileged relations holding on the one hand between states and (some of) the individuals who reside in the territory they govern and on the other hand among individuals who are members of the same political community. Because the state is integral to both these aspects of citizenship, competing accounts of citizens' qualifications, rights, and responsibilities typically have been embedded in larger theories about the proper functions of the state.[1] At the beginning of the twenty-first century, however, the state is becoming less central in political life, and the seeming decline in its importance generates a multitude of new questions for political philosophy.[2] Here, I consider the recent emphasis on civil society as a terrain of democratic empowerment and begin exploring the implications of this emphasis for rethinking citizenship in the twenty first century.

This essay was written originally for a conference on Women and Citizenship, organized by Marilyn Friedman and held at Washington University in St. Louis, Missouri, in April 2002. I am very grateful for helpful comments made by participants in that conference, by two anonymous reviewers for the *International Journal of Feminist Politics*, and by Kathleen B. Jones, editor of the journal.

1. When the state was regarded as designed primarily to guarantee internal and external security, the rights and responsibilities of citizens were seen as concerned primarily with promulgating, administering, and obeying the law and serving in the military. When the responsibilities of the state were expanded to include social welfare, especially in the twentieth century, citizenship came to be seen as including social entitlements. For instance, in South Africa in the 1990s, "social citizenship" came to include the rights of everyone to schools, jobs, health-care and housing (Kaplan 1997:14).

2. As the mandates of international trade and financial institutions increasingly constrain their sovereignty, many states in practice are no longer the ultimate sources of political power in the lands that they administer. As millions migrate across borders, many people no longer live in the territory of the state whose citizenship they hold, and most lands contain many residents who are not citizens of the states that govern them. Finally, as ever more of people's basic needs, even their need for physical security, are met through either the market or the voluntary associations of civil society, states no longer appear as the primary guarantors of citizens' safety and well-being.

Feminists Rechart the Terrain of Citizenship

Throughout Western history, citizenship has been gendered masculine. Citizen identity has been limited to (some) men, and citizens' relations with each other have been conceived as fraternal bonds. The activities regarded as characteristic of citizens—fighting, governing, buying and selling property, and eventually working for wages—have all been viewed as masculine, as have been the social locations where these activities are undertaken. Thus, the battlefield, the state, and (later) the market have been constituted as the public realm, the arenas in which citizenship is performed. Although the boundaries of the public have been variously defined, they have always demarcated the public from the private realm of home, family, and community. The private has been a symbolically feminine sphere, whose inhabitants—slaves, servants, women, and children—have often lacked the privileges of citizenship and have been viewed as needing protection and control by citizens.[3] Although the activities carried out in the private sphere have always been recognized as indispensable to the reproduction of human life, they have typically been viewed as closer to nature, less fully human, and so less valuable than the activities that distinguish citizenship.[4]

Early Western feminists demanded that women too should be accorded the status of citizens. They argued that women were as capable as men of fulfilling the responsibilities of citizenship and therefore deserved its full privileges. Women should have the same rights and responsibilities as male citizens and should be able to participate equally with men in the activities characteristic of citizenship. The public sphere should no longer be a masculine preserve. However, in addition to dominant versions of feminism, which argued for including women as citizens in the traditional sense, other currents of feminist thinking have brought traditional conceptions of citizenship into question, often via challenges to established assumptions about the characteristic activities of citizens and the social locations in which those activities are undertaken. The rest of this section sketches some of those challenges.

---

3. Of course, the symbolic world may diverge from the real world; in practice, women have always been active in the public sphere and men in the private.

4. Different Western theorists have, of course, drawn and evaluated the distinctions between public and private spheres in different ways. In both the civic republican and the liberal traditions, the public sphere is understood as consisting of primarily the institutions of the state, which are seen as separate from the private realms of the economy, the family, and other social institutions, but these two traditions diverge in their valuations of public and private life. Civic republicans regard individuals as becoming fully human and free only when they abandon preoccupation with their petty private affairs and substitute concern for the larger *res publica*. By contrast, liberals view citizens as "possessive individuals," for whom politics is a means of promoting private interests, and they see human fulfillment as possible only outside politics, which they regard as an often dirty business of bargaining, striking deals, and sometimes trickery and manipulation. Participatory democrats share the civic republican view that citizens should participate directly rather than indirectly in government and also the idea that political activity is honorable and fulfilling. However, they regard the sites of democratic participation as extending beyond the state to include the community and especially the workplace.

One set of challenges derives from Western feminist criticisms of symbolically masculine styles of citizenship. Nineteenth-century Western feminists drew on gendered stereotypes of women as pure and as housekeepers to argue that if women received the vote, they would clean up the dirty world of public politics. In the twentieth century, organizations of women such as Mothers Against Drunk Driving (MADD) in the United States and the Mothers of the Plaza de Mayo in Argentina have drawn on the symbolic power of the maternal to develop practices of citizenship that are widely viewed as feminine (Ruddick 1989; Tronto 1993.) Arguments that the culturally feminine values of purity, care, and responsibility should infuse public as well private life suggest that political and domestic realms are continuous rather than separate.[5]

A second set of challenges to traditional conceptions of citizenship emerges from feminist disappointment that, even after attaining the formal rights of citizens, women are still underrepresented at the highest levels of government and industry—not to mention the military. Seeking to explain women's limited participation in these arenas, some feminist theorists have challenged the masculine norm embedded in many modern conceptions of citizenship, which define citizens' rights and responsibilities in ways that make it difficult for women to be full citizens. For example, civic republican conceptions of citizenship are so demanding that citizen responsibilities can be met only by people who belong to a relatively leisured elite—an elite that, on the prevailing gender division of labor, is likely to be disproportionately male.[6] Similarly, feminists have charged that the liberal model of citizenship, which relies on an implicitly masculine understanding of the citizen as soldier and as worker, makes it especially difficult for women to be full citizens, because their socially assigned care-taking responsibilities pose obstacles to women's working for wages or serving in the military.[7] The

---

5. Classic liberal theorists, such as John Stuart Mill and John Rawls, also regarded the home as the school of citizenship, but they treated it as outside politics and did not advocate that culturally feminine values should be introduced into political life.

6. In the premodern city-states where civic republican citizenship emerged, the exclusion of the majority of the population from citizenship was not simply contingent. Instead, a necessary condition for a few men to fulfill the extensive and culturally masculine responsibilities of citizenship, namely, being a warrior and holding political office, was that most of the socially necessary work should be done by slave and/or female labor.

7. This understanding is especially strong in the versions of liberal citizenship current in the United States, as opposed to the European social democracies. In the military forces of the United States, women (and "out" male homosexuals) are excluded from "frontline" combat, an exclusion said to consign women (and gay men) to a second-class citizenship status defined as weak, infected, and needing protection (Allen 2000; Carter 1996) In addition, first-class citizens in the United States are expected to be (or once to have been) economically "independent" and "productive" "social contributors." This expectation is reflected in a distinction between two kinds of government payments. Some payments, such as unemployment insurance, veterans' benefits, and social security, are considered to have been earned by citizens' previous social contributions through their paid work or military service, whereas others, such as payments to families or the disabled, are regarded as unearned and as a kind of charity. Feminists charge that this distinction between kinds of government payments relies on arbitrary and gender-biased understandings of "independence," "productivity," and "social contribution" that consign all those unable to work for wages to a "dependent" and second-class citizenship status (Fraser and Gordon 1997; Kittay 1999; Young 1995).

participatory democratic model of citizenship is less elitist than the liberal and civic republican models and more respectful of the dignity of labor, because it regards the workplace as one arena for citizen participation; however, participatory democrats typically envision workplaces as sites in which people work for pay and ignore the vast amount of unpaid labor performed by women in the home and the community.[8] One way that feminist theorists have responded to women's de facto exclusion from full citizenship, traditionally defined, is by challenging the disproportionate assignment of unpaid caring labor to women, which deprives women of the time and energy to participate fully in citizens' distinctive activities. Alternatively, however, a few theorists have argued that women's caring labor should be recognized as a distinctive practice of citizenship, performed in the domestic arena.[9]

Additional challenges for established understandings of citizenship are raised by reflection on women's community activism in bread riots, tenant organizations, and agitation for school reform or in opposition to environmental hazards. This activism is often motivated not by narrow self-interest but rather by women's concern for threats against their families and communities (Kaplan 1997). Martha Ackelsberg contends that women's community activism reveals a need to revise prevailing, especially liberal, conceptions of citizenship so as to recognize that citizens are not always isolated individuals but instead may act as members of class, ethnic, or cultural communities. She further argues that democratic citizenship is revealed not only in a narrow range of behaviors undertaken by those relatively few citizens who seek to influence the formal structures of government for their own benefit but also in community activism generated by the concerns of everyday life and characterized by the values of community and connection (Ackelsberg 1988).

Many Third World feminists argue that women's community organizing promotes the political as well as the economic empowerment of women in the global South.[10] Grassroots organizations, initially formed to address such immediate practical needs as those for food, shelter, water, income, medical care, and transportation, often come to recognize that immediate needs are generated by larger systems of inequality, not only between genders but also among classes and nations. Members of these organizations may then turn away from an exclusive focus on the local and the immediate and move to creating longer term strategies directed against structural inequalities, perhaps challenging unjust laws or seeking

---

8. The participatory-democratic model of citizenship draws its inspiration from both town meetings in the United States and the socialist idea of worker self-management.

9. An obvious danger of this response is that it risks essentializing and naturalizing the gender division of labor, reinforcing the idea of women as breeders and care-takers of citizens and consigning them to forms of citizenship that are different from and subordinate to masculine varieties.

10. Talk about the global North and the global South often now replaces talk about the First, Second, and Third Worlds, but many women activists in the global South, as well as some women of color in the global North, continue to refer to themselves as Third World feminists. For them, the designation "Third World" refers to their anticolonial politics as much as to their economic or geographical locations.

greater control over the activities of multinational corporations (Kabeer 1994; Moser 1991; Sen and Grown 1987).[11] Some Third World feminists regard this self-help and bottom-up approach to development as more genuinely democratic and more empowering to women as citizens than government-initiated forms of development.

Perhaps the most direct feminist assault on traditional conceptions of citizenship is implicit in the slogan emblematic of Western second-wave feminism, "The personal is political."[12] This slogan asserts that so-called personal or private life is shaped by power inequalities that are rooted not only in individual characteristics but also in social structures. Thus, apparently individual problems often have systemic causes, and many so-called personal decisions about issues of sexuality, appearance, consumption, and family life have political implications. The slogan has often been interpreted to mean that working to change the institutions that shape personal life should be recognized as a form of political activism.

Each of the foregoing strands of argument draws attention to activities occurring outside those arenas traditionally recognized as constituting the public realm—activities focused on the social, the domestic, and the personal rather than on the state and the market. The theorists highlighting these activities destabilize traditional understandings of the spaces in which citizenship is performed, understandings that have assumed a separation between the social on the one hand and "politics and questions of citizenship" on the other (Kaplan 1997:184). Such feminist work challenges older conceptions of citizenship by suggesting not only that citizens may be female but also that women and men may often *do* citizenship differently from each other and do it in different locations.

From Civil Society to NGOs

Feminist interest in arenas of citizenship beyond the state and the market chimes with recent valorizations of civil society promoted by nonfeminist theorists. Hegel was the first Western philosopher to articulate the notion of civil society as a semi-autonomous and nonpolitical realm of life under the protection but not the explicit direction of the state.[13] For Hegel, civil society was constituted primarily by the

11. Often-cited examples of such organizations include GABRIELA in the Philippines, the Forum Against the Oppression of Women in Bombay, and SEWA (the Self-Employed Women's Association) in Ahmedabad, India.

12. This slogan may be seen as a feminist appropriation of older anarchist and New Left ideas about the need to democratize everyday life.

13. In recognizing that people may achieve some unity or coordination outside the political structure, Hegel's idea of civil society idea builds on Locke's earlier postulation of a prepolitical state of nature. However, Locke used the term "civil society" to refer not to the state of nature but rather to the political society that succeeded the state of nature. McBride reflects that the general sense that civil society is something good is probably encouraged by the fact that "civil" can mean not only "organized" but also "decent" or "civilized." He also remarks that the fact that many European languages have a word with more or less the same two meanings probably reflects two ancient divisions, one between town and country and a corresponding one between the civil and uncivil or uncouth (McBride 2001:49).

self-regulating entrepeneurial economy, but today, the term "civil society" usually excludes the economy and refers instead to a terrain of voluntary associations existing between the economy and the state (Phillips 1999:56). These associations include families, social movements, and voluntary, nonprofit associations, often referred to as nongovernmental organizations (NGOs). None of them is controlled directly by the state, though all exist within the regulative framework that the state provides. Whereas the state is said to coordinate action through the medium of its authorized coercive power and the economy to coordinate action through the medium of money, civil society is said to coordinate action through the medium of communicative interaction (Cohen and Arato 1992).[14]

Several developments in the 1980s and 1990s encouraged Western political theory to give new attention to civil society. In the industrialized nations, new social movements, such as the peace and environmental movements, were regarded as opening up spaces of democratic practice outside the state (Cohen and Arato 1992; Offe 1985).[15] Meanwhile, neoliberal governments in the United States, United Kingdom, and elsewhere wanted to reduce the state's responsibility for various social welfare functions and to "deregulate" the economy, especially reducing governmental control over large corporations. Spokespersons for these governments lauded the ability of civil society to meet social needs through voluntary action, without the coercion of state power, and more efficiently than when hampered by government regulation. At the same time, many left-wing and semianarchist groups, such as Germany's Green Party, were resisting both the bureaucratic control of the state and the technical efficiency of the market and extolling the virtues of interdependence, free association, local democracy, self-reliance, and spontaneity, all of which they associated with civil society. Finally, activism in civil society was given much credit for undermining authoritarian regimes in Eastern Europe, South Africa, and Latin America and eventually causing their collapse. In response, many Western theorists in the 1990s agreed that the best hope for establishing democracy in regions previously governed by authoritarian rule lay in limiting the state's control over social life and in encouraging the emergence of a vibrant civil society. Citizenship was redefined "as the active exercise of responsibilities, including economic self-reliance and political participation. Implicit in this redefinition is a dismantling of the ostensibly 'passive' citizenship associated with the postwar, so-called 'statist,' period" (Shild 1998:94).

14. Because the liberal tradition has always been concerned to limit the power of the state, it has tended to look favorably on civil society as a space of freedom, in which individual happiness and fulfillment might be found. By contrast, the state-centered socialist regimes of Eastern Europe sought to bring all aspects of social life under direct government regulation. Marx thought that the idea of civil society functioned within liberal theory as a rationale for insulating the powers of capital from explicitly political scrutiny, and he rejected the idea that civil society was politically neutral. McBride reports that Marx almost spat when he pronounced *buergerliche Gesellschaft*, the German words for *bourgeois civil society* (McBride 2001:147).

15. New social movements were seen "as actively creating alternative spaces for new democratic practices" (Ewig 1999:77). They were welcomed as "disruptors of sedimented, limiting social identities and narrow understandings of the political, and hence as capable of opening up new spaces of democratic practice and, often, of even bypassing the state altogether" (Schild 1998:96).

In the last decades of the twentieth century, Western theorists discussed civil society in terms that were almost entirely positive.[16] Writers on both right and left of the political spectrum portrayed civil society as operating on a higher ethical plane than either politics or the economy, since it was characterized by activities that were voluntary rather than required by law and undertaken for altruistic reasons rather than motivated by profit. It became widely regarded as the realm of community, equality, creativity, and full human development, and "the dogma that strengthening civil society is the key to creating or sustaining a healthy polity (came) to dominate the thinking of major charitable foundations, as well as human rights and humanitarian organizations" (Rieff 1999:12). Civil society was characterized in terms of diversity, tolerance, mutual aid and solidarity, responsiveness, and democracy, and its associations were "presented as the solution to problems of welfare service delivery, development and democratization" (Fisher 1997:41). The discourse of autonomy, accountability, and responsibility promoted by the new civilian governments in Latin America and elsewhere referred to "the qualities expected not only of bureaucracies but also of citizens and of civil society in general" (Schild 1998:99).

Women were largely excluded from civil society as Hegel had described it, but more contemporary understandings identify civil society with a social realm that, since the nineteenth century, has often been regarded as feminine (Riley 1988:50).[17] Anne Phillips suggests that feminists are especially likely to be attracted to civil society activism because feminism is radically pluralistic, and pluralism flourishes better in civil society than in either family or state (Phillips 1999:56). She asserts that locally based associations are more accessible to women than the formal channels of state power and that the informality and openness of many associations in civil society encourage the emergence of previously unheard voices, the exposure of previously unchallenged biases, and the articulation of previously neglected issues. Phillips reports that many feminists "have expressed reservations about centralized state power, talked of the risks of co-option and betrayal, and presented state institutions as actively patriarchal or peculiarly unresponsive to human need" (Phillips 1999:57).[18]

16. "Within the works of Western democratization experts . . . (t)he cultivation of civil society is said to be beneficial because it encourages citizens to organize to promote their interests and fosters ties among like-minded people across divisions of race, class, ethnicity, and gender. Private interest organizations create alternative power centers outside the state, provide an opportunity for learning leadership and developing political skills, and can provide not only a means of political communication but also a mechanism for tracking government performance and holding governments accountable. . . . Such an account of civil society sounds uniformly beneficial" (Hawkesworth 2001:228).

17. Although the realm of the social has often been regarded as feminine, Anne Phillips observes that, insofar as "civil" often implies a contrast with natural or familial, whereas "woman" still suggests an association with nature or family, civil society often conjures up a masculine realm (Phillips 1999:56). Nancy Fraser argues that the bourgeois public sphere (as conceived by Habermas) has been inhospitable to women because, in the absence of social equality, formal political equality is not enough for women to make their voices heard.

18. For example, Phillips observes many feminists have preferred self-financing and self-regulating community nurseries to nurseries provided by the local government and funded by taxation. Even though physical facilities may be worse in the community nurseries, more opportunities exist for developing nonsexist ways of caring for children, promoting healthy diets, and so on.

By contrast, she asserts that civil society offers more scope for identifying and exploring nonsexist, egalitarian ways of doing things and contends that "the battle for sexual equality has to be won in civil society, for there is a limit to what can be achieved through the 'right' legislation alone" (Phillips 1999:58).

In the 1980s, Western discussions of civil society tended to focus on what were called the new social movements, but in the 1990s the focus shifted to NGOs. "NGOs may be a part of social movements, such as the women's environmental, and fundamentalist movements, but by definition an NGO is narrower in scope, constituency, and impact" (Silliman 1999:154). NGOs are nonprofit, nonparty organizations whose goal is to serve a social purpose in the public interest. They are typically created and managed by their members in order to produce or distribute benefits to others. "NGOs include a broad spectrum—from unstructured associations with no funds comprised of a handful of volunteers who espouse a social cause, to elaborate organizations with broad membership bases, large budgets, professional staff, and considerable political clout. There are both 'David' and 'Goliath' NGOs" (Silliman 1999:135).

In the 1990s, NGOs became celebrated as means by which local communities could empower themselves and enable people who had been previously marginalized or silenced to participate in the everyday decisions that shaped their lives. Because women are represented disproportionately among the marginalized and silenced, many feminists came to see NGOs as grassroots democratic vehicles for achieving feminist goals. Civil society has long been regarded as a school of citizenship, but in the 1990s it came to be regarded not only as a training ground for citizens but also as an arena in which citizenship was practiced.[19] For instance, the development of a "feminist curriculum" by the Chilean women's movement has been described as a "struggle to promote new forms of citizenship for women." "Without calling it such, the women's movement was engaged in undermining Chile's authoritarian political culture by promoting a redefinition of citizenship and more generally the concept of the political" (Schild 1998:109).

Recent activism in civil society by women and feminists reinforces older feminist suggestions that there should be more to citizenship than governing, fighting, buying, selling, and working for pay. It also suggests that the arenas in which citizenship should be performed extend beyond the state, the battlefield, and the market. I agree that classic Western understandings of the terrain of citizenship have been narrow and gender biased and that a more inclusive model is required to recognize many of women's distinctive contributions as citizens—not to mention providing an expanded model of citizenship for men. However, I also worry that undue emphasis on activism in civil society may sometimes restrict rather than expand women's empowerment as citizens. In the next section, I offer a counterbalance to uncritical valorizations of civil society by describing some of the ways in which women's involvement in this arena has muffled or

---

19. Participation in the women's movement certainly made Brazilian women feel more empowered, a feeling that "guides them both in questioning domestic relationships and in changing state agencies and the services they provide" (Caldeira 1998:83).

marginalized their voices as citizens and thwarted rather than promoted feminist goals.

NGOs and Women's Citizenship

Nongovernmental organizations vary widely not only in their size, goals and membership but also in their sources of funding.[20] Local NGOs often raise money through member initiatives, such as benefit concerts or bake or garage sales, while larger NGOs may receive funds from philanthropic foundations, religious organizations, or businesses. In the countries of the global South, NGOs frequently receive money from wealthy donors who wish to avoid channeling their foreign aid through Third World governments that they regard as inefficient or corrupt or who wish "to strengthen 'civil society' and promote 'citizen participation'" (Schild 1998:99). Some NGOs receive money from their own governments. In Africa and Latin America, some NGOs have contracts from their governments to provide women's health services. In Germany, many women's shelters, women's centers, and feminist job training institutions are funded by the state (Lang 1997:112). The source of an NGO's funding obviously influences the sorts of services it provides, as well its ability to challenge the policies of its donors, whether corporate or governmental.[21] Rather than prioritizing the expressed practical needs of their clients, much less their clients' longer term needs for structural change, some NGOs have become "women's auxiliaries" for government or business, abandoning "the kinds of projects they closely associated with their feminist commitments."[22]

Even when donors have no corporate or governmental agendas, NGOs' projects are shaped by the demand for fiscal accountability, which often pushes NGOs to select narrow, "realistic" projects, whose outcomes are accessible to measurement.[23] "The impact of an NGO trying to change power structures or dominant social values cannot be easily quantified through standard evaluation procedures to fit neatly into a project report for a funding agency or government" (Silliman

20. Many types of NGOs have been identified, including community-based organizations (CBOs), grassroots organizations (GROs), people's organizations (POs), membership support organizations (MSOs), GONGOs, QUANGOs, DONGOs,[A] and the like. Unfortunately "the creation and use of acronyms remains inconsistent within the field" (Fisher 1997:447).

21. In the 1970s, I worked with a Cincinnati women's organization that sought funding from the United Way. The price of this funding was that our organization should refrain from providing referrals to services for abortion and for lesbians. The NGOs that take corporate money are the contemporary incarnation of the nonprofit civic associations of the nineteenth-century United States, which were conceived and funded by entrepreneurs such as Andrew Carnegie and John D. Rockefeller (Hall 1992).

22. Examples of feminist projects "promote consciousness raising through a 'feminist curriculum' (the various workshops on topics such as sexuality, women's rights, and leadership training)" (Schild 1998:106).

23. "A common complaint on the part of the NGO professionals is that their approach to social programs highlights 'process,' while (government) agencies emphasize 'outcomes' and 'products' (for example, the number of streets paved, or the number of women trained in a particular skill)" (Schild 1998:105).

1999:138). Nevertheless, in order to survive, many "NGOs must adapt to this commodification of their purposes" (Schild 1998:105).

Because NGOs often mediate between social movements and the state, they may "translate needs claimed by oppositional movements 'into potential objects of state administration'" (Silliman 1999:155), in some cases even replacing grassroots mobilizations.[24] The reduction of feminist constituencies to professional "expert publics" "results in the exclusion of a larger public and in the controlled and restrictive appropriation of a feminist agenda for state policies" (Lang 1997:115–6). Within some NGOs, feminist discourses become "tamed, selected, and resignified, losing radicalism and transformative power" (Caldeira 1998:80).[25]

The demand for accountability to their donors limits not only the goals of many NGOs but also their internal democracy. Writing requests for funding is not something easily undertaken by poor and already overworked women, who may well have limited literacy skills. In order to win grants and demonstrate their accountability, NGOs are forced to develop formal organizational structures and hire professional staff, rather than encouraging local women to organize and speak for themselves. "In this process of becoming more 'accountable,' many women's NGOs have come to replicate the corporate model of organization" (Silliman 1999:139). Working on formal structures and paying for professional staff may consume much of NGOs' organizational time, energy, and funds.

The professionalization of NGO services also operates to transform some women into clients of others. For instance, feminist NGOs in Nicaragua are dedicated to helping poor and working-class women improve their health, but "reaching out to women of the poor and working classes is not the same as allowing these women to participate in making decisions about the NGO's goals or operation" (Ewig 1999:97). Many professionalized NGOs reproduce class inequalities and limit the internal democracy of the women's movement (Ewig 1999:96).[26] Some NGOs resist the pressure to professionalize; in Nicaragua, "the smaller and less-professionalized NGOs are the ones that tend to encourage greater participation and are likelier to succeed in incorporating women of different classes" (Ewig 1999:97). However, it is precisely the "activist NGOs that are closest to the grass roots" that lose out in the competition for funding (Schild 1998:106).

Some NGOs attempt to bridge the gap between their clients and their well-educated, middle-class professional staff by utilizing so-called participatory research

---

24. "German women's movements have metamorphosed from over-arching movements into small-scale professionalized organizations. They no longer focus on mobilizing feminists for the re-building of a democratic public sphere but have turned into women's nongovernmental organizations (NGOs) with strong ties to the state" (Lang 1997:102).

25. "As NGOs become the main form under which women organize, they may be losing important spaces for transforming their everyday lives and practices" (Caldeira 1998:84).

26. In Chile, "the clientization of some poor and working-class women, carried out by others in the name of advancing the cause of women, is in effect undermining the possibility that poor and working-class women will come together to articulate their own needs" (Schild 1998:108). In Brazil, "the rapid professionalization . . . provoked by the proliferation of NGOs break(s) down the traditional connections that many middle-class feminists have maintained with working-class women for a long time, alienating the latter from the movement's new activities, most clearly from transnational networking" (Caldeira 1998:80).

methods, such as the World Bank's "Beneficiary Assessment," "Social Analysis," and "Participatory Rural Appraisal" (PRA), all of which seek to discover how local communities perceive their own needs (Francis 2001:72). However, Mohan charges that the "primitivist discourse" of PRA tends to promote a view of "communities" as harmonious while romanticizing and essentializing "the poor" (Mohan 2001:159-60).[27] Kothari notes that supposedly participatory research often relies on a moralistic and simplistic use of binary oppositions, such as uppers/lowers, North/South, professional/local knowledge, micro/macro, margins/center, local/elite, and powerless/powerful (Kothari 2001). In situations of inequality, clients' so-called participation in NGOs may provide simply "the 'sense' and warm emotional pull of participation without its substance" (Taylor 2001:125). Similarly,

> development agencies may allow an NGO to "represent" indigenous people at decisions taken in Washington, DC, or elsewhere, but the selection of some NGO to stand in for people is quite different from ensuring that decisions affecting the lives and resources of indigenous people are not taken without their informed consent. (Fisher 1997:455)

Deborah Mindry notes that women's and feminist NGO discourse relies heavily on terms such as "local," "community," "grassroots," "empowerment" "development," "enterprise," "self-help," "education," and (in South Africa) "uplift." She observes that the language of grassroots empowerment is often used in ways that tend to replicate earlier colonial relations, "constituting some women as benevolent providers and others as worthy or deserving recipients of development and empowerment" (Mindry 2001:1189). "Poor, rural, black and brown ("third-world") women have been idealized and objectified as a worthy category of intervention. Often portrayed as innocent victims of oppression, poverty, and "ignorance" (construed as something akin to political naivete), they are represented as helpless, apolitical in their misery, and needy of representation" (Mindry 2001:1203). By contrast, the needs of young and urban women are neglected, perhaps because they are less "helpless, humble and virtuous" (Mindry 2001:1207).

Critics of the contemporary emphasis on civil society and NGOs argue that addressing social problems through private rather than public channels depoliticizes the poor. Involvement in "self-help" microprojects encourages poor women to exhaust their scarce energies in developing ad hoc services or products for the informal economy rather than mobilizing as citizens to demand that the state utilize their tax monies for the provision of public services (Petras 1997). Thus, even though NGOs create programs that involve and serve women, their private provision of services tacitly acquiesces in the state's shedding or, as Canadians call it, "downloading" its public responsibilities.[28] For example:

> Muhammad Yunus, the founder of the Grameen Bank, has announced that the bank is working with the government to replace the nationalized health care system with a

---

27. Mohan also observes that "community" is a term most often used by the state or by outsiders — or by those who wish to impose yet more care-taking responsibilities on women.

28. For instance, Veronica Schild argues that in Latin America NGOs are being used to implement "social adjustment" strategies as well as for developing new forms of citizenship (Schild 1998).

system for poor people on a "cost recovery basis.". . . The privatization of health care and dismantling of government programs . . . are in line with the political goals and orientation of neoliberal economic agendas (Silliman 1999:145)[29]

Anne Phillips asserts that the voluntary associations of civil society belong only to their members, but this assertion is too simple (Phillips 1999:57). Although many NGOs are self-supporting, many rely on outside funding. The rhetoric of accountability surrounding NGOs ignores the fact that "the structure of an NGO requires accountability to outside actors such as international funders, rather than to the membership or even its target population. This arrangement inhibits horizontal democratic participation" (Ewig 1999:97). Some critics argue that foreign-funded NGOs are a new form of colonialism because they create dependence on non-elected overseas funders and their locally appointed officials, undermining the development of social programs administered by elected officials accountable to local people.[30] Kalpana Mehta observes that, in India, "NGOs could be said to be running a parallel government in the country, with priorities determined abroad and with no accountability to the people" (Mehta 1996:49, quoted in Silliman 1999:147).

That women's NGOs use the language of inclusion, empowerment, and grassroots democracy provides no guarantee that in practice they empower local women as citizens, enhance their political influence, or promote feminist goals. Because NGOs often must tailor their projects to what funding agencies find acceptable rather than to what clients say they need, they often contain grassroots mobilization and forestall challenges to the structural status quo. Moreover, rather than maximizing poor women's democratic participation in and control of community development projects, the professionalized *modus operandi* of many NGOs disempowers their clients and further marginalizes them as citizens. When women's struggles "are no longer conceived as struggles for citizenship rights but framed as disputes for private resources" (Caldeira 1998:80), the work of NGOs may undermine the social citizenship entitlements of poor women and weaken the legitimacy of Third World states. As Silliman puts it, expanding civil society may shrink political spaces. In such circumstances, participation in civil society does not enhance women's citizenship but rather eviscerates it.

Heterogeneous and Interdependent Arenas of Citizenship

Do these problems mean that feminist activists should curtail their work in civil society and return to more traditional state-centered understandings of the practice

---

29. "The Nicaraguan women's centers are caught in a vicious cycle: by providing low-cost health services to the public and free consultation to the state, they are playing into the hands of neoconservatives who minimize the state's responsibility to its people." The centers do not want to let the state "off the hook," but "if (they) insisted that only the state should provide these services, given the state's current spending limits under structural adjustment, the movement would risk worsening the already severe health risks that Nicaraguan women face" (Ewig 1999:94–5).

30. "In India, NGOs with foreign connections have sometimes been regarded as antinationalist agents of capitalism and Western political and cultural values" (Fisher 1997:454, citing Karat 1988).

and terrain of citizenship? This question, like much of the civil society literature, relies on static and dichotomous understandings of state and civil society and indeed the economy. A more adequate conception of citizenship must begin by recognizing that civil society, state, and economy are each quite heterogeneous. Moreover, although each is partially autonomous, none is entirely separate from the others but instead presupposes them. Civil society, state, and economy are not discrete spheres but rather overlapping and interlocking, not independent but rather interdependent, not separate but rather inseparable.

Not-for-profit associations in civil society are often contrasted with profit-driven business organizations, but the division between civil society and market economy is not as sharp as this contrast suggests. The goal of some NGOs "is to help the poor and marginalized access the market by financing small social and economic infrastructure programs" (Schild 1998:105), and many labor, professional, consumer, and even environmental organizations direct their activities toward influencing or limiting the market in other ways. Conversely, many businesses use donations to influence or limit the agendas of nonprofit organizations. Many NGOs employ paid staff who regard their work as a "job" (Lang 1997:114), and many sell products to raise money and promote their causes. Membership and influence in many voluntary organizations reflects existing inequalities in power and in access to resources such as money, information, contacts, and time, inequalities that are typically rooted in market relations (Phillips 1999:58). In addition, the fact that nonprofit organizations must compete with each other for funding creates pressure for many to develop a corporate culture, characterized by "glossy publications, high-powered seminars, and workshops conducted in lavish NGO quarters around the world" (Silliman 1999:139). Thus, civil society does not exist independently of the market but instead is enmeshed with it in a complex and changing web of relationships that are variously oppositional and symbiotic. According to John Keane, "where there are no markets, civil societies find it impossible to survive"; equally, "where there is no civil society, there can be no markets" (Keane 1998:19).

The contrast between civil society and the state is also frequently overdrawn, even though the associations of civil society are often referred to as nongovernmental organizations and the voluntary nature of their activities is often contrasted with the coercion associated with the state. Civil society is just as intertwined with the state as it is with the market.[31] Many organizations in civil society exist in order to influence the state; conversely, they, like all social institutions, are regulated by the state, even though they are not under its direct control.[32] Sometimes governments give money to NGOs, but sometimes they take money from them.[33] Individuals' opportunities

31. The distance between civil society and the state varies, according to the context. In the period of Nicaraguan dictatorship, civil society and state were far apart, but in the 1980s, under the Sandinista government, they were very close (Ewig 1999:78).

32. The extent of permissible or desirable state regulation over "private associations" is a matter of frequent controversy. For instance, should Catholic universities be allowed to discriminate against non-Catholics or Boy Scouts against homosexuals?

33. The main government agency for women in Chile, the Servicio Nacional de la Mujer (National Women's bureau, or SERNAM), is almost entirely funded from abroad (Schild 1998:105).

for political equality and full citizenship are often affected by their positions in civil society; for instance, leaders of NGOs directed to serving women are frequently hired as "gender-expert" consultants to corporations, states, or UN agencies (Hawkesworth 2001:231).[34] Some NGOs, called by their critics "para-statal" organizations (Schild 1998:105), have become simply vehicles for the delivery of state services. Other organizations, which replace state activities in the social sector and function as repair networks for economic and political disintegration processes, are less accurately described as nongovernmental than as semigovernmental organizations (Lang 1997:112). Thus, civil society does not exist as a sphere separate from the state; instead, it is necessarily enmeshed with the state, as it is with the economy, in a complex, changing, and interdependent web of relationships that are both oppositional and symbiotic.

Although the associations of civil society typically invoke ethical values, they possess no "natural innocence" (Lang 1997:103). Civil society is penetrated by power derived from the economy and the state, and its leaders and associations are often coopted by government or business. Thus, even when NGOs represent themselves as invoking ethical standards that exist above or outside the political arena, their judgments and activities are not apolitical or politically neutral (Fisher 1997:458). Many associations of civil society are undemocratic and exclusionary, and some, such as the Ku Klux Klan, promote values worse than those upheld by their government.[35] As William F. Fisher observes, "there is no simple or consistent story of good NGOs confronting evil governments" (Fisher 1997:452).

Because civil society is not the sphere of a higher ethical consciousness, activism in this arena is not necessarily "cleaner" or more virtuous than activism in formal politics. Moreover, because civil society is only partially autonomous of the state and the market, activism within it is often continuous with more traditional forms of political and economic activity. For these reasons, women's empowerment as citizens often depends less on whether we choose formal politics or civil society—or, indeed, the economy—as our arena of activism and more on the nature of our work within each arena. Most important is that, in every arena, our work should sustain a commitment to both democratic empowerment and social equality.

Commitments to democratic empowerment and social equality can and indeed must be pursued through the organizations of civil society, including NGOs. The relationship between NGOs and social movements is dynamic (Fisher 1997:541), and although some NGOs may limit social movements, some promote their goals. Nira Yuval-Davis asserts that "NGOs, like other political organizations, have to be judged according to their specific projects and practices rather than *en*

---

34. In South Africa in the mid-1990s, "leaders of NGOs were being drawn into positions of political power at national and regional levels in the new African National Congress (ANC)-led democratic government [and] it was clear that the route to power was through NGOs" (Mindry 2001:1191).

35. David Rieff reports that pregenocide Rwanda was viewed by development experts as having one of the most developed civil societies in Africa (Rieff 1999:15). In "Bad Civil Society," Simone Chanbers and Jeffrey Kopstein discuss civil society organizations that deny the value of reciprocity, which "involves the recognition of other citizens, even those with whom one has deep disagreement, as moral agents deserving of civility" (Chambers and Kopstein 2001:839).

bloc as positive or negative phenomena" (Yuval-Davis 1997:121).[36] Naila Kabeer offers several criteria for identifying NGOs that promote the genuine empowerment of their members.[37] Her criteria are designed primarily for NGOs intended to promote economic development for women in the global South, but they may well be more widely applicable. However, no matter how well an NGO succeeds in promoting internal democracy and economic development, Kabeer contends that the longer term empowerment of poor women ultimately requires that such women should not only participate at the project level but also have a voice in the broader policy-making agenda. Feminists cannot remain content with activity that promotes democracy and improves women's lives only within parameters that remain unquestioned.

Some organizations of civil society succeed in challenging those parameters. Iris Young distinguishes three levels of associative activity in civil society. Private associations, such as families and social clubs, primarily exist for the benefit of their members; civic associations aim to improve "the collective life of the neighborhood, city, country, or world"; political associations focus self-consciously on "claims about what the social collective ought to do" (Young 2000:161–2). Many feminist criticisms of NGOs may be recast as complaints that some of them operate too much as civic or even private associations, focusing too exclusively on meeting women's practical gender needs and neglecting the larger context of their strategic gender needs. However, innumerable examples exist of NGOs taking on larger policy issues. In the 1970s, the Bombay Forum Against Oppression of Women campaigned on the issue of homelessness, which was an acute problem for women deserted or abused by their husbands, raising awareness of the male bias in inheritance legislation and succeeding in placing these issues on the mainstream political agenda (Moser 1991:109). In the United States, many women's organizations have worked for reforms in the areas of reproductive rights or welfare legislation.[38] In these and many other cases, activism in civil society has articulated group consciousness, provided a voice for the excluded, and expanded political agendas (Young 2000:165).

Activism in civil society supplements and enriches traditional state-oriented political activity, but it cannot replace it. One feminist development NGO asserts that

> although NGOs can effectively influence the direction of public policies, and can implement exemplary programs, no amount of service provision by non-governmental

---

36. Following Clarke (1996), Fisher suggests "conceiving NGOs as 'an arena within which battles from society at large are internalized' rather than as a set of entities" (Fisher 1997:449). He advises attention to the ideology and politics of both the associations and the analysts (Fisher 1997:447).

37. The more empowering NGOs organize "around the participatory modes of needs identification and prioritization rather than through the imposition of their own priorities on those who have traditionally had no voice in influencing the course of development." Their rules and practices endeavor to "compensat(e) for the exclusionary implications of most conventional institutions of resource distribution . . . [and] to provide women with access to new kinds of resources." Finally, they position women not as needy clients but rather as socially constrained but competent actors with "the ability to evolve their own agendas rather than merely implementing predetermined ones" (Kabeer 1995:261–2).

38. In Nicaragua, NGOs drew on the global feminist concept of integral health-care to shape an alternative health-care model for the state (Ewig 1999:79, 85). In Chile they influenced the constitution.

organizations can substitute for the state in some of these critical areas referring to good health, education, clean water and fuel, child care and basic nutrition at reasonable cost for the majority of people. (DAWN 1995:43–4, quoted in Silliman 1999:143)

David Rieff observes: "Without a treasury, a legislature or an army at its disposal, civil society is less equipped to confront the challenges of globalization than nations are, and more likely to be wracked by divisions based on region and the self-interest of the single-issue groups that form the nucleus of the civil society movement" (Rieff 1999:14). Although twentieth-century feminists often found that states promoted conservative political agendas, these feminists also relied on states to enforce laws against discrimination and promote social welfare. Twentieth-century women achieved their highest status on many measures within the welfare states of Africa, Australia, and Europe, especially Scandinavia.

Events in the last quarter of the twentieth century showed that strong civil societies are indispensable for resisting oppressive states and for promoting democracy and government accountability. However, the increase in inequality and poverty, especially among women, that accompanied governments' worldwide retreat from the social welfare responsibilities they had assumed in the first three-quarters of the century demonstrated that civil society is not able to substitute for the state. Civil society may sometimes be "bad," oppressive, and undemocratic, and improving it may require promoting more just social and economic arrangements (Chambers and Kopstein 2001). In Iris Young's view, civil society and state (as well as the economy) must be kept in balance: civic associations should be neither tied so closely to state institutions that they are unable to hold them accountable nor so influential that they lose "a generalized vision of the co-ordinated action of the whole society" (Young 2000:195). A "good" state and a "good" civil society each require the other.

Chilean feminists have debated the split between the *politicas*, feminists who believe that the struggle for women's greater equality must be fought through the state, and the *autonomias*, who fear that appealing to the state will undermine feminists' autonomy and the transformative-emancipatory potential of the women's movement (Schild 1998:100). In fact, the achievement of democratic empowerment and social justice requires what Chileans call *doble militancia*, activism in the arenas of both state and civil society (Schild 1998:100). Fortunately for women, who have too often been called on to work double or even triple shifts, the interpenetration of civil society and state means that sometimes it may be possible to fulfill the responsibilities of citizenship in both arenas simultaneously.

Citizenship in a Global Context

Recognizing that civil society is an indispensable, though not exclusive, arena for citizen activity is an important step toward developing a richer conception of citizenship that is more adequate for the twenty-first century. However, the arenas of citizenship are not limited to national civil societies, states, and markets, because these arenas are no longer—if they ever were—insulated from external pressures, including other states and global institutions. When decisions made in one country have far-reaching consequences for people's lives elsewhere, citizens can no longer define the public good exclusively in terms of the interests of their compatriots. At the beginning of the twenty-first century, many arenas of citizenship have become global as well as national, and citizens' rights and responsibilities, privileges, and duties must be rethought in this global context. Just as civil society is enmeshed with the state, so the global and national are not separate arenas but interpenetrate on many levels.

One manifestation of the interconnection between national and global arenas of citizenship is the emergence of many transnational feminist movements and organizations. In the last quarter of the twentieth century, a number of UN conferences encouraged women and feminists to work together across borders, and transnational feminist networks have opposed violence against women and promoted their rights (Keck and Sikkink 1998). Such transnational networks include the Latin American and Caribbean Women's Health Network, Women Living Under Muslim Laws, and ABANTU for Development (Ewig 1999:83; Yuval-Davis 1997:121). In this context, the foreign funding of women's NGOs has not always been imperialistic. Yuval-Davis reports that many NGOs in the global South have been able to survive and resist local pressures through the aid provided from overseas, "as well as the more personal support and solidarity of feminist organizations in other countries." She observes: "it would be a westocentric stereotype to view women associated with NGOs in the South as puppets of western feminism" (Yuval-Davis 1997:120–1). Over the past twenty-five years, transnational feminist NGOs have provided voices for many hitherto excluded women and placed their issues on global agendas. Civil society has become increasingly a terrain of global as well as local activism, addressing not only states but also international institutions.

The inseparability of national and global is also evident in the disproportionate effects that the policies and actions of some states have on others. Generalizations about "the state" suggest that all states are similar, obscuring profound differences, and especially inequalities, among them. States are strong or weak not only in relation to their own citizens but also in relation to each other, and only the citizens of the most powerful states can afford to ignore these inequalities. Feminist citizens of the United States may sometimes wish that their government would take a stronger domestic role, for instance in providing social benefits, but they benefit daily, if not voluntarily, from the overwhelming power that their state wields abroad.

The intersection between the national and the global is strikingly revealed by the enormous number of foreign-born residents in many countries, especially, though not only, the wealthy countries of the North Atlantic.[39] Lacking citizenship in the country where they reside and sometimes any citizenship at all, such migrants are extremely vulnerable. This is especially true of women migrants, whose

---

39. Large numbers of refugees also reside in several poor countries, often overwhelming their resources.

residence may depend on male family members (Bakan and Stasiulis 1994; Narayan 1997a, 1997b). The precarious situation of many migrants clearly demonstrates that the possession of citizenship remains crucial to individuals' safety, security, and well-being. Conceptions of citizenship for the twenty-first century must reflect on the phenomenon of large-scale migration and develop nonsexist and nonracist criteria for achieving full citizenship.

Repelled by masculinist and imperialist nationalisms, some Western feminists have sought to distance themselves from their states.[40] Virginia Woolf famously declared: "as a woman, I have no country. As a woman, I want no country. As a woman, my country is the whole world" (Woolf 1938). However, the privileges of citizenship in powerful Western states remain substantial, and the responsibilities of such citizens cannot be met by disassociating ourselves from our countries.[41] Just as activism in civil society is not an exclusive alternative to traditional state-centered politics, so global feminist citizenship is not an alternative to national citizenship. Instead, it is an insistence on holding our own state accountable for the impact of its policies on women all over the world (Cf. Zajovic 1994).

References

Ackelsberg, Martha A. 1988. "Communities, Resistance, and Women's Activism: Some Implications for a Democratic Polity." In *Women and the Politics of Empowerment*, ed. Ann Bookman and Sandra Morgen. Philadelphia: Temple University Press.

Allen, Holly. 2000. "Gender, Sexuality and the Military Model of U.S. National Community." In *Gender Ironies of Nationalism: Sexing the Nation*, ed. Tamar Mayer. London: Routledge.

Bakan, Abigail B. and Daiva Stasiulis. 1994. "Foreign Domestic Worker Policy in Canada and the Social Boundaries of Modern Citizenship." *Science and Society* 58:1, 7–35.

Braidotti, Rosi. 1992. "The Exile, the Nomad, and the Migrant." *Women's Studies International Forum* 15:1, 7–10.

Caldeira, Teresa P. R. 1998. "Justice and Individual Rights: Challenges for Women's Movements and Democratization in Brazil." In *Women and Democracy: Latin America and Central and Eastern Europe*, ed. Jane S. Jaquette and Sharon Wolchik. Baltimore: Johns Hopkins University Press.

Carter, April. 1996. "Women, Military Service and Citizenship." In *Gender, Politics and Citizenship in the 1990s*, ed. Barbara Sullivan and Gillian Whitehouse. Sydney: University of New South Wales Press.

Chambers, Simone, and Jeffrey Kopstein. 2001. "Bad Civil Society." *Political Theory* 29:6, 837–65.

Clarke, G. 1996. "Non-Governmental Organizations (NGOs) and Politics in the Developing World." Pap. Int. Dev. no. 20. Swansea, Wales: Centre for Development Studies.

---

40. By contrast, feminist citizens of many Third World states may have reason for "polycentric" (rather than androcentric) nationalist loyalties, despite those states' past betrayals of women (Herr 2003).

41. Uma Narayan asserts that "bigoted and distorted nationalisms must be fought with feminist attempts to *reinvent* and *reimagine* the national community as more genuinely inclusive and democratic." (Narayan 1997c:36).

Cohen, Jean, and Andrew Arato. 1992. *Civil Society and Political Theory*. Cambridge: MIT Press.

Cooke, Bill, and Uma Kothari. 2001. *Participation: The New Tyranny?* London: Zed Books.

Development Alternatives with Women for a New Era (DAWN). 1995. *Markers on the Way: The DAWN Debates on Alternative Development*. DAWN's Platform for the Fourth World Conference on Women, Beijing, China. Barbados: West Indies.

Ewig, Christina. 1999. "The Strengths and Limits of the NGO Women's Movement Model: Shaping Nicaragua's Democratic Institutions." *Latin American Research Review* 34:3, 75–102.

Fisher, William F. 1997. "Doing Good? The Politics and Antipolitics of NGO Practices." *American Review of Anthropology* 26, 439–64.

Francis, Paul. 2001. "Participatory Development at the World Bank: The Primacy of Process." In Cooke and Kothari 2001.

Fraser, Nancy, and Linda Gordon. 1997. "A Genealogy of 'Dependency': Tracing a Keyword of the Welfare State." Chapter 5 of *Justice Interruptus: Critical Reflections on the "Postsocialist" Condition*. New York: Routledge.

Hall, Peter Dobkin. 1992. *Inventing the Nonprofit Sector and Other Essays on Philanthropy, Voluntarism, and Nonprofit Organizations*. Baltimore: John Hopkins University Press.

Hawkesworth, Mary E. 2001. "Democratization: Reflections on Gendered Dislocations in the Public Sphere." In *Gender, Globalization and Democratization*, ed. Rita Mae Kelly, Jane H. Bayes, Mary E. Hawkesworth, and Brigitte Young. Lanham, Md.: Rowman and Littlefield.

Herr, Ranjoo S. 2003. "The Possibility of a Feminist Nationalism." *Hypatia: A Journal of Feminist Philosophy* 18:3, 135–160.

Kabeer, Naila. 1994. *Reversed Realities: Gender Hierarchies in Development Thought*. New York: Verso.

Kaplan, Temma. 1997. *Crazy for Democracy: Women in Grassroots Movements*. New York: Routledge.

Karat, P. 1988. *Foreign Funding and the Philosophy of Voluntary Organizations: A Factor in Imperialist Strategy*. New Delhi: National Book Centre.

Keane, John. 1998. *Civil Society: Old Images, New Visions*. Stanford: Stanford University Press.

Keck, Margaret E., and Kathryn Sikkink. 1998. "Transnational Networks on Violence Against Women." In *Activists Beyond Borders: Advocacy Networks in International Politics*. Ithaca, N.Y.: Cornell University Press.

Kittay, Eva Feder. 1999. *Love's Labor: Essays on Women, Equality and Dependency*, New York: Routledge.

Kothari, Uma. 2001. "Power, Knowledge and Social Control in Participatory Development." In Cooke and Kothari 2001.

Lang, Sabine. 1997. "The NGOization of Feminism: Institutionalization and Institution Building within the German Women's Movements." In *Transitions, Environments, Translations: Feminisms in International Politics*, ed. Joan W. Scott, Cora Kaplan, and Debra Keates. New York: Routledge.

McBride, William L. 2001. *From Yugoslav Praxis to Global Pathos: Anti-Hegemonic Post-Post-Marxist Essays*. Lanham, Md.: Rowman and Littlefield.

Mehta, Kalpana. 1996. "Population or Development: Search Conference Organized by UNFPA in India." In *Political Environment: A Publication of the Committee on Women, Population and the Environment*, no. 4 (summer-fall). Hampshire College, Amherst, Mass.

Mindry, Deborah. 2001. "Nongovernmental Organizations, 'Grassroots,' and the Politics of Virtue." *Signs* 26:4, 1187–1211.

Mohan, Giles. 2001. "Beyond Participation: Strategies for Deeper Empowerment," in Cooke and Kothari 2001.

Moser, Caroline O. N. 1991. "Gender Planning in the Third World: Meeting Practical and Strategic Needs." In *Gender and International Relations*, ed. Rebecca Grant and Kathleen Newland. Bloomington: Indiana University Press.

Narayan, Uma. 1997a. "'Male-Order' Brides: Immigrant Women, Domestic Violence and Immigration Law." In *Feminist Ethics and Social Policy*, ed. Patrice DiQuinzio and Iris Marion Young. Bloomington: Indiana University Press.

———. 1997b. "Towards a Feminist Vision of Citizenship: Rethinking the Implications of Dignity, Political Participation and Nationality." In *Reconstructing Political Theory: Feminist Perspectives*, ed. Mary Lyndon Shanley and Uma Narayan. University Park: Pennsylvania State University Press.

———. 1997c. *Dislocating Cultures: Identities, Traditions, and Third-World Feminism.* New York: Routledge.

Offe, C. 1985. "New Social Movements: Challenging the Boundaries of Institutional Politics." *Social Research* 52:4 (winter), 817–68.

Offe, C., and V. Ronge. 1984. "Theses on the Theory of the State." In *Contradictions of the Welfare State*, ed. J. Keane. London: Hutchinson.

Petras, James. 1997. "Imperialism and NGOs in Latin America." *Monthly Review* (December), 10–27.

Phillips, Anne. 1992. "Must Feminists Give Up on Liberal Democracy?" *Political Studies* 40, 68–82.

———. 1999. "Who Needs Civil Society? A Feminist Perspective." *Dissent* (winter), 56–61.

Rieff, David. 1999. "The False Dawn of Civil Society." *Nation*, February 22, 11–6.

Riley, Denise. 1988. *"Am I That Name?" Feminism and the Category of "Women" in History.* Minneapolis: University of Minnesota Press.

Ruddick, Sara. 1989. *Maternal Thinking: Towards a Politics of Peace.* Boston: Beacon Press.

Schild, Veronica. 1998. "New Subjects of Rights? Women's Movements and the Construction of Citizenship in the 'New Democracies.'" In *Cultures of Politics/Politics of Cultures*, ed. Sonia E. Alvarez, Evelina Dagnino, and Arturo Escobar. Boulder, Colo.: Westview Press.

Silliman, Jael. 1999. "Expanding Civil Society, Shrinking Political Spaces: The Case of Women's Nongovernmental Organizations." In *Dangerous Intersections: Feminist Perspectives on Population, Environment, and Development*, ed. Jael Silliman and Ynestra King. Cambridge: South End Press.

Taylor, Harry. 2001. "Insights into Participation from Critical Management and Labour Process Perspectives." In Cooke and Kothari 2001.

Tronto, Joan. 1993. *Moral Boundaries: A Political Argument for the Ethics of Care.* New York: Routledge.

Woolf, Virginia. 1938. *Three Guineas.* New York: Harcourt Brace.

Young, Iris M. 1995. "Mothers, Citizenship and Independence: A Critique of Pure Family Values." *Ethics* 105 (April), 535–56.

———. 2000. *Inclusion and Democracy.* Oxford: Oxford University Press.

Yuval-Davis, Nira. 1997. *Gender and Nation.* Thousand Oaks, Calif.: Sage.

Zajovic, Stasa. 1994. "I Am Disloyal." In *What Can We Do for Ourselves?* Proceedings of the East European Feminist Conference. Belgrade: Centre for Women's Studies, Research and Communication.

6

Multiple Subjectivities

Chicanas and Cultural Citizenship

AÍDA HURTADO

As awful as it is to say, it has become trite to mark all events in our lives by "before and after September 11, 2001." The crumbling of the New York City's twin towers signified the end of innocence and the sense of this nation's childlike belief in its invulnerability. Political pundits, academics, and public intellectuals, regardless of political persuasion, embraced this nation's right to defend itself and many brought out their flags and proudly displayed them on their windows, SUVs, and on their bodies. A president who got to be president not by popular vote but by dubious political maneuvering and with the help of a cowardly Supreme Court enjoys unprecedented job approval. Even poking himself in the eye with his glasses as he choked on a pretzel is perceived as charming. But do we all feel the same way? Was this temporary suspension of internal differences for the sake of the war effort felt as uniformly or as deeply as *Newsweek, Time*, the *Wall Street Journal*, the *New York Times*, and all television news outlets led us to believe? What are the underground rumblings of discontent with the whitewashing of the war in Iraq and of the suppression of counterhegemonic discourses? How might these differences in perceptions be the result of a different conception of what constitutes a "nation?" And are the differences in definition of "nation" related to the troubled history of the United States and its colonizing policies?

It is noteworthy that among the most outspoken critics of this "new patriotism" have been women (Butler 2004; Gates 2001; Roy 2001; Sontag 2001). Arundhati Roy wrote, on November 11, 2001, a widely circulated editorial against the war on terror, saying:

Correspondence regarding this essay should be addressed to Aída Hurtado, Psychology Department, University of California, Santa Cruz, Social Science II, Santa Cruz, CA 95064 Cruz; e-mail: aida@cats.ucsc.edu.

> Terrorism as a phenomenon may never go away. But if it is to be contained, the
> first step is for America to at least acknowledge that it shares the planet with other
> nations, with other human beings, who, even if they are not on TV, have loves and
> griefs and stories and songs and sorrows, and, for heaven's sake, rights.

After reading these words out loud to me, my partner told me: "I hope she has a
bodyguard and has no listed address"—that's how transgressive her sympathy could
be perceived as being, in a country that thrives on pretending that cultural and
social and economic assimilation into the "American way" is the solution to the
world's troubles. In spite of the failure of assimilationist policies, the United States
subscribes to the myth, and we've yet to fully understand how cultural, gender, class,
and sexuality are related to our definitions of citizenship and its attendant privileges
(Benmayor 2002).

In this essay, I want to propose that the theoretical writings of Chicana feminists, as well as other feminists of Color, help us understand diversity in its most
profound sense and begin to give us a roadmap toward a more global definition of
citizenship. I also want to draw on a recent national study I just concluded of 101
Mexican-descent Latinas between the ages of twenty and thirty who have attended
higher education. Many of these young women are in the most prestigious graduate programs and professional schools in the country. As such, they voice the
future of what a small number of elites propose as the shape of our participation in
this society that does not honor diversity in the core of its definition of who has
rights as citizens.

The Changing Backdrop to Who We Are as a Nation

The United States has undergone a demographic revolution in the last twenty
years. The notion of a coherent "mainstream" or a coherent "dominant culture" is
becoming increasingly remote (Flores and Benmayor 1997). This is not to say that
the top echelons of the power structure have been substantially integrated but
rather that people's lived experience has become increasingly diverse. One could
argue that perhaps the illusion of coherence was plausible prior to the 1960s, when
there was not such a complex view of what constitutes "family" and where there
seemed to be much more consensus about what constitutes basic "American"
values. But even this is a contested assumption (see Coontz 1992, for the complexities of families through time). Since the 1960s, however, there have been
enormous changes in the basic unit of society. Dominant families no longer look
the way they did in the 1950s or early 1960s (Staples and Mirandé 1980, 892).
Massive cultural and economic changes modified white families to look more like
ethnic and racial families: more female-headed households, higher rates of divorce, more children living in poverty, and higher school dropout rates (Staples
and Mirandé 1980). Married white women are now entering the labor force at a
rate that, until recently, was seen exclusively among women of Color (Baca Zinn
1990; Smith 1987). As a result, different family arrangements have mushroomed,
creating such alternatives as nonmarital cohabitation, single-parent households,
extended kinship units and expanded households, dual-wage-earner families,

commuter marriages, gay and lesbian households, and collectives (Baca Zinn 1990, 71). All of these factors increase the number of overlapping social categories between groups.

Moreover, the old definition of nation rested on having a white majority population and a minority population composed of various groups of Color. This has obviously changed in many areas of the United States, especially California, the most multicultural state and where the majority of Latinos reside. For example, in 1940, Latinos were indeed a minority, constituting only 6 percent of California's population, or approximately 374,000 California residents. By 1980, however, the Latino population reached four million and had nearly doubled by 1990 to over seven million. By the year 2000, nearly one-third of the state was Latino. Nationwide, by the year 2050, only 53 percent of the population is projected to be white, down from 74 percent today (Preston 1996).

As recently as 1960, Latino immigrants were relatively rare; less than 20 percent of Latinos were foreign born. By 1980, however, 37 percent of Latinos were foreign born, with increasing numbers of immigrants from all parts of Mexico and other countries of Latin America. Since 1980, immigration from Latin America has continued at a rapid pace. The 2000 census shows that immigrants make up the majority of California's Latino adult population. Furthermore, the majority of immigrants are Latinos, and the majority of immigrant Latinos are of Mexican descent (Portes and Rumbaut 1990). Mexican immigrants are characterized by their extensive contact with their communities of origin through family visits, through phone calls, and by encouraging immigration of members of their extended family. This is a situation quite different from the one experienced by European immigrants at the turn of the last century, when an ocean and unreliable modes of communication often meant cutting all ties with their native countries—at least for a generation or two (Alvarez 1973). Extensive and frequent contact with Mexico leads Latino immigrants to increase their cultural vitality and renew and modernize their Spanish language skills—a situation that is less likely to lead to complete assimilation (Gurin, Hurtado, and Peng 1994).

Furthermore, under the demographic conditions of a white majority and a nonwhite minority, citizenship rights were based on the concepts of assimilation and acculturation, processes that were facilitated by having immigrants distance themselves from their countries of origin. The majority of immigrants are now Latinos, who have extensive contact with their native countries through the ease of air travel, a 2000-mile border, and the availability of Spanish mass media. Most immigrants do not see assimilation as desirable, and it has become increasingly less necessary as they navigate a multicultural world.

It is within this context that Chicana feminist writers make their proposals for what constitutes cultural citizenship.

The Importance of History and Culture

Chicana feminist writers claim a multiplicity of histories—they readily acknowledge their United States–based Americanness at the same time that they assert their indigenous roots and Mexicanness. Their experience of subordination also makes them natural allies with Third World movements, as well as liberation movements all over the world. As Sonia Saldivar-Hull claims in the preface to her book *Feminisms on the Border*:

> The feminism on the border that I have begun to discuss is more than a theoretical position; it is also an articulation of political solidarity between Third World women in the United States and women such as the Bolivian Domitila Barrios of Chungara, Rigoberta Menchú of Guatemala, and Elvia Alvarado from Honduras. . . . I can now name myself a Chicana feminist scholar—a Third World woman raised at the periphery of the First World, the border region of South Texas. I use *Third World feminism* to indicate how our histories as Chicana/Latina feminists force us to examine geopolitics as well as gender politics. As our alignment with women of the Third World indicates, our subject position exists in the interstices of national borders. (54–55)

Yet theirs is not a commitment to a global ideology akin to what we saw in the 1960s, when young people of all races and ethnicities became Marxists, joining what they perceived as a global class struggle that deemphasized other aspects of social life, such as profound differences in language, culture, religions, and sexuality. The allegiance to global struggles is centered on Chicanas' own cultural, historical, linguistic, and religious specificity.

Chicana feminists writers think of themselves as having lived between and betwixt cultures, languages, nation-states, and intersectionalities of oppression. They openly claim "la frontera"—the borderlands—as permeating all aspects of their being. Fragmentation, however, is a luxury (Hurtado 2003). Rather, coherence is sought *at the same time* that fragmentation is used to gain a deeper understanding of the arbitrary nature of all social and political categories. Chicana feminists as a group align themselves with social justice as *embodied* in the daily lives of people, mostly women, and mostly women of Color (Pérez 1999). Their cultural and historical specificity does not mean they do not question their roots, but it is a questioning that takes place within a commitment and solidarity to stay within their communities even if those communities reject them. As Gloria Anzaldúa says:

> Not me sold out my people but they me. So yes, though "home" permeates every sinew and cartilage in my body, I too am afraid of going home. Though I'll defend my race and culture when they are attacked by non-mexicanos, conosco el malestar de mi cultura [I know my culture's ailments]. I abhor some of my culture's ways, how it cripples its women, como burras [like beasts], our strengths used against us, lowly burras bearing humility with dignity. The ability to serve, claim the males, is our highest virtue. I abhor how my culture makes macho caricatures of its men. No, I do not buy all the myths of the tribe into which I was born. . . . I will not glorify those aspects of my culture which have injured me and which have injured me in the name of protecting me. . . . So, don't give me your tenets and your laws. Don't give me your lukewarm gods. What I want is an accounting with all three cultures—white, Mexican, Indian. I want the freedom to carve and chisel my own face, to staunch the bleeding with ashes, to fashion my own gods out of my entrails. And if going home is denied me then I will have to stand and claim

my space, making a new culture—una cultura mestiza [a hybrid culture]—with my own lumber, my own bricks and mortar and my own feminist architecture. (1987, 21–22)

Chicana feminisms adhere to a *relational* analysis of power (Hurtado 1996a) where all claims of oppression have to be taken seriously to dismantle the existing status quo. The respondents in my study resonated with this analysis as they fought on multiple fronts against inequality. Nina D. Sánchez, as a heterosexual woman, participated as an intern in an organization fighting for gay and lesbian rights. Alicia Granillo attended the meetings of the W. E. B. Du Bois society while at Harvard University to expand her political consciousness. Frida had been politically involved since she was in elementary school and saw her affiliation with women of Color and Third World feminisms. Many of my respondents were reluctant to rank "the oppressions" because they wanted to further the goal of an "authentic, non-hierarchical connection among oppressed groups."

Chicana feminists claim a geographical rootedness to the American Southwest—in particular, to the territory colonized by the United States as a result of the 1848 Treaty of Guadalupe y Hidalgo by which Mexico lost over fifty percent of its territory and is now the five U.S. states of Arizona, California, Colorado, Nuevo Mexico, and Tejas. This territory literally had one nation-state with an Indo/Hispanic/Mexican culture and language layered by another nation-state. The history of colonization and racism did not lead to assimilation and amalgamation but rather to a hybridity that is difficult to miss. It is on the basis of these historical and geographical interstices that Chicana feminists claim *las fronteras* (the borderlands) as the metaphor for their social and cultural citizenship. As Gloria Anzaldúa explains:

> The actual physical borderland that I'm dealing with...is the Texas-U.S. Southwest/Mexican border. The psychological borderlands, the sexual borderlands and the spiritual borderlands are not particular to the Southwest. In fact, the Borderlands are physically present wherever two or more cultures edge each other, where people of different races occupy the same territory, where under, lower, middle and upper classes touch, where the space between two individuals shrinks with intimacy. (1987, preface)

Many of my respondents were invested in crossing borders to expand who they were and to cultivate their critical consciousness about oppression. The borderlands as metaphor was further reinforced as many of my respondents regularly traveled to Mexico, and other Latin American countries. They, as bilingual, multicultural subjects, were socialized into multilayered social meanings that gave them insight into the constructed nature of all social categories. They understood this well when they traveled to Mexico and all of a sudden received male attention, whereas they were not considered physically attractive by many people in the United States. Others worked with coworkers of different racial and ethnic backgrounds, and their own ethnicity and race was read differently according to context. And still others saw the advantages and disadvantages of all the cultural and social systems they were exposed to. My respondents were "hurdle jumpers" (Cuádraz 1989), border crossers (Anzaldúa 1987), and "internal exiles" (Judy Baca, quoted in Anzaldúa 1990, 25–26) who used *las fronteras* to further their understanding of who they were as citizens.

My respondents' travels were not only academic, as tourists, or exploratory—rather, they were visiting a former homeland, trying to find a long-lost familial connection, or trying to make a rediscovery of a cultural and linguistic past that had been beaten out of them in U.S. schools. Their guts literally churned as they entered other social worlds in countries they could have grown up in but for a twist of fate. Their skin color, facial features, and sometimes fluency in the language gave them a reconnection to what they considered the homeland of their ancestors and further contributed to blurring the arbitrary political lines drawn by nation-states.

The Importance of Language

When we speak of the importance of language, it is not simply about speaking in a non-English language, usually Spanish, but also about language having multiple meanings. In 1991 Emma Pérez wrote about Chicana feminist production:

> Our works emerge from *un sitio y una lengua* [a space and language] that rejects colonial ideology and the by-products of colonialism and capitalist patriarchy—sexism, racism, homophobia, etc. The space and language is rooted in both the words and silence of Third-World-Identified-Third-World-Women who create a place apart from white men and women and from men of color. . . . Chicanas seize sociosexual power [to create] our own *sitio y lengua* [space and language]. [I move] from deconstructing male centralist theory about women to reconstructing and affirming a Chicana space and language in an antagonistic society. (161–162)

Emma Perez's phrases "un sitio" (a space) and "una lengua" (a language) capture the essence of the Chicana feminists' project to construct their definition of cultural citizenship. Both parts of the phrase—space and language—have multiple layers of meaning. Claiming *a lengua* meant claiming a language, a tongue, and a discourse. Claiming *a sitio* involved a historical place, a geographical location, and a philosophical space.

Chicanas reclaim their native language, Spanish. Reclaiming Spanish is a public acknowledgment of the linguistic limbo many experience as they are socialized in Spanish at home and then confront language repression when they enter school (Hurtado and Rodríguez 1989). Learning the "colonizer's language" was a traumatic event for many Chicana feminist writers and one that deeply influenced their thinking about the meaning of having their own "*lengua*" [language]. As Emma Pérez related:

> Like many tejanas/os [Texans] who attended Anglo schools through grade school, I too was punished for speaking my parent's tongue on playgrounds and classrooms. Spanish set my brother and me apart. Anglo teachers peered at us when we spoke Spanish, the way white women peer at me now when they try to interfere in a circle of Chicanas speaking together in Spanglish, reaffirming our *mestizaje* [hybridity/mixed race]. As a child in Anglo schools, I realized quickly that I had to

learn English, to pronounce it accurately, precisely. I was ridiculed for my accent, I was pushed into dark closets, disciplined for calling a student *gringo*. I practiced at night, staring up at the ceiling in my bedroom, reciting the alphabet. In English. Forgetting *la lengua de mi gente* [the language of my people]. Not knowing that the loss of language is loss of memory. (1991, 174)

The loss of their native *lengua* [language] and the shame around those who retained it propelled Chicana feminists' understandings of the political nature of all discourse. Sonia Saldívar-Hull (2000) refused to translate, italicize, or otherwise mark the shift between English and Spanish in the first few chapters of her book. She wanted non-Spanish readers to experience the disjuncture felt by many monolingual Spanish speakers, especially children, as they are thrown into mainstream circles not understanding English:

> In a consciously political act, what Gloria Anzaldúa calls "linguistic terrorism," I will not italicize Spanish words or phrases unless they are italicized in direct quotations. I invite readers not fluent in Spanish to experience a sense of life on the border as we switch from English to Spanish. Sometimes we translate, at other times we assume the nonnative speaker will understand from the context. Many Chicanas/os speak only English. Reading Chicana texts puts several demands on the reader, including the expectation that the reader will be knowledgeable in multiple Chicana and Chicano linguistic, cultural, and historical contexts. While most contemporary Chicana writers and critics have been formally educated in the United States and are fluent in English and Spanish, many of the writers code-switch between the two languages in a conscious act of identity politics. . . . My political practice as a transfrontera border feminista informs my linguistic acts of "identitarian collectivities." Once I have given the non-Spanish-literate reader a sense of "alien" disorientation in the text, I move toward more inclusionary tactics and offer translations in [later chapters]. (2000, 173)

Having access to multiple discourses in two languages—from formal English, to Spanglish, to Caló—provides insight into the political nature of how intellectual "merit" is defined. Many Chicana feminists who came from working-class backgrounds experienced the derogation of their parents by schools and other institutions because their parents did not speak English.

> When I entered the first grade, I cried each day after school. I lay my head on my mother's lap, a woman who was denied the right to read and write the language of the colonizer in a land that belonged to her ancestors. She brushed my hair back, comforting me. I couldn't articulate what I say so easily now. I couldn't say that the woman who comforted me, the woman who held power, beauty, and strength in my eyes, that Anglos dismissed her because she couldn't fill out their damn forms. I couldn't say that the school was infested with white students, so alien to me. And that day the white teacher shoved me against a wall because I didn't recite the "Pledge of Allegiance." I didn't know it. But I knew "El Rancho Grande." (Pérez 1991, 177–178)

The use of Spanish by Chicana feminists in intellectual production became a political assertion of the value of their heritage and the means to create a feminist discourse directly tied to a Chicana experience.

Claiming a Tongue

> this tongue of mine
> sets fires
> licking hot
> all in its path
> scorches the old
> announces the new
>
> this tongue of mine
> breaks through walls
> setting free
> imagery of feelings
> odors of dreams
> tasting the bitter
> the rancid
> quenching the thirst
>
> —Elba R. Sánchez, "A Gift of Tongues" (1992)

Another translation for *lengua* is "tongue" — capturing the sexuality implicit in the word. Claiming sexuality has been central to the Chicana feminist project. Chicana feminists have written explicitly about sexual pleasure to counteract the silence and repression around sex in Chicano communities. Central to this has been the recognition that although Chicanas experience sexual repression in their communities and although virginity is highly valued (Hurtado 1996a, 59), within these spaces of restriction they also seek pleasure (Zavella, 2003).

Some of the most prolific Chicana feminist writers openly claim their lesbianism. They also are the best known in mainstream circles. Writers like Cherríe Moraga, Gloria Anzaldúa, and Emma Pérez have been pivotal in making sexuality a central part of Chicana feminist theorizing. Chicano communities have been as homophobic as white mainstream communities, and Chicana feminists who expose and defend lesbianism profoundly challenge the status quo (Saldívar-Hull 1991, 214). It is important to highlight the fact that progressive politics in Chicano communities are practiced by individuals deeply committed to maintaining the cultural integrity of Chicano culture as a counterchallenge to the dominant hegemony of cultural, linguistic, and economic assimilation. Most lesbian Chicana writers have an intense loyalty to their communities of origin, to Chicano culture, to the Spanish language, and to working-class issues. As such, to propose that homophobia should be challenged even among the working class is a deeply courageous act.

Claiming a Discourse

> Foucault transcribes historical documents to ventilate the power of discourse. He argues that through discourse power-knowledge is realized. Language, after all, is power. Third World people know that to learn the colonizer's language gives one access to power and privilege, albeit controlled, qualified power. (Perez 1991, 165)

"Discourse" is yet another meaning for *lengua*. Chicana feminisms use a Foucauldian definition of discourse, where "groups of statements and rules exist historically and change as the material conditions for their possibility also change" (Childers and Hentzi 1995, 84). Furthermore, "discourse informs and shapes subjectivity, including the possible activities and knowledge of the individual" (85). Chicana feminisms proclaim that creating and controlling their own discourse is essential to decolonization and to their definition of cultural citizenship. Passive silence has been the enemy that allowed others to construct who Chicanas are, what they can and cannot do, and what they are capable of becoming. Claiming discourse is claiming power to construct themselves.

The lack of access to academic writing erased Chicanas from the white feminist intellectual landscape. Chicana feminists recuperated the wisdom of their foremothers by reconstituting what was considered valid discourse in the academy. As Lorna Dee Cervantes claims, "I come from a long line of eloquent illiterates / whose history reveals what words don't say" (1981, 45); Sonia Saldívar-Hull exhorts us to go beyond the "dominant discourse" and look in "nontraditional places for our theories" (2000, 46); and Alvina Quintana advocates the use of literary texts written by Chicanas as "cultural self-ethnographies" (1996, 34).

Chicana feminists struggle to decolonize language, to burst open discourse to allow for the possibility of a liberatory consciousness (Sandoval 2000). They reject the dichotomization of discourse between "high" theory and everyday discourse.

> We speak our history to each other now just as our ancestors used oral tradition. A tradition which is minimized. We must write in accomplished English to legitimize our work. We must master the language of the colonizer before our studies are read. *Gringos y gringas* censure our real language which is often born from rage. (Pérez 1991, 175–176)

Chicana feminists claimed women's discourse within their communities. They validate women's bonding through sharing stories of defeat and resistance within their families as worth recording and writing about. No longer is women's gossip outside the purview of academic theorizing. It was through the sharing inherent in "gossiping" that women subverted the silence around abuse by husbands, lovers, parents, and other authority figures. If it was spoken about, it existed in the memory of others—accountability was at least possible, if not viable.

Chicana feminists have self-consciously fashioned a rhetoric that integrates different genres—poetry (Cervantes 1981; Cisneros 1994; Villanueva 1978), spoken word (Gonzalez and Habell-Pallan 1994), *teatro* (theater; Broyles-González 1994; Yarbro-Bejarano 1986), *declamación* (oratory; Cantú 1995), short stories (Serros 1993, 2000; Viramontes 1993), artistic performance (Broyles-Gonzalez 2001; Najera-Ramirez 2003)—to explicate the content and form of their civic participation. Many Chicana feminist writers align themselves with cultural theorists who examine discourse to uncover the dynamics of power (Alarcón 1994; Chabram 1990; Fregoso 1990; Sandoval 2000).

Chicana feminisms talk back to feminisms that do not speak to their historical and socioeconomic experiences, to the colonizing discourses of the academy, and to parts of their cultural practices in their own communities that are politically regressive. The targets of their speaking back include the progressive men in the Chicano movement who have not been willing to acknowledge women's issues. Because silent, passive women who are willing to sacrifice everything on behalf of their families have represented the ideal of womanhood in Chicano communities, there was a backlash when Chicanas claimed their outspokenness against the men in their communities.

Chicana feminisms' emphasis on class issues (Pesquera 1991; Romero 1992; Segura 1994; Zavella 1987) stems from the high participation of Chicanas in work outside the home, as well as with their association with the Marxist-infused Chicano movement of the 1960s and 1970s (Córdova 1994, 175, 188–189; Segura and Pesquera 1992). They have appropriated a discourse that challenges multiple constituencies and that consciously allies itself with progressive political causes in the United States and internationally.

Sitios (Spaces)

Claiming a Historical Space

> Here [the conquest of Mexico], the sexual, political, social, and psychological violence against *la india*—the core of the Chicana—is born. This core has been plundered from us through conquest and colonization. We reclaim the core for our woman-tempered *sitio y lengua.* (Perez 1991, 168)

Chicana feminisms openly fight the "loss of memory" (Pérez 1991, 174) through the recuperation of history—not only of women but of their ethnic and racial group as a whole—to carve out a geographical and philosophical space where their complexities are not ignored or elided. A central part of the project is debunking the stereotypes that portrayed Chicanas as nonagents in the creation of history, especially in political struggles around labor issues (Córdova 1994).

An integral part of the recuperation of history was to revise the official narrative of the historical events surrounding the colonization of *mexicanos*. Chicanos, as a group, originated from an act of war and eventual conquest that was codified in the treaty of Guadalupe Hidalgo that ended the Mexican American War of 1848. This history of colonization affects all Mexican descendants whether they were part of the conquered territory or not. Mexico as a nation still feels the loss of its former territory. Much of the Southwest still bears the visible signs of having belonged to Mexico through city and street names, the presence of Catholic missions and other historical buildings, and in the vibrant cultural practices that are very much alive.

This, however, was not the first experience of conquest. La Malinche, an indigenous woman, was a pivotal figure in the conquest of the Americas in 1519 by the Spanish. La Malinche was the ultimate traitor of Mexico, because she allegedly facilitated Hernán Córtes's conquest of the Aztec empire by acting as translator between the Spanish and the different Mixteca tribes. Norma Alarcón notes that "Malintzin [La Malinche] comes to be known as *la lengua*, literally meaning the tongue. *La lengua* was the metaphor used, by Cortés and the chroniclers of the conquest, to refer to Malintzin the translator" (1989, 59). Modern Mexico was born from this betrayal both figuratively and literally, since La Malinche converted to Catholicism *and* bore the children of Hernán Córtes's soldier Jaramaillo (Pérez 1993, 61). Although Chicana feminists did not choose La Malinche as the defining figure in their conception of historical subjects, many male writers made La Malinche and her betrayal iconic. (See Paz [1961] as a prime example of this tendency.) All Mexicana/Chicana women are potential Malinches capable of betrayal if they are not under the watchful eye of patriarchy. Chicana feminists have engaged the polemics around La Malinche either to redeem her, to commiserate with her, or to appropriate her as a feminist hero (Alarcón 1989). Other female historical figures have been embraced as potentially mapping specifically Chicana feminist cultural citizenship, including La Virgen de Guadalupe (Castillo 1996),[1] Sor Juana Inés de la Cruz (Gaspar de Alba 1992),[2] La Llorona (Cisneros 1991; Mora 1996, 91; Saldívar-Hull 2000),[3] and Frida Kahlo,[4] among others (Córdova 1994, 193). These historical figures had an engagement with gender struggles and also with struggles around labor and social revolutions against repressive governments. Their actions are emblematic of Chicanas' definition of citizenship.

The historical experience of conquest by the Spaniards and the imposition of Catholicism on indigenous people produced culturally specific definitions of womanhoods—what cultural theorists have called gendered subject positions for Chicanas. According to Chicana feminists, Marianismo and Malinchismo dichotomized women's womanhood into the "good woman" and the "bad woman," according to their sexuality (Hurtado 1996a). Definitions of womanhood in turn influence Chicanos' views of their citizenship. *Marianismo* is the veneration of the Virgin Mary (NietoGomez 1974, 37). Her Mexican version, La Virgen de Guadalupe, is the role model for Chicana womanhood—she is the mother, the nurturer, she had endurance for pain and sorrow, and willingness to serve (37). These values form the basis for the construction of Chicana womanhood (Córdova 1994, 175) and are rooted in the practice of Catholicism. To be a "good woman" is to remain a virgin until marriage and to invest devotion, loyalty, and nurturance in the family, specifically Chicanos' definition of family, which included extended networks of kin, as well as friends and parts of their communities (Baca Zinn 1975, 13).

Other ethnic and racial groups have similar models of idealized womanhood (members of the Christian Right are a good example). For many Chicanos,

1. Chicana feminists appropriated La Virgen de Guadalupe as a symbol of Chicanas' racial hybridity and recognition of women's sacrifices on behalf of their families as essential to the group's economic and cultural survival.

2. Sor Juana Inés de la Cruz, a seventeenth-century Mexican nun, was a scholar, poet, playwright, and intellectual who in her work addressed the unfair condition of women.

3. La Llorona refers to a legendary figure that first appeared in sixteenth-century colonial Mexico and has persisted to the present in Mexico, as well as in Chicano communities in the United States. According to the legend, La Llorona (the Weeping Woman) wanders the streets at night wailing over the loss of her children, whom she killed by drowning after her husband betrayed her with another woman (Limón 1990, 414–415).

4. Kahlo was a committed Marxist and political activist (Herrera 1983).

however, commitment to these values has been a source of solace and strength to fight racism and resist oppression by the dominant group. Women's dedication to their families and many men's commitment to upholding their side of the bargain by hard work in the agricultural fields, dehumanizing work in factories, and low-paying, unskilled labor have made it difficult for Chicana feminists to challenge them. Chicana feminists critique the inherent sexism in dichotomizing their womanhood between Malinchismo and Marianismo at the same time that they recognize the courageous work of women and men who have fought to preserve their families against brutal racist state intervention—challenges that have not always been successful. Among the critics are Chicanas who do not see the advantages of challenging patriarchy and others who consider it a betrayal to join *any* feminist cause. Within U.S. Chicano communities, there are several definitions of cultural citizenship that are vying for recognition and are constantly contested.

The debates around deconstructing these subject positions and their impact on definitions of citizenship were especially heated during the Chicano Movement of the 1960s and the 1970s. When Chicana feminists questioned their roles in the Chicano movement, they were perceived by both men and women as not only attacking unequal gender practices but also as questioning the Catholic underpinnings of *all* Chicano culture and of the unity necessary to obtain citizenship rights. Consequently, the emerging Chicana feminist consciousness was perceived as a betrayal, and Chicana feminists were labeled "anti-family, anti-cultural, anti-man and therefore an [*sic*] anti-Chicano movement" (NietoGomez 1973, 35). Ironically, they were called Malinchistas and attacked as "selling out" to white feminism. As part of the attack, they were labeled lesbians, because they were supposedly privileging their sex above the unity of the Chicano movement in its struggle for social justice.

There are rewards for women who comply and punishments for those who rebel against the model of a "good woman." But as in white mainstream culture, the power of patriarchy to enforce norms can occasionally be expressed by the father or husband with little or no accountability. Women who rebel openly pay the price. Punishment, which can include banishment from Chicano communities, has been especially harsh for women who openly declare their lesbianism. To sexually prefer women is viewed as the ultimate rejection of patriarchy. Furthermore, the strong Catholic underpinnings of Chicano culture make it a "mortal sin." Many Chicana lesbians find refuge in white lesbian communities and in activism on behalf of gay and lesbian issues. These gay activists, however, never completely disengage from their Chicano communities or from political work on behalf of Chicano issues (Trujillo 1991). The political and theoretical sophistication gained from participation in this broader political movement has infused much of the theorizing about Chicanas' gender issues.

White women, as well as other non-Latina women, are not held accountable to the demands of these subject positions, because they are not the descendants of La Malinche. Non-Chicana feminisms were not completely helpful to Chicana feminists to deconstruct subject positions that had historical specificity and were based on the material conditions of Chicanos as a group.

Claiming a Geographical Place

I have rights to my space. I have boundaries. I will tell you when you cross them.
I ask that you respect my request. (Perez 1991, 178)

The site of colonization also had geographical specificity—the southwestern
United States. It was in *la frontera* that Chicanas situated their feminisms, as well
as their claims to cultural citizenship, to highlight a particular border culture and
language that stood between two nation-states—Mexico and the United States—
but not belonging fully to either. Chicana feminists have been at the forefront of
theorizing from *la frontera* as their *sitio* (space) (Anzaldúa 1987; Mora 1993).

The geographical area represented by *la frontera* has become the guiding
metaphor for all of the border crossings Chicanas do on a daily basis—class, race,
ethnicity, sexuality. They have to fight different battles because of the multiplicity
of boundaries they have to cross. Maintaining a core self and preventing others
from invading their boundaries is a constant battle.

The history of conquest, which basically layered another country over a preexisting nation, gave Chicana feminists the knowledge of the temporality of nation-
states (Klahn 1994). The political line dividing the United States from Mexico did
not correspond to the experiential existence on the border. Many Chicana feminists declare the border as the geographical location (*lugar*) that created the ap-
erture for theorizing about subordination and about citizenship from an ethnically
specific Chicana/*mestiza* consciousness (Anzaldúa 1987). It was at the border that
Chicanas/*mestizas* learned the socially constructed nature of all categories. By standing on the U.S. side of the river, they saw Mexico and they saw home; by standing
on the Mexican side of the border, they saw the United States and they saw home.
Yet they were not really accepted on either side. Their ability to "see" the arbitrary
nature of all categories but still take a stand challenges Chicana feminists to
exclude while including, to reject while accepting, to struggle while negotiating.
Chicana feminists variously called this "facultad" (ability) a "*mestiza* consciousness" (Anzaldúa 1987), "differential consciousness" (Sandoval 1991, 2000), and
"conscientización" (Castillo 1995, 171). The basic concept involves the ability to
hold multiple social perspectives while simultaneously maintaining a center that
revolves around concrete material forms of oppression.

More recently, some Chicana feminists have pointed out that the *facultad* to
cross "borders" is not easily exercised, nor is it often without pain and retribution by
authority figures (Lamphere, Zavella, and Gonzalez, with Evan 1993) who require a
"false" unified self. True enough—those who exercised *la facultad*, especially in
writing, were the outliers (Hurtado 1996b), who, by definition, ran the risk of ex-
pulsion from their communities. There were, however, those who exercised *la
facultad* (the faculty) without writing and without calling it a feminist consciousness, who imparted their lessons to younger women, and who resisted gender
subordination through everyday acts of rebellion (Steinem 1983) and guerrilla war-
fare of the mind (Hurtado 1989; Sandoval 1991, 2000). Chicana feminists' commitment to work across differences, finding dimensions of similarity through
strategic suspensions (Hurtado 1996b), allowed them feminisms and definitions of
citizenship that defied "geopolitical borders" (Saldívar-Hull 1991, 211).

La frontera is also the geographical area that is most susceptible to hybridity that is neither fully Mexico nor fully the United States. As Gloria Anzaldúa claims, *la frontera* is where you "put chile in the borscht / eat whole wheat tortillas / speak Tex-Mex with a Brooklyn accent" (1987, 195). The borderlands denote that space in which antithetical elements mix, not to obliterate each other or to get subsumed by a larger whole but rather to combine in unique and unexpected ways.

The combination of colonization and situating their citizenship in *la frontera* makes Chicana feminisms deeply aware of their racial mixture—their *mestizaje*. The borderlands are a space of *mezclas* (mixtures, hybridity) of all kinds, including racial. Chicana feminists address issues of racism within their communities based on skin color and Indian heritage as determined by phenotype (Anzaldúa 1987, 21; Broyles-González 1994; Castañeda 1990, 228). Male scholars have as well (Arce, Murguía, and Frisbie 1987; Forbes 1968; Telles and Murguía 1990, 1992). Expanding on this work, Chicana feminists specifically analyze how racialized physical features are used to define desirable standards of beauty and womanhood (Anzaldúa 1981). They reclaimed *mestizaje*—the mixture of European, African, and Indian "races"— to resist the racist standards adopted in Chicano communities in preferring lighter skin and European features, especially for women (Saldívar-Hull 1991, 214–215). Exposed also were the negative racist judgments of darker skinned, Indian-looking women and the derogation of their womanhood even by otherwise progressive men (Anzaldúa 1987; Broyles-González 1994). By speaking to the internal racism of Chicano communities and of progressive Chicano men, Chicana feminists turned the critical lens inward. Their use of standpoints reveals how the dynamics of prejudice influence relations in Chicano, as in all other, communities (Ochoa and Teaiwa 1994, ix). Importantly, the analysis of *mestizaje* was *woman-centered* rather than relying on male scholars' paradigms for studying racism.

Claiming a Philosophical Space

Ya no me van a robar mi sitio y mi lengua.[5] They live inside my soul, with my mother, my sisters, *mis hermanas del tercer mundo.* (Perez 1991, 179)[6]

Chicana feminists agree with white feminists that patriarchy oppresses them and does not allow them full citizenship. They diverge, however, from white feminisms, because philosophically their analysis of patriarchy does not stem from claiming *individual rights* denied to them by men. Instead, Chicana feminisms propose that their subordination is the result of the intersection of multiple systems of oppression that include gender, race, ethnicity, class, and sexuality. It is from this *bocacalle* (intersection) that they construct their feminisms. The interlocking systems of oppression stem from the historical specificity of colonization, first of native peoples by Spain and second by the conquest of Mexico by the United States. Chicana feminisms take the history of the Americas as the bedrock on which

---

5. The translation from Spanish is "They will no longer steal my space and my language."
6. The translation from Spanish is "my sisters of the Third World."

they theorize their condition as *mestizas* (hybrids, mixed-race women). Unlike Virginia Woolf's claim to "a room of one's own" as the means to liberation, Chicanas claim a space to congregate with others like them as liberatory. The space envisioned is a nurturant space where cultural and language differences do not have to be constantly explained. It is also a space of replenishment from the daily interactions in which Chicanas negotiate a fragmented self. Chicana feminisms theorize about *collective* liberation against all kinds of oppression. Chicana feminisms do not only focus on men as individual potential oppressors but also on systems of oppression that converge into what Emma Perez calls the "subject" who holds "sociosexual-racial power" over marginalized others that include her and others like her; "I see you, who hold sociosexual-racial power, as the subject who objectifies the marginal other—me....I sense you as invasive, conquering and colonizing my space and my language. You attempt to 'penetrate' the place I speak from with my Chicana/Latina *hermanas* [sisters]" (1991, 178).

The "subject" oppressing Chicanas and preventing them from having full citizenship rights is sometimes white men, other times white women, and still other times men of Color and other members of their communities. Regardless of this *relational* analysis of power, Chicana feminists still put Chicanas and Third World women at the center of their analysis. As Emma Pérez claims:

> I prefer to think of myself as one who places women, especially Third World women and lesbians, in the forefront of my priorities. I am committed to women's organizations because in those spaces we revitalize, we laugh, we mock the oppressor, we mock each other's seriousness and we take each other seriously. This is a process of support, this is living the ideal, if only momentarily, to give, to nurture, to support each other in a racist, sexist, homophobic Western society. I speak at this moment of historical consciousness as a Chicana survivor who has survived much more than I speak of here, just as we, women of color survive daily. (1991, 178)

Chicana feminists think of themselves as multiply positioned because of the interlocking nature of their oppression. It is from this philosophical space that they develop political proposals for coalitions to accomplish social justice. Chicana feminists' commitment to coalition politics stems theoretically from their knowledge that "women of Color," or "African American women," or "Chicana women" are racialized subjects that have been constructed through historical events and material conditions (Davis and Martínez 1994). Rather than adhering to an essentialist notion of racial or gender identity, Chicana feminists struggle with implementing standpoint theory through coalition building. Ultimately, Chicana feminisms' core value, to accomplish social justice by building successful coalitions, is part of their theoretical and political agenda.

In summary, what would educated feminist Chicana writers and the young women inheritors of this intellectual legacy see as the contours of their cultural citizenship? First of all, precisely because theirs is a historical experience tied to the loss of land, culture, and language, they know how important these are to the definition of a people while *simultaneously* knowing that the loss does not entail loss of allegiance to one's group, or that the loss is permanent. They also adhere to a relational definition of cultural citizenship where loss and conquest leads to insight for its devastating effects on a people, *regardless* of their cultural and historical specificity. The ability to switch back and forth between ethnic and racial specificity and universality while simultaneously remaining anchored in their own group's contours, I think, will be necessary as economic and cultural globalization increases. Chicanas' existence in the United States has created what the art critic Jennifer Gonzalez calls a "baroque intelligence." She argues that many mainstream art critics do not understand Chicano art generally and Chicana art in particular because they apply the perceptual principles of mainstream aesthetics that do not map onto a Chicano aesthetic based on a subaltern existence of layering many different cultural and linguistic influences while simultaneously kneading it into a specific, albeit varied, Chicano/a aesthetic.

Chicanas' views on cultural citizenship are also important because of their commitment to social justice for all rather than to interest-group politics. Theirs is a paradigm for social change rather than promotion of a particular political and cultural agenda. As such, they privilege change, chaos, and revision. It is a turbulent perspective, constantly reinventing and deconstructing itself, not for the sake of adolescent rebellion but for the sake of cultural, political, and economic transformation. A bedrock in Chicana feminist perspectives is the invention of paradigms that increase participation of all that are excluded, not as political ploy but as a profound recognition that one is not free until everybody is. Will they be successful? Even this question is not relevant; most would say that it is in the struggle where success lies. Whether it succeeds or not is irrelevant to the higher power of fighting, even as the goals and successes get defined as they go along.

Bibliography

Alarcón, Norma. 1994. "Conjugating Subjects: The Heteroglossia of Essence and Resistance." Pp. 125–138 in *An Other Tongue*, ed. Alfred Arteaga. Durham, N.C.: Duke University Press.

———. 1989. "*Traductora, traidora*: A Paradigmatic Figure of Chicana feminism." *Cultural Critique* 13: 57–87.

Alvarez, R. 1973. "The Psycho-Historical and Socioeconomic Development of the Chicano Community in the United States." *Social Science Quarterly* 53(4): 920–942.

Anzaldúa, Gloria. 1987. *Borderlands—La Frontera: The New Mestiza*. San Francisco: Aunt Lute.

———. 1990. "The Theoretical Subject(s) of This Bridge Called My Back and Anglo-American Feminism." Pp. 356–369 in *Making Face, Making Soul: Haciendo Caras*, ed. Gloria Anzaldúa. San Francisco: Aunt Lute Foundation Books.

Arce, Carlos H., Edward Murguía, and W. Parker Frisbie. 1987. "Phenotype and Life Chances among Chicanos." *Hispanic Journal of Behavioral Sciences* 9: 19–32.

Baca Zinn, Maxine. (1990). "Family, Feminism, and Race in America." *Gender and Society* 4(1): 68–82.

———. 1975. "Political Familism: Toward Sex Role Equality in Chicano Families." *Aztlan* 6(1): 13–26.

Benmayor, Rina. 2002. "Narrating Cultural Citizenship: Oral Histories of First-Generation College Students of Mexican Origin." *Social Justice* 2002 (29): 96–121.

Broyles-González, Yolanda J. 1994. *El Teatro Campesino: Theater in the Chicano Movement.* Austin: University of Texas Press.

———. 2001. *Lydia Mendoza's Life in Music, La Historia De Lydia Mendoza.* Oxford: Oxford University Press.

Butler, Judith. 2004. *Precarious Life: The Power of Mourning and Violence.* New York: Verso.

Cantú, Norma E. 1995. *Canícula: Snapshots of a Girlhood En La Frontera.* Albuquerque: University of New Mexico Press.

Castañeda, Antonia I. 1990. "The Political Economy of Nineteenth Century Stereotypes of Californians." Pp. 213–236 in *Between Borders: Essays on Mexicana/Chicana History,* ed. Adelaida R. Del Castillo. Encino, Calif.: Floricanto Press.

Castillo, Ana, ed. 1996. *Goddess of the Americas, La Diosa De Las Americas: Writings on the Virgin of Guadalupe.* New York: Riverhead Books.

———. 1995. *Massacre of the Dreamers.* New York: Plume Book.

Cervantes, Lorna Dee. 1981. *Emplumada.* Pittsburgh: University of Pittsburgh Press.

Chabram, Angie. 1990. "Chicana/O Studies as Oppositional Ethnography." *Cultural Studies* 4(3): 228–247.

Childers, Joseph, and Gary Hentzi. 1995. *The Columbia Dictionary of Modern Literary and Cultural Criticism.* New York: Colombia University Press.

Cisneros, Sandra. 1994. *Loose Woman.* New York: Knopf.

———. 1991. *Woman Hollering Creek, and Other Stories.* New York: Random House.

Córdova, Teresa. 1994 "The Emergent Writings of Twenty Years of Chicana Feminist Struggles: Roots and Resistance." Pp. 175–202 in *The Handbook of Hispanic Cultures in the United States,* ed. Félix Padilla. Houston: Arte Público Press.

Coontz, S. 1992. *The Way We Never Were: American Families and the Nostalgia Trap.* New York: Basic Books.

Cuádraz, Gloria Holguin. 1989. "I Want to Be Known as a Hurdle-Jumper, Not as a High-Achiever." *Revista Mujeres* 6(2): 69.

Davis, Angela, and Elizabeth Martínez. 1994. "Coalition Building among People of Color." *Inscriptions* 7: 42–53.

Flores, William V., and Rina Benmajor. 1997. *Latino Cultural Citizenship.* Boston: Beacon Press.

Forbes, Jack. 1968. "Race and Color in Mexican-American Problems." *Journal of Human Relations* 16(1): 55–68.

Fregoso, Rosa Linda. 1990. "The Discourse of Difference: Footnoting Inequality." *Critica* (2)2: 182–187.

Gaspar de Alba, Alicia. 1992. "Juana Ines." Pp. 1–15 in *New Chicana/Chicano Writing,* ed. Charles M. Tatum. Tucson: University of Arizona Press.

Gates, David. 2001. "The Voices of Dissent." *Newsweek,* November 19, 66–67.

Gonzalez, Jennifer A., and Michelle Habell-Pallan. 1994. "Heterotopias and Shared Methods of Resistance: Navigating Social Spaces and Spaces of Identity." *Inscriptions* 7: 80–104.

Gurin, Patricia, Aída Hurtado, and Timothy Peng. 1994. "Group Contacts and Ethnicity in the Social Identities of Mexicanos and Chicanos." *Personality and Social Psychology Bulletin* 20(5): 521–532.

Hurtado, Aída. 2003. "Theory in the Flesh: Toward an Endarkened Epistemology." *International Journal of Qualitative Studies in Education* 16(2): 215–225.

———. 1996a. *The Color of Privilege: Three Blasphemies on Feminism and Race.* Ann Arbor: University of Michigan Press.

———. 1996b. "Strategic Suspensions: Feminists of Color Theorize the Production of Knowledge." Pp. 372–392 in *Knowledge, Difference and Power: Essays Inspired by*

Women's Ways of Knowing, ed. Nancy Goldberger, Jill Tarule, Blythe Clinchy, and Mary Belenky. New York: Basic Books.

———. 1989. "Relating to Privilege: Seduction and Rejection in the Subordination of White Women and Women of Color. *Signs* 14(4): 833–855.

Hurtado, Aída, and Raúl Rodríguez. 1989. "Language as a Social Problem: The Repression of Spanish in South Texas." *The Journal of Multilingual Multicultural Development* 10: 401–419.

Klahn, Norma. 1994. "Writing the Border: The Languages and Limits of Representation." *Journal of Latin American Cultural Studies* 3(1–2): 29–55.

Lamphere, Louise, Patricia Zavella, and Felipe Gonzales with Peter B. Evan. 1993. *Sunbelt Working Mothers: Reconciling Family and Factory.* Ithaca: Cornell University Press.

Mora, Pat. 1996. "Coatlique's Rules: Advice from an Aztec Goddess." Pp. 88–89 in *Goddess of the Americas/La Diosa de las Americas: Writings on the Virgin of Guadalupe*, ed. Ana Castillo. New York: Riverhead Books.

Nájera-Ramírez, Olga. 2003. "Unruly Passions: Poetics, Performance and Gender in the Ranchera Song." Pp. 184–210 in *Chicana Feminisms: Disruptions in Dialogue*, ed. Gabriela Arredondo, Aída Hurtado, Norma Klahn, Olga Nájera-Ramírez, and Patricia Zavella. Durham, N.C.: Duke University Press.

NietoGomez, Anna. 1973. "La Feminista." *Encuentro Femenil* 1(2): 28–33.

———. 1974. "La Feminista." *Encuentro Femenil* 1(2): 34–47.

Ochoa, María, and Teresia Teaiwa. 1994. "Enunciating Our Terms: Women of Color in Collaboration and Conflict." *Inscriptions* 7: 1–155.

Paz, Octavio. 1961. *Laberinto de la Soledad [The Labyrinth of Solitude: Life and Thought in Mexico]*, trans. Lysander Kemp. New York: Grove Press.

Pesquera, Beatriz M. 1991. "'Work Gave Me a Lot of Confianza': Chicanas' Work Commitment and Work Identity." *Aztlán* 20(1–2): 97–118.

Pérez, Emma. 1999. *The Decolonial Imaginary: Writing Chicanas into History.* Bloomington: Indiana University Press.

———. 1991. "Sexuality and Discourse: Notes from a Chicana Survivor." Pp. 159–184 in *Chicana Lesbians: The Girls Our Mothers Warned Us About*, ed. Carla Trujillo. Berkeley: Third Woman Press.

———. 1993. "Speaking from the Margin: Uninvited Discourse on Sexuality and Power." Pp. 57–71 in *Building with Our Hands: New Directions in Chicana Studies*, ed. Adela de la Torre and Beatríz M. Pesquera. Berkeley: University of California Press.

Portes, Alejandro, and Rubén Rumbaut. 1990. *Immigrant America: A Portrait.* Berkeley: University of California Press.

Preston, S. H. 1996. Children Will Pay. *The New York Times Magazine*, 96–97.

Quintana, Alvina E. 1996. *Home Girls: Chicana Literary Voices.* Philadelphia: Temple University Press.

Romero, Mary. 1992. *Maid in the U.S.A.* New York: Routledge.

Roy, Arundhati. 2001. *San Francisco Chronicle*, November 11, D6.

Saldívar-Hull, Sonia. 2000. *Feminism on the Border. Chicana Gender Politics and Literature.* Berkeley: University of California Press.

———. 1991. "Feminism on the Border: From Gender Politics to Geopolitics." Pp. 203–220 in *Criticism in the Borderlands: Studies in Chicano Literature, Culture, and Ideology*, ed. Hector Calderón and Jose David Saldívar. Durham: Duke University Press.

Sánchez, Elba Rosario. 1992. *Tallos de Luna / Moon Shoots.* Santa Cruz, Calif.: Moving Arts Press.

Sandoval, Chela. 1991. "U.S. Third World Feminism: The Theory and Method of Oppositional Consciousness in the Postmodern World." *Genders* 10 (spring): 1–24.

———. 2000. *Methodology of the Oppressed.* Minneapolis: University of Minnesota Press.

Segura, Denise. 1994. "Beyond Machismo: Chicanas, Work, and Family." Paper presented at the Sixth European Conference on Latino Cultures in the United States, Bordeaux, July 7–10.

Segura, Denise A., and Beatriz M. Pesquera. 1992. "Beyond Indifference and Antipathy: The Chicana Movement and Chicana Feminist Discourse." *Aztlán* 19(2): 69–91.

Serros, Michele M. 1993. *Chicana Falsa: And Other Stories of Death, Identity, and Oxnard.* Valencia, Calif.: Lalo Press.

———. 2000. *How to Be a Chicana Role Model.* New York: Riverhead Books.

Smith, D. E. (1987). "Women's Inequality and the Family." Pp. 23–54 in *Families and Work,* ed. N. Gerstel and H. E. Gross. Philadelphia: Temple University Press.

Sontag, Susan. (2001). "Talk of the Town." *New Yorker,* September 24.

Staples, Robert, and Alejandro Mirandé. 1980. "Racial and Cultural Variations Among American Families: A Decennial Review of the Literature on Minority Families." *Journal of Marriage and the Family* 42(4): 887–903.

Steinem, Gloria. 1983. *Outrageous Acts and Everyday Rebellions.* New York: Holt, Rinehart, and Winston.

Telles, Edward, and Edward Murguía. 1990. "Phenotypic Discrimination and Income: Differences among Mexican Americans." *Social Science Quarterly* 71(4):682–93.

Trujillo, Carla. 1991. *Chicana Lesbians: The Girls Our Mothers Warned Us About.* Berkeley, CA: Third Woman Press.

Viramontes, Helena Maria. 1993. "The Moths." Pp. 117–124 in *Growing Up Chicana/O,* ed. Tiffany Ann Lopez. New York: W. Morrow.

Villanueva, Alma. 1978. *Mother May I.* Pittsburgh: Motheroot.

Yarbro-Bejarano, Yvonne. 1986. "The Female Subject in Chicano Theater: Sexuality, 'Race,' and Class." *Theater Journal* 38(1): 389–407.

Zavella, Patricia. 1987. *Women's Work and Chicano Families: Workers of the Santa Clara Valley.* Ithaca, N.Y.: Cornell University Press.

———.2003. "Talkin' Sex: Chicanas and Mexicanas Theorize about Silences and Sexual Pleasures." Pp. 228–253 in *Chicana Feminisms: A Critical Reader,* ed. Gabriela F. Arredondo, Aída Hurtado, Norma Klahn, Olga Nájera-Ramírez and Patricia Zavella. Durham, NC: Duke University Press.

7

Care as the Work of Citizens
A Modest Proposal

Joan Tronto

Care is a fundamental aspect of human life. Care consists of "everything we do to continue, repair, and maintain ourselves so that we can live in the world as well as possible" (Fisher and Tronto 1990, 41). Most of us think about care in the intimate relationships of our lives: care for ourselves and our families and friends. In its broadest meanings, care is complex and multidimensional: it refers both to the dispositional qualities we need to care for ourselves and others, such as being attentive to human needs and taking responsibility to meet such needs, as well as to the concrete work of caring. To care well requires that both of these elements be present: a disposition to care and care work. Care thus always involves thinking about who is responsible for what caring, and about what that responsibility means (Tronto 1993). Many political theorists, moral philosophers, sociologists, and others have demonstrated the value of using care as a perspective from which to think about human life. Despite the burgeoning literature on care, and especially on its usefulness as a framework to guide moral, political, and policy decisions, though, critics of the care perspective persist in insisting that there are some questions that require a more universal perspective from which to think about broader political and moral questions. To such critics, since care is always (to use Nel Noddings's 2002 book title) "starting at home," it is necessarily limited in its ability to make arguments beyond the most intimate and local level. In response to such critics, many of us have argued that care is the better perspective because it asks us to think differently about the nature of the problem and the nature of the solutions. As a perspective from which to think about social and political life, a care perspective demands that, as we try to make moral and political judgments, we use the concrete

My thanks to Deborah Kaufman for research assistance in preparing this essay, and to anonymous reviewers of this manuscript. I am also grateful for comments received at the conference at Washington University where this essay was first presented and from which this volume grows, and for comments received at a conference organized by Kari Waerness at the University of Bergen, Norway.

and contextual to support our more general political, social, and moral judgments.[1] An ethic of care is in this way a subset of what Margaret Walker has called "an ethics of responsibility" (Walker 1998). There are critical moral and political questions for us to ask in determining who is responsible for the ways that care work is done, and what caring work is done and what caring work is left undone.

In this essay, I would like to consider a global problem, the international commodification of care work. While my approach is limited, situated in the politics of the United States, nevertheless I hope to argue that the care perspective can help us to understand not only the nature of the problem but also the nature of the solution. Thus, the point of this essay is to demonstrate that, despite criticisms that it is not a universal ethical framework from which to derive principles, a care perspective can help us to think usefully about how to resolve genuine political problems.

My short solution to the problem of the international commodification of care is the modest proposal of the title: that we should think of care as a ground for conferring citizenship. Among other things, care is the work of citizens. In a world in which we took the centrality of care more seriously, we would define citizens as people engaged in relationships of care with one another. Care itself would thus become a possible qualification for citizenship. It might seem, then, that it would be a very modest proposal to suggest that we adopt such a definition of citizenship; in fact, we shall see that it requires a radical rethinking of political values for the United States. I shall first try to describe why this problem emerges, and then consider how to solve it.

The Problem: The Care Crisis

One aspect of Thomas More's *Utopia*, written in 1516, seems especially disturbing. Thomas More resolved the question of care work by assigning the "dehumanizing" work of Utopia, such as cleaning up, taking care of children, and slaughtering animals, to slaves. Such slaves would come from the small criminal element within the society itself and from abroad:

> Another type of slave is the working-class foreigner who, rather than live in wretched poverty at home, volunteers for slavery in Utopia. Such people are treated with respect, and with almost as much kindness as Utopian citizens, except that they're made to work harder, because they're used to it. If they want to leave the country, which doesn't often happen, they're perfectly free to do so, and receive a small gratuity. (More [1516] 1965, 103)

If people are willing to volunteer for "slavery," is it a moral and political problem? Since the eighteenth century, virtually all political philosophers have

---

1. A number of scholars have written on the value of care as a kind of political perspective; see, *inter alia*, Folbre 1994, 2001, Schwarzenbach 1996, Sevenhuijsen 1998, Stone 2000, White 2000, Waerness 1990.

agreed that slavery so affronts human dignity that no one can justly be enslaved, even if they so "volunteer." Perhaps More's description of such foreign working-class workers willing to do the drudgery as slaves will shock our modern consciences, but throughout the industrialized world, there is an increasing reliance upon the same solution that More created. Although care workers are no longer slaves, care work does not automatically make someone a citizen who is not a citizen to begin with. They are workers for whom work is not enough to make them into citizens, and who only enjoy the partial benefits of what Rhacel Parreñas (2001) calls "partial citizenship."

How did this situation come into existence? Why does it persist? To answer this question, we need to consider the current crisis in care in the United States, a fateful choice about how to proceed, and a political strategy to make the more moral but politically unlikely prospect come to pass.

The Care Crisis

Not-So-Simple Justice

The traditional association of caring with women rested on a social order that excluded women from many parts (or all) of the public sphere. Women (and for that matter slaves, servants, and often working-class people), as well as care activities, were relegated outside of public life. One of the great accomplishments of the second wave of feminism was to break the caste barriers that excluded women from the public sphere. As Judith Stacey has argued, it was not only the push from feminists but also the pull from the new economy that led to the great victory of second wave feminism (Stacey 1990).

Eliminating caste barriers may seem to be a matter of simple justice. Increasingly, though, I think that we must reflect seriously upon the political economy of injustice. There is no such thing as a matter of simple justice. Unjust institutions serve social functions, as do just institutions. The result is that if one simply changes unjust institutions without paying attention to the functions that they performed in society, then in eliminating injustice one also may create new forms of social dislocation and dysfunction. Allowing women full and equal access to the workplace, second wave feminism contributed to such an outcome by removing women as the primary caregivers for nuclear families. Failing to acknowledge how these two pieces are connected together, feminists have not fully addressed the moral and political consequences of their success.

The Care Worker Crisis

That Americans now face a crisis in care cannot be denied. Here are some obvious pieces of that crisis.

1. Workers now work too much. Globalization is sometimes understood in terms of the mobility of capitalism. We can also understand it, however, in terms of the ways that it represents a new kind of capitalism. David Harvey argues, for

example, that while modern capitalism has always controlled workers in space and time in order to exploit their labor, postmodern capitalism operates on smaller margins of exploitation. This new capitalism must take advantage of a profound *time-space compression*. He observes that the general speedup in the turnover times of capital accentuates volatility and ephemerality of commodities and capital. "The volatility, of course, makes it extremely difficult to engage in any long-term planning. Indeed, learning to play the volatility right is now just as important as accelerating turnover time" (Harvey 1990, 286–287). In order to play such volatility right, workers need to be available, flexible, and willing to bend their schedules to match the requirements of global capital. Intensive labor in the "new economy" that has as its primary function to take advantage of fluctuation in capital requires that workers be available all the time ("24/7/365," as the new locution puts it).

A second and related effect of globalized, restless capital is that it makes it possible for capitalism to make greater demands on the physical time of those in the service-oriented working class than was possible even for industrial workers. There was a natural limit to the demands of industrial work on workers: at some point their physical bodies became too battered, weary, and spent for them to be effective workers. The obvious physical toll upon them also meant that workers could and did recognize and organize around their physical needs for rest and leisure (indeed, such a right is included in article 24 of the Universal Declaration of Human Rights).

Workers who are constantly on the move, always available, have less distance from work, not more. "Knowledge workers" are working more and in more different locales than before (Gould Ellen and Hempstead 2002). One of the leading arguments made for worker flex-time is that it allows workers to do *more* work (Hill, Hawkins, et al. 2001). And work they do; the average American family added four weeks of paid work in the 1980s and continued to work more throughout the 1990s (Francis 2001).

2. The other side of this trend is that, while knowledge workers spend more of their time working, a huge gap opens in the care work that they used to do (especially for women but also for men). The United States faces a care worker crisis, in traditional caring occupations such as teaching and nursing, and in rapidly expanding care fields as well, such as nursing and day-care work (Pear 2002; Perrera 2002; Schlinkmann 2002; Trapps 2001). Ninety percent of the nursing homes in the United States have inadequate numbers of workers (Pear 2002). We are often warned of the coming crisis in teacher shortages.[2]

3. It is no surprise, either, that these occupations reflect shortages, because, among other factors, they offer relatively less attractive places to work. Care work is the core of the "pink collar ghetto"; traditional women's jobs are less well paid and less well supported than are other occupations. In addition, there are several aspects of care work that make care workers especially vulnerable to exploitation

---

2. By 2011, the shortfall nationwide is expected to reach two million teachers, with nearly 300,000 positions in California's public schools going unfilled (Trapps 2001).

in this setting. One set of such vulnerabilities was discussed at length by Diemut Bubeck: care work is always subject to exploitation (Bubeck 1995). In the first place, because care work requires the creation and nurturance of relationships, it is difficult for care workers to pull themselves out of their work situation when they are being treated poorly and not lose entirely the sense and value of their work. Furthermore, because care workers often work in "private" locations or in the informal economy, they are subject to exploitation and not protected by labor law (Bakan and Stasiulis 1997; Chang 2000; Hondagneu-Sotelo 2001; Romero 1992).

4. The end result of the confluence of all of these factors is that care work is becoming an *imported* commodity (see Parreñas 2001; Trapps 2001). The care crisis is the obverse of capital mobility, which is matched by labor mobility. Third World/Southern world workers are now moving into the "First World" and the rest of the developing world to do care work. Care labor is the new basic raw material imported from the developing world to the developed world, as Rhacel Perreñas observes. Parreñas observes that "designated export-based nations in the global labor market such as the Philippines, Bangladesh, and Sri Lanka...export the bodies of their citizens to induce foreign currency into their economies" (51). Throughout the globe, the rise in women's immigration to developed countries (and women are now the majority of illegal immigrants in the United States) is a result of the need for someone to do the caring work that was once done by members of the home population. Some of these workers are professionals—for example, nurses—but many of them are unskilled domestic workers. In many countries outside the United States, by the way, these circumstances are not always better and are often worse. These workers, especially those who work as domestics, are treated extremely badly, as little better than chattel. Their immigration status is often different from the status of other immigrants (for example, in Canada, see Cohen 2000) and at the point at which they cease being useful as domestic servants (for example, by becoming pregnant) they are subject to immediate deportation (in Singapore, for example, pregnant women are deportable, even if their pregnancy was caused by their employer (Bakan and Stasiulis 1997).

Fateful Directions

The fateful directions that will resolve this crisis depend in part upon how Americans think about the crisis. On the one hand, if Americans think of the crisis in care workers as primarily an issue of scarce resources and their allocation, Americans will come to one set of conclusions. On the other hand, if Americans think of this crisis as a call to rethink collectively how Americans allocate responsibility for care, then Americans will come to a very different conclusion.

If Americans understand the current situation in terms of economic scarcity, then neoliberals can delight in its solution. If care work is scarce, the solution to the problem is to allow the market to dictate the allocations. We can imagine a situation in which the overall solution to the problem of care work is to privatize care work as much as possible. The second alternative is to figure out a way to make care work more public and a widely shared social good, that is, to socialize care work.[3] The difference between these two solutions may seem abstract, but in concrete terms it determines whether individuals and their care-takers will hire and supervise and control the organization of care or whether such organization will be done through wider social institutions and practices. Hiring a nanny is an example of a private solution to the problem of child-care; using a day-care center is an example of a public or social solution to the problem of child-care.

Privatization

Privatization would involve the use of as many care workers in individual and private settings as possible. By this model, moreover, the more an individual can pay to receive care, the better the care the individual will receive.

In this model, individuals receive as much care as they can pay for, allowing also for the prudent to provide for their own future caring needs through various insurance plans to guarantee their future care. By this logic, if parents have children and cannot locate adequate day care, it is their problem, since they should have determined that such care would be available before they became parents. This solution fits very well with the ideological direction that neoliberalism has imposed upon the United States and throughout the globe (Tronto 2001).

The problem with this solution is that it allows the most unjust and exploitative forms of care to flourish. We can easily determine that, if Americans allow the private market to serve as the basis for the allocation and distribution of care, these practices will have effects contrary to the interests of justice. (Why this is so is somewhat intuitively obvious,[4] but I will explore this point at greater length later.)

Socialization

Increased socialization of care requires that Americans acknowledge, in the first place, the importance of care as a public resource and responsibility. By this account, the government (and ideally, in the United States, the federal government) would become responsible for the provision of basic necessary care. Government would become responsible for insuring a base level of health care, housing, day care, and elder care, as well as continuing its responsibility for education. It would require adoption of the kinds of policies for family support and institutions for health and welfare that characterize virtually all other industrial states.

---

3. E. E. Schattschneider, the American political scientist, faced a similar terminological problem; he decided that the opposite of privatization was socialization. To publicize, or publicization, does not mean the opposite of privatization, so, despite the fact that my emphasis is not so much on "society," I will follow Schattschneider's use.

4. Consider the sentiments of a working mother, quoted in a consumer-oriented article in the *New York Times*: "You want someone who puts the children before herself," said Judy Meyers, thirty-seven, a mother of two in Briarcliff Manor, N.Y., who works for a health insurance company. "But to find someone for the right amount of money is not so easy" (Rubenstein 1993).

It also requires that Americans redefine citizenship so that immigrants who make important contributions to public care be eligible for citizenship. One of the great difficulties faced by immigrant workers is that they are only permitted "partial citizenship" (Parreñas 2001, 37). Since care work is often organized informally, paid "off the books," and so forth, the legal regulations controlling citizenship should change to reflect the real work that immigrant care workers do. The problem of making care workers into "citizens" is a problem not only of legal citizenship but also of what Rena Benmayor labeled "cultural citizenship" (Benmayor 1992); that is, of creating a sense of entitlement to full participation.

This is a radical idea. It is radical, in the first place, because "care" has not traditionally been among the concerns that made one into a citizen. But changing our understanding of citizenship, while a crucial piece in making care more public, is not the only crucial piece. In order to make care more valued publicly, a change will be required in our fundamental notions of responsibility, so that the problems faced by others in organizing their care work are seen not simply as "their" problem but also as a social and political concern. Insofar as caring is seen as a private concern, this seems to require a fundamental change in our approach to caring.

Which Way to Turn?

What will determine whether we should privatize or socialize care? I shall argue that though morality might dictate a preference for public care, politically it is unlikely that such a change will occur.

Morally Speaking, Public Care Seems More Desirable than Further Privatization of Care

The moral choice is clearly to go in the direction of public care. Morally, it is difficult to argue that privatization is better. Many of the effects of greater privatization of care exacerbate existing problems of justice. This is so for a number of reasons, as follows.

1. Privatization of care increases social inequality. Insofar as receiving adequate care prepares one for, or enhances, success, then those who already have command of more resources will also be able to command more care resources as well. Social inequality violates our notions of justice as fairness, if not in itself, then insofar as it translates into unequal opportunity.

2. Privatization increases the chances that workers will be exploited. The opportunity for care workers to be exploited is always great, as Diemut Bubeck has argued. When we add to this situation a condition of "partial citizenship," economic inequality, privatized work places that make it difficult to organize workers, and so forth, the likelihood of exploitation grows (Tronto 2002a).

3. Privatization creates the conditions for an "epistemology of ignorance" around this exploitation. In general, people do not like to view their activities as exploitative toward others. The only way, often, to engage in such exploitation, then, is to remain willfully ignorant of the damage that one is doing to others.

Charles Mills labels this kind of ignorance "the epistemology of ignorance" (1997) and condemns it as contributing to ongoing injustice. In this case, we may speculate that people of adequate means will think that they are doing a favor for the workers they hire who are illegal immigrants or whose immigration status is uncertain.[5]

4. Privatization does not allow a social dialogue about "necessary care." Here is another problem with care that privatization does not allow us to solve: not all caring needs are equally important and worthy of being met. Kari Waerness distinguished between "necessary care" (care that one cannot provide to oneself, such as the care provided by doctors to patients or the protection that day-care workers provide to children in their charge) and "personal service" (which is the care that one could provide for oneself but chooses not to provide, such as when one hires a laundress or when a husband expects his wife to keep track of his clean clothing) (Waerness 1990). If we think about this distinction from the standpoint of an account of justice, we would probably be able to argue that urgent forms of necessary care take moral precedence over others' "personal service" needs. Nonetheless, in a society in which caring needs are met by private resources, there is no way to have a public discussion about this question.

However, most people are not moved by such moral arguments, and powerful people are not likely to give up the advantage of being able to get more care.

As if self-interest and greed were not strong enough incentives to avoid a more public account of care, in some ways the care perspective, paradoxically, lends itself to the privatization solution. If one is competing in a world of limited care, then is it not proper, given one's greater care responsibilities to those who are nearest and dearest to one, to grab for them all the care that one can? If so, is there anything wrong with hiring a nanny, a housecleaner, Sylvan tutors, to make certain that one's own children are a leg up, or a private-duty nurse to make certain that one's loved one is adequately cared for in a public hospital (Tronto 2002b)?

Americans have created a system of care, then, that rewards only those with resources. It pays no attention to the question of desert (i.e., who deserves what kinds of care) or justice (i.e., how to provide care in accordance with principles of justice) or to thinking more broadly about what care would look like in a good society.

Is there some way to change the political outcome, then?

Political Reality Suggests That Privatization Is the More Likely Outcome

Politically, there are many reasons to expect the outcome to be greater privatization. The American political system is probably not amenable to any of the kinds of changes that I have suggested might be required by the interests of justice and improved care. Let us just recall a few basic facts: the American political system

---

5. Indeed, many workers are sponsored for Green Cards by their employers. This benefit seems, on the one hand, to be support for such workers. On the other hand, employers often use the threat of withholding sponsorship to take further advantage of their workers. For a discussion, see, *inter alia*, Hondagneu-Sotelo 2001.

reflects the interests of citizens and not immigrants. The political system reflects the concerns of well-educated, higher income individuals more than the concerns of working-class people. Political leaders seem reluctant to consider even the most modest measures that might call attention to the existing care crisis (e.g., the Bush administration refused to provide any guidelines for nursing home care; Pear 2002).

Care concerns are not organized as a part of public life but are viewed by individuals as their own problem. As Piven and Cloward long ago observed, fundamental political change is only possible when people perceive the disorder in their world not as being of their own making but as something mutable and addressable through public, political means (Piven and Cloward 1978).

Creating Political Change: Rethinking Citizenship and Care

Care and Citizenship

Although care has often been relegated to the private sphere of life, the conditions of the postmodern age make care and its provision into a more central part of our collective concerns. Americans face a fateful moment in the future direction of democratic life in our society. Americans may decide that we should continue to allocate responsibility for care along lines that continue to reinscribe the split between public and private life and to leave care as a concern that extends only within our personal sphere. Or Americans may determine that care is a public concern, and may change their set of political values and priorities accordingly. In this essay I argue that understanding the current care crisis and the alternatives that we face provides us with one slim hope for creating a more just global society.

But such a definition would confound many aspects of current conceptions of citizenship. Citizenship signifies political membership. In this essay, I focus on the moral and political problems that arise when we think of citizenship as an exclusionary practice. Citizenship is determined by the people who live in a nation-state, who set the rules for membership. Like a private club that understands the value of its exclusionary rules for inclusion, citizenship can function as a kind of barrier that reflects and protects the political power of those who are already insiders. Citizenship is not always determined, then, by what is moral and just. The question of citizenship is quintessentially a political question, and political questions call for political solutions.

Furthermore, questions about citizenship are inevitably local questions. They concern the decisions about membership that are made by the closed circle of those who are already members. Citizenship is thus best understood as a privilege, and though arguments about international human rights might come into play in embarrassing or convincing a nation's citizens into rethinking some of its membership rules (e.g., in some African states, such as Botswana),[6] discussions about

6. Until a recent court challenge, for example, the children of a married Botswanan mother and a noncitizen father were not permitted citizenship in Botswana. See Dow 2001.

citizenship must always then be local and political, and cannot only be made in universal and moral terms.

Models of citizenship define the boundaries between public and private life and determine which activities, attitudes, possessions, and so on are to be considered worthy in any given state.[7] Citizenship shapes, and is shaped by, our most deeply held values about justice and fairness in determining what good citizens in our society do. And models of citizenship also include an implicit account of what citizens are like before they come to the public arena. States exclude children and others who have not been thought to have achieved "majority" from active citizenship. In previous historical eras, property or arms were conditions of citizenship. Through inclusion and exclusion of some people, citizenship reflects winners and losers in the political game with the highest stakes, a political game in which the deck is stacked, since one can only win by achieving the favor of previous winners, who dilute their victory by allowing others to join them as winners.

Societies conceive of citizens in terms of the contributions that they make to the society. Historically, citizens have been conceived as warriors, as burgher-merchants, as farmers, as artisans (Isin 1997). The chief discourse on citizenship in welfare states has followed the lead of T. H. Marshall in identifying citizens primarily as workers (see, among others, Marshall and Bottomore 1992 [1950]). It is instructive, perhaps, to recall here the Aristotelian model of the citizen as one who participates in public life but whose actual conditions of life presuppose a separate realm of existence for both economic activity and care work (see, among others, Stiehm 1984; Yak 1993). Thus, the Aristotelian citizen "floats" his (*sic*) citizenship on previously accomplished work that is beneath the observance of political institutions but nonetheless essential for his life.

Whereas property was once conceived as a necessary prerequisite for independence and thus for citizenship, that model of the citizen has by now faded (Isin 1997). As many astute observers have noted, the conception of the welfare state that informs postwar life presumes a particular model of citizens (e.g., Bussemaker and van Kersbergen 1994; Knijn and Kremer 1997; Lister 1997; Pateman 1988). This model presumes a citizen worker and a "support staff," traditionally conceived as the wife in a nuclear family, whose task it is to perform the "reproductive labor" of "the other side of the paycheck" (Bridges 1979; Schwarzenbach 1996).

This model of the household is no longer an accurate description of the way most people live, but the notion that citizenship attaches to work remains. If anything, recent welfare reform in the United States has reinforced the view that citizenship depends upon paid labor. Indeed, the second wave of feminism has, as one of its profoundest consequences, the increase in the participation of women in the paid labor force. Yet, as many more women now work, they are caught in a bind, the "double shift," in which they must do both their previously assigned caring work and the paid work outside of the household. Although men have made minor increases in their contributions to work within the household, the main

---

7. There is a huge and burgeoning literature on this topic of citizenship. See, *inter alia*, the new journal *Citizenship Studies* (1997–), Lister 1997, Turner 1997, Vogel 1994.

effect of the universalizing of the citizen-as-worker model is to leave inadequately answered the question: Who shall do the care work?

Questions about citizenship remind us that, even though the world economy is globalizing, nation-states still exert some forms of power. The rules governing formal citizenship in the United States have changed but remain somewhat constant over the past forty years. The extension by the courts of certain forms of legal rights to immigrants in the 1960s and 1970s perhaps removed some of the urgency of re-thinking rules of citizenship. In recent years, however, as many immigrants have come to the United States[8] and as national security threats have grown more ominous, the courts and Congress have begun to erode these protections for noncitizens. The question of what an immigrant should do to qualify as a citizen of the United States, then, is no longer a settled question but one that should be before decision-makers. That the current wave of immigrants includes a high proportion of women makes this an urgent question as well for feminists.[9]

Historically, definitions of citizenship change when there is a political move-ment by noncitizens that sufficiently threatens existing members into changing their definitions of citizenship. Usually, the threatening non- or partial citizens are already in residence, and a crisis makes their presence and contributions apparent. Such were the incentives to rethink the citizenship status of women in the United States in the aftermath of World War I, of African Americans after the Civil War and World War II. To raise the question of citizenship at the present moment, when issues of globalization and the perception of greater hostility in the world are at the forefront, poses some interesting challenges.

Changing the Political Calculus to Make It Conform to Morality: A Care Movement

In an American context, it is very difficult to know how to proceed. While argu-ments for equality, social justice, and solidarity carry weight in northwestern Europe, such arguments are not powerful in the United States. My hope is that, by asking Americans to think about care needs and the noncitizens who currently do a great deal of care work, the rethinking of citizenship and care will open new possibilities for thinking about immigrants' lives, the nature and value of care, and the costs and advantages of globalizing care work.

The solution is for Americans to recognize that they need to take collective action to improve the conditions for care in the United States. Deborah Stone

8. According to the National Immigration Law Center, "between 1970 and 2000, the naturalized citizen population increased by 71 percent," and "according to the 2000 census, there are over 30 million immigrants in the United States, representing 11 percent of the total population" (National Immigration Law Center 2004).

9. "Federal investigators have said that 45,000 to 50,000 women and children are brought to this country both legally and illegally each year by employers who promise opportunity but exploit them sexually or force them into servitude" (Harden 2002). Immigrant workers are most likely to be found doing unskilled work: "Immigrants—legal and illegal—now make up 13 percent of the nation's workers, the highest percentage since the 1930's ... and hold 35 percent of the unskilled jobs." (Parker 2001).

issued a call for a care movement in the *Nation* (Stone 2000). She used this instructive analogy: just as clean air and water are basic for human survival but people had to organize into an environmental movement to attain them, so too care is a basic human need but requires political clout if it is to be taken seriously politically. Stone sees the need for a care movement arising out of an alignment of a great proportion of the people as a whole: she includes care-givers, care-receivers, and family members who would otherwise have to care or concern themselves with such care as people who share a common interest in making certain that there are adequate numbers of well-trained and well-employed care workers.

Within a care movement, Americans need to set priorities on fundamental change, not piecemeal reform. We need a way to bring professional and non-professional workers together. There are, further, some broad aspects of public care that we need to consider: we need to make certain that care is organized with a proper balance among the interests of those who need care, those who give care, and those whose lives are made easier if others receive care.[10]

In calling for a care movement, Americans need also to disrupt the gendered and privatized assumptions that are usually made about care in our society. In what ways can caring count as a public activity?

Many scholars, including me, have argued that care is largely private. I argued, wrongly I now think, that care is generally accorded a place either above or below politics (Tronto 1996). I argued that care is not political, on the one hand, because it is too lowly and banal to be a part of politics and thus more attached to a realm of "necessity" than to a realm of "freedom." On the other hand, care is not political because it is too exalted to be a part of politics and thus more attached to a realm of charity that transcends politics. Both of these accounts, however, accept the realist view about the proper realm of politics and ignore the long-existing benevolent aspects of politics that provide for making citizens' lives easier and more comfortable. Although it is thus wrong to equate a noncaring approach as essential to all politics, this has been the way to emphasize the realist, and masculinist, account of politics. This realist view of politics has been extremely important both in using and maintaining gender domination in political life.[11]

Nevertheless, as a description of why realists find it useful to obscure the role of care in political life, I would now modify that argument. The historical process by which care's political role is obscured is more complicated and involves a more complicated shaping of the relationship of gender, care, and politics. It involves, in the first analytic instance separating "care" from what men do, and then ignoring the ways in which work ascribed to men is part of the realm of care. In this way, work that has been designated as "care" is marked as feminine and is placed

10. If such a balance is not considered, we may end up creating institutions for care that are really serving peripheral rather than basic needs. For example, Jan Poppendieck (1998) argues that the emergency food system gives donors a sense of their generosity, and that this latent function of the system is really more important than solving the problem of hunger.

11. For two interesting accounts of "realist" politics, see Bologh 1990, Pitkin 1984.

outside of the public realm, either above it or below it, but work that is left within the public realm is never called "care."

Among such "noncaring" care (i.e., "men's work" that is actually care) is the work that was called in the eighteenth century "police." The "police powers" still extend broadly to include provisions for public health, safety, and education. Modern policing has become militarized and masculinized and receives unquestioned public support, but it is a kind of care work. The care work that has been marked as "feminine" is the care work that has been only suspiciously associated with public life. Indeed, perhaps one reason why there was no objection to making education public is that, at the time of debates about publicizing education, men taught school. It was only when it became clear that women could be hired for considerably less money that this occupation was turned over to women and became a "natural" extension of the maternal, rather than the paternal, role.

There is another aspect to the distinction between "masculine" and "feminine" care, however, that is relevant to the nature of citizenship, and it concerns the question of who receives these two different types of care. Recipients of "masculine" care are perceived, by their nature, to be citizens who, for one reason or another, find themselves *in extremis*. Recipients of "feminine" care, on the other hand, are people who are somehow dependent: children, the disabled, the ill and infirm, the elderly. As long as most American citizens are able to delude themselves into thinking that they do not receive care, then they are able to exclude the "needy" from full citizenship and their care-givers from full citizenship (see Kittay 2001). Not until Americans recognize that we are "care receivers all" is there any hope of changing our political vision to make care more a collective concern.

A care movement is necessary, then, to redefine care as a concern that is neither feminine nor masculine but human. It is necessary to overcome the indifference of a political system that benefits the well-to-do, who currently benefit from the availability of inexpensive care assistance at their beck and call. A care movement is necessary to change the way that Americans think about themselves as public actors, and to include the provision of what Americans need to live as a part of what they need to live as citizens.

Conclusion

Citizenship reflects values. Our society does not now and never has adequately valued care. Focusing on citizenship requires us to think about the most fundamental aspect of defining who is a member of a political community. It is a key way to begin to reframe the meaning of care as a public issue and to reopen the public debate about the nature of our responsibilities toward others, both within our own society and around the globe.

Including immigrant care workers as citizens is also the least that Americans can do to right the injustices done to exploited care workers. But I do not wish to make the argument of this essay depend upon our sense of justice. Although it requires us to change the way that Americans think about their interests, it is also the case that changing the public value of care is in all of our broader interests. The relentless drive to force us into becoming nonstop workers means that the caring that we do for ourselves and each other is mediated increasingly by market relations. It marks a new form of alienation, but one that has been cleverly thrust out of the workplace and back into the home. If Americans instead realize that part of their responsibilities as citizens is to think about how they need to care for "public things," then they will be able to start thinking about the relationship of public and private caring. In an age in which societies are so integrated, it is difficult to start to think about the public good and not understand that our interests are connected to the flourishing of all others, not just those closest to us.

Capitalism and globalization will not end because we believe these processes to be unjust. But national political actors have been able to mitigate against some of the more vicious effects of capitalism: worker safety laws, for example, exist because workers demanded them. So, too, as producers of national and corporate wealth, we all can demand that in our collective lives together we recognize our needs to care for ourselves, those closest to us, and all others.

Politics, said Max Weber, is the slow boring of hard boards. The process of political change requires, above all else, that we get people to think differently about their most fundamental interests. Asking Americans to rethink their reliance on care workers, or to at least acknowledge their reliance, asks that we rethink our interests in providing and distributing care. It requires that we return to an earlier framework in which people understood that care work is fundamentally public.

Bibliography

Bakan, Abigail B., and Daiva Stasiulis. 1997. "Not One of the Family: Foreign Domestic Workers in Canada." Toronto: University of Toronto Press.

Benmayor, Rena. 1992. *Responses to Poverty Among Puerto Rican Women: Identity, Community and Cultural Citizenship.* New York: Centro de Estudios Puertorriqueños, Hunter College.

Bologh, Roslyn Wallach. 1990. *Love or Greatness: Max Weber and Masculine Thinking—A Feminist Inquiry.* Boston: Unwin Hyman.

Bridges, Amy. 1979. "The Other Side of the Paycheck." In *Capitalist Patriarchy and the Case for Socialist Feminism*, ed. Z. Eisenstein. New York: Monthly Review Press.

Bubeck, Diemut. 1995. *Care, Justice and Gender.* Oxford: Oxford University Press.

Bussemaker, Jet, and Kees van Kersbergen. 1994. "Gender and Welfare States: Some Theoretical Reflections." In *Gendering Welfare States*, ed. D. Sainsbury. London: Sage.

Chang, Grace. 2000. *Disposable Domestics: Immigrant Women Workers in the Global Economy.* Boston: South End Press.

Cohen, Rina. 2000. "'Mom Is a Stranger': The Negative Impact of Immigration Policies on the Family Life of Filipina Domestic Workers." *Canadian Ethnic Studies* 32: 76–88.

Dow, Justice Unity. 2001. "How the Global Informs the Local: The Botswana Citizenship Case." *Health Care for Women International* 22: 319–331.

Fisher, Berenice, and Joan C. Tronto. 1990. "Toward a Feminist Theory of Caring." Pp. 36–54 in *Circles of Care*, ed. E. Abel and M. Nelson. Albany: SUNY Press.

Folbre, Nancy. 1994. *Who Pays for the Kids? Gender and the Structure of Constraint.* New York: Routledge.

———. 2001. *The Invisible Heart: Economics and Family Values.* New York: New Press.

Francis, David. 2001. "The Dollars and Cents of America's Work Ethic." *Christian Science Monitor,* June 27, 2001: 1.

Gould Ellen, Ingrid, and Katherine Hempstead. 2002. "Telecommuting and the Demand for Urban Living: A Preliminary Look at White-collar Workers." *Urban Studies* 39(4): 749–766.

Harden, Blaine. 2002. "Case of Princess Accused of Pushing Maid Down Stairs Reveals a Failing of a New Law." *New York Times,* July 2, A14.

Harvey, David. 1990. *The Condition of Postmodernity. An Enquiry into the Origins of Cultural Change.* Oxford: Blackwell.

Hill, E. Jeffrey, Alan J. Hawkins, Maria Ferris, and Michelle Weitzman. 2001. "Finding an Extra Day a Week: The Positive Influence of Perceived Job Flexibility on Work and Family Life Balance." *Family Relations* 50(1): 49–58.

Hondagneu-Sotelo, Pierrette. 2001. *Doméstica: Immigrant Workers Cleaning and Caring in the Shadows of Affluence.* Berkeley: University of California Press.

Isin, Engin F. 1997. "Who Is the New Citizen? Towards a Genealogy." *Citizenship Studies* 1: 115–132.

Kittay, Eva Feder. 1999. *Love's Labor: Essays on Women, Equality and Dependency.* New York: Routledge.

Knijn, Trudie, and Monique Kremer. 1997. "Gender and the Caring Dimension of Welfare States: Toward Inclusive Citizenship." *Social Politics* 4: 328–361.

Lister, Ruth. 1997. *Citizenship: Feminist Perspectives.* London: Macmillan.

Marshall, T. H., and Tom Bottomore. 1992 [1950]. *Citizenship and Social Class.* Concord, Mass.: Pluto Press.

Mills, Charles. 1997. *The Racial Contract.* Ithaca, N.Y.: Cornell University Press.

More, Thomas. [1516] 1965. *Utopia.* Repr., trans. with an introduction by Paul Turner. New York: Penguin.

Noddings, Nel. 2002. *Starting at Home: Caring and Social Policy.* Berkeley: University of California Press.

National Immigration Law Center. 2004. Facts about Immigrants. Los Angeles: National Immigration Law Center (July). Available online at: http://www.nilc.org/immspbs/research/pbimmfacts_0704.pdf.

Parker, Laura. 2001. "USA Just Wouldn't Work without Immigrant Labor." *USA Today,* July 23, 1.

Parreñas, Rhacel Salazar. 2001. *Servants of Globalization: Women, Migration and Domestic Work.* Palo Alto, Calif.: Stanford University Press.

Pateman, Carole. 1988. *The Sexual Contract.* Palo Alto, Calif.: Stanford University Press.

Pear, Robert. 2002. "Nine of Ten Nursing Homes Lack Adequate Staff, Study Finds." *New York Times,* February 18, A11.

Perrera, Andrea. 2002. "Nurses Across State Cash in on Shortage." *Los Angeles Times,* February 17, 8.

Pitkin, Hanna Fenichel. 1984. *Fortune Is a Woman: Gender and Politics in the Thought of Niccolò Machiavelli.* Berkeley: University of California Press.

Piven, Frances Fox, and Richard A. Cloward. 1978. *Poor People's Movements: Why They Succeed, How They Fail.* New York: Vintage.

Poppendieck, Janet. 1998. *Sweet charity? Emergency Food and the End of Entitlement.* New York: Viking.

Romero, Mary. 1992. *Maid in the U.S.A.* New York: Routledge.

Rubenstein, Caren. 1993. "Consumer's World: Finding a Nanny Legally." *New York Times,* January 28, C1.

Schlinkmann, Mark. 2002. "In Meeting at Child-Care Center Here, Senators Hear of Need for Trained Workers; Carnahan Plans Bill Aimed at Easing Shortage." *St. Louis Post-Dispatch*, January 30, C4.

Schwarzenbach, Sibyl A. 1996. "On Civic Friendship." *Ethics* 107: 97–128.

Sevenhuijsen, Selma L. 1998. *Citizenship and the Ethics of Care*. London: Routledge.

Stacey, Judith. 1990. *Brave New Families: Stories of Domestic Upheaval in Late-Twentieth-Century America*. Berkeley: University of California Press.

Stiehm, Judith. 1984. "Our Aristotelian Hangover." In *Discovering Reality*, ed. M. Hintikka and S. Harding. Amsterdam: Elsevier.

Stone, Deborah. 2000. "Why We Need a Care Movement." *Nation*, March 13, 13–15.

Trapps, Tynisa. 2001. "Teacher Shortage Expected to Worsen, Especially in California." *Los Angeles Times*, August 15, 22.

Tronto, Joan C. 1993. *Moral Boundaries: A Political Argument for an Ethic of Care*. New York: Routledge.

———. 1996. "The Political Concept of Care." In *Revisioning the Political: Feminist Reconstructions of Traditional Concepts in Western Political Theory*, ed. N. Hirschmann and C. Di Stefano. Boulder, Colo.: Westview Press.

———. 2001. "Who Cares? Public and Private Caring and the Rethinking of Citizenship." In *Women and Welfare: Theory and Practice in the United States and Europe*, ed. N. J. Hirschmann and U. Liebert. New Brunswick, N.J.: Rutgers University Press.

———. 2002a. "The 'Nanny Question' in Feminism." *Hypatia* 17: 34–61.

———. 2002b. "The Value of Care." *Boston Review* 27(1): 16–17.

Turner, Brian S. 1997. "Citizenship Studies: A General Theory." *Citizenship Studies* 1: 5–18.

Vogel, Ursula. 1994. "Marriage and the Boundaries of Citizenship." In *The Condition of Citizenship*, ed. B. van Steenbergen. London: Sage.

Waerness, Kari. 1990. "Informal and Formal Care in Old Age: What Is Wrong With the New Ideology in Scandinavia Today?" In *Gender and Caring: Work and Welfare in Britain and Scandinavia*, ed. C. Ungerson. London: Harvester, Wheatsheaf.

Walker, Margaret Urban. 1998. *Moral Understandings: A Feminist Study of Ethics*. New York: Routledge.

White, Julie Anne. 2000. *Democracy, Justice and the Welfare State: Reconstructing Public Care*. University Park: Penn State University Press.

Yak, Bernard. 1993. *The Problems of a Political Animal*. Berkeley: University of California Press.

III

Grounds of Citizenship in Culture and Civil Society

8

The Kin Contract and Citizenship in the Middle East

Suad Joseph

Kin and Citizen

Scholarship theorizing the culturally and historically specific intersections between women and citizenship in the Middle East has been limited by conceptual obstacles to linking family and politics in the discourses of citizenship—discourses inherited mostly from Western liberalist theory (Pateman 1988). "Family" as an idea and an institution and families as relationships and practices are the outcomes of multilayered processes that are highly political (Donzelot 1997, Elshtain 1982). Family and families are critical mediating mechanisms for state political institutions. Indeed, family and state can be said to be mutually constitutive (Cott 1995). In the Middle East, family and families are central to understanding states' social and political organizations and actions. Yet relatively few major theoretical breakthroughs in understanding family and families in relation to politics in the Middle East have been made (Barakat 1993, Doumani 2003, Joseph 1999a, 2002a, Sharabi 1988), despite Peter Gran's urging that the family be "studied as a part of politics, if for no other reason than the fact that the state invests a great deal of its resources in upholding its conceptions of an ideal family" (1996, 77). I propose to examine the relations between the family and the gendering of citizenship in Middle Eastern countries by analyzing what I call the "kin contract."

I have used the term "kin contract" to describe formal and informal understandings that underpin state/citizen relationships in Lebanon, but key parameters of the kin contract are found in all Middle Eastern countries (Joseph 2000). The kin contract is organized around the notion that all citizens belong to families prior to membership in the state and that families claim the primary and primordial loyalties of citizens. Membership in and a priori commitment to families is assumed equally for male and female citizens. Families, however, are presumed to be patriarchal (gender and age hierarchies), giving males and seniors privileges in relation to females and juniors. The kin contract presumes that males and females, seniors and juniors are engaged in complex webs of rights and responsibilities to and for each other. Within the kin contract, family includes not only nuclear members but extended kin, often many degrees removed, with the patrilineage awarded most rights and responsibilities vis-à-vis their members. The a priori standing of these kin rights and responsibilities is often formalized into law, receiving the endorsement and formal enforcement of the state legal apparatus. The kin contract receives further authorization through local religious doctrines that sanction familial rights and responsibilities. While state and religious institutions subsidize family and families, they also make critical use of family and families to underwrite their own structural priorities that may, at times, be at odds with family relations and practices.

Elements of the kin contract can be found in kin/state relations in many countries. As Jacqueline Stevens argues, "The Reformation-era notion of the family as pre-political is one that has continued to inform liberal and radical views of the relation between marriage and the state," even in the United States (Stevens 1999, 213). Many elements of the kin contract are not unique to the Middle East, and Middle Eastern societies are not exceptional in their interweaving family/families and politics. Indeed, as Susan Moller Okin aptly observed, "defenders of both autocratic and democratic regimes have recognized the political importance of different family forms for the formation of citizens" (Okin 1989, 18). Rather, it is the systemic and institutionalized positioning of family/families in politics in the Middle East that stands out in relationship to the West. It is the broad-based public acceptance of the political salience of kin idioms and morality and the public acceptance of the transporting of family practices and relationships into political life that stands out. It is this institutionalization of the kin contract, found to varying degrees in all Middle East countries, that, I suggest, undergirds the gendering of citizenship.

Despite the centrality of kin to state in the Middle East, the relationships of kin to state have been undertheorized. This could be, paradoxically, because they are so important that they are taken as givens in the social sciences of the Middle East, and while frequently discussed, these relationships are rarely problematized (Joseph 2002b).[1] One step toward a more critical analysis of women and citizenship in the Middle East is to situate women's citizenship within the kin contract and to view family and families through the lens of politics. Politics writ large, and politics as daily experiences of the ways in which self and society are constituted within relations of power and empowerment, shed light on the intersections among gender, citizenship, family, and state dynamics, highlighting the specificities and commonalities of the conditions of women as citizens in the Middle East.

---

1. In the nearly four years of the Arab Families Working Group (AFWG) since its founding in Cairo in May 2001, its fifteen scholars, policy-makers, and planners and four research assistants researching Egypt, Lebanon, and Palestine have found and compiled an extensive bibliography of work that refers to family and families in Arab societies. Relatively little of that work, however, is based on critical empirical research or offers critical theorization of family and families. The bibliography will be available on the AFWG website, which is under construction.

The recognition of the centrality of family to politics, state, and society in the Middle East can and has led to an essentialization that presumes that "the family" is pretty much the same throughout the Middle East or in key sections of the Middle East (such as the notion of "the Arab family," Barakat 1993, Sharabi 1988). Family forms and practices are varied throughout the region. The family and families are highly contested domains of action internally and externally. Family members may act against each other in specific actions; who counts as family is renegotiated at given times and places; lines of identity, alliances, and loyalties within families continually change; what family members think of themselves and each other in familial terms is always under construction; and what external actors and agencies think of and act on as "family," and how they do so, is always shifting.

Nevertheless, the family as idea and institution does occupy a central terrain in the political and legal landscape and significantly mediates women's relationship to the state and to the laws and practices of citizenship. What is persistent is the enmeshing of family in politics and in almost all arenas of social life.[2] Therein lie important continuities that mark women as second–class citizens in Middle Eastern countries. It is to that political condition (rather than the specific structures of families) that I refer in arguing that we must understand the relationships among family/families and state, mediated through the kin contract, to understand the realities of women as citizens in the Middle East. The question addressed here, therefore, is of the impact of the political positioning of family as idea and institution on women as citizens with its consequences for families as practices and relationships.

False Binaries, Family Fault Lines, and Citizenship

The binary between public and private in classical Western liberalist discourses definitively situated citizenship in the realm of the "public"—the realm of law, governance, and the state. Indeed, as Seyla Benhabib argued, for Hegel, the strict separation of public and private was part and parcel of the decline of political patriarchy (Benhabib 1992, 248). The private has had less clarity, at times referring to nongovernmental organizations understood as "civil society," at times to nongovernmental businesses and the marketplace, and at other times to the "domestic," "kinship," or "family." For analytical clarity, replacing the public/private binary, minimally with government, nongovernment, and domestic (Joseph 1997, Yuval-Davis 1997) offers conceptual tools for locating women in relationship to citizenship issues.

The public/private binary is a product of state-level discourses and theorizing (Benhabib 1992, Joseph 1997, Reiter 1975). The binary, in Western political theory, created an arena for the operations of the family, distinct from the operations of law. For Hegel, Benhabib contended, "the legal system stands at the beginning and

---

2. Family is crucial to the markets, economies, popular culture, literature, and many other arenas of social life in the Middle East. For the purposes of this argument, however, I focus on the intersections of family, state, law, and religion as critical to the gendering of citizenship.

end of the family; it circumscribes it but does not control its internal functioning or relations" (Benhabib 1992, 248). The family, in Hegel's vision, was crucial to the constitution of the modern state "because it is the sphere in which the right of the modern individual to particularity (Besonderheit) and subjectivity (Subjektivitat) is realized," including, she argued, the rights of women to become legal-juridical subjects (248).

As the idea of citizenship and the public/private binary are inventions of state societies, so also is the idea of "family" an invention of state societies. Not only is the family, I suggest, central to political imagination and to political practices, but the idea of "family" may be seen as having emerged in state-level societies as a concomitant of the state. The structures, dynamics, idioms, and moralities of the family and of families must be viewed in the context of the nature of the states of which they are a part. It has not only been Middle Eastern states who have invested heavily in their notions of the ideal family (Gran 1996); virtually all states invest in their notions of the ideal family through their regulation of marriage, divorce, children, inheritance, child labor, and a variety of practices that have direct impact on family practices and relationships (Olsen 1985, Stevens 1999). As Stevens notes, "law constitutes marriage" (Stevens 1999, 215) and does so actively, not passively reflecting some preexisting marital norms. Nancy Cott goes further in arguing: "the institution of marriage and the modern state have been mutually constitutive. As much as (legal) marriage does not exist without being authorized by the state, one of the principle means that the state can use to prove its existence—to announce its sovereignty and its hold on the populace—is its authority over marriage (Cott 1995, 109). In so doing, law constitutes family. In effect, the state constitutes family. The birthing of these conceptual tools of statehood is tied to the carving out of domains for state authority and the mobilization of citizens into structures of governance.

Western states have fostered the development of social spheres that are legally required to be different from each other. The notions of "civil society" or nongovernmental arena make sense only in the context of the carving-out of an arena of the governmental. The idea of "the domestic" or kinship or family as a "thing" unto itself is understandable only in the context of a different/separate arena that belongs to the state (Joseph 1997, Yuval-Davis 1997). These constructions were critical to classical contractarian and liberalist Western notions of governance. The conceptual invention of separate spheres (necessary to create and contain a domain of state power), over time, came to have legal authority. With the weight of law behind them, the boundaries between spheres became naturalized. Law constructs its own subjects (Collier, Maurer, and Suarez-Navaz 1995, Ong 1996). The autonomy of the spheres became an anchor point of democratic society discourse. Boundary-making in the service of constructing spheres of social life has been a key project of Western state-building. A major contribution of critical feminist political theory has been to expose the historicity of these spheres and how that historical construction remanded women to secondary citizenship status (Benhabib 1992, Nedelsky 1989, Pateman 1988).

In most Middle Eastern societies, government, nongovernment, and domestic spheres are closely interwoven, both in imaginative discourses and in reality. The flow of people, rights, and responsibilities between and among these arenas is considered to be natural and normal. It is the small numbers of intellectuals and activists who worry about the fluid movement of relationships and resources among these domains. And it is the relationships and rationalities of family/families, I suggest, that are the most powerful motor and morality behind the ease of movement between/among social spheres discursively constructed as "separate."

Women were so scripted out of the "public" in classical Western liberalist discourses of citizenship (Pateman 1988, Stevens 1999, Voet 1998) that recognition of women's vital roles in the "public" in non-Western societies has been hindered by the uncritical application of Western scholarly assumptions about the "public" to non-Western societies. As definitively as citizenship has been housed in the public in Western liberalist discourses, women have been housed in "the domestic." The resistance to the insertion of women into the public (and therefore citizenship) is only partly linked to political ambivalence about gender. It is also partly linked to ambivalence in the West about the relationship of "family" to politics. As Jacqueline Stevens observed, even today, many people still assume "there is something natural about kinship" (Stevens 1999, 210) and therefore take for granted that there is a divide between the family, "which is natural and political society, which is artificial" (211). In the Middle East, however, there is less uncertainty about the relation of family to politics. The family is squarely at the center of politics and, therefore, of citizenship issues.

The Domestic: Domain or Dominion

The processes by which the "domestic" comes to be marked as a separate domain (Deleuze 1997, x) contribute to women's secondary citizenship in both Western and Middle Eastern states. If, as I argue, the idea of the "domestic" as a separate sphere is an invention of the state, then historical research is need to trace the process by which the "family" came to fill the space of "the domestic" in specific societies (where it has). No doubt, this was partly the result of efforts by states to mobilize their citizens into manageable and mobile units, pliable for labor market needs yet consolidated for social control.

Prestate societies tend not to delimit a domestic arena or equate domestic with family. Nor do they identify family, the domestic, or kinship with women. David M. Schneider argued that the very idea of "kinship" and the "social" is a relatively modern invention (1984). During the French Revolution, "the most obvious material at hand for thinking politically was the family, not the family as some kind of modal social experience, but the family as an imaginative construct of power relations," according to Lynn Hunt (1992, 196). Disregarding early imaginative political uses of the family, much of Western classical liberalist theory bracketed family off from politics (Benhabib 1992, Lister 1997). The shift from linking to delinking of family and politics is partly the story of the development of the public/private binary in Western liberalist theories of citizenship.

In most Western countries, states managed to consolidate "family" as a distinct domain. This was partly accomplished by reducing the services families provide and the control families have over their members, thus diminishing the space family occupies. Most Middle Eastern states, on the other hand, have allowed extensive space for families to occupy, have subsidized the services families provide to their members and the control families have over their members, and have absorbed family structures, moralities, and idioms into the body politic. This difference is significant for understanding the differences in the gendering of citizenship in Western and Middle Eastern states, underwritten both by different allocations of "space" and differing forms of patriarchy.

Carole Pateman (1988) argued that the development of Western classical liberalism and social contract theorists represented a shift from paternal to fraternal patriarchy, from rule of the "fathers" to rule of the "brothers." For Pateman, political liberalism privileged men as men rather than men as kinsmen. The distinction between Pateman's notion of a Western fraternal patriarchy and Middle Eastern kin-based patriarchy is crucial for understanding the specificities of the gendering of citizenship in many Middle Eastern states. The power of Middle Eastern patriarchy is its rooting in kinship—a kinship system that permeates all spheres of life: private/public, state/civil society, religion/nation. Kin-based patriarchy has been transported into political, economic, social, and religious dynamics, weaving threads through all domains of Middle Eastern societies; producing a porosity in movements of practices, relationships, and resources; and constructing social idioms and moralities that rationalize the connectivity of the societal fabric.

The authority of kin-based patriarchy in the Middle East rests partly on what I have called, in the Lebanese case, the "kin contract." Unlike the liberalist social contract (which assumes autonomous, unattached, separative, bounded, and gender-neutral subjects willingly engaging in the contract) and unlike the fraternal sexual contract (which Pateman, 1988, argues assumes men as brothers as the contracting actors and all subjects as gendered and partnered), the kin contract assumes that men and women equally commit to membership in the kin group that is prior to membership in the state. The kin unit, in the kin contract, is not only assumed to precede state entities but is assumed to preempt the state in specific rights over their members and in responsibilities members have to their kin. The state both defers certain authorities over its political subjects to kin units as well as uses the authority it gives to kin over their members to mediate its own relationships to its citizens—similar to the relationship that Deniz Kandiyoti describes as the "patriarchal bargain" (Kandiyoti 1988). The kin contract is played out in the administering of state laws, and especially family law, in the privileged relationships between religion and kin entities, and in the everyday practices of citizens and state agencies. The kin contract engages not only small, immediate, nuclear families but large extended families of grandparents, uncles, aunts, cousins many times removed who have rights and responsibilities toward each other.

The kin contract, while privileging men, aims to discipline men as well as women. It commands men to fulfill familial obligations, including submitting to the authority of their elders (which might include females). Linked to a culturally specific form of patriarchy that I call "patriarchal connectivity" (see hereafter), the kin contract presumes the priority of the family over and above family members, such that sacrifice of the self on behalf of other family members is an expectation (though not always a practice). Unlike fraternal patriarchy, which privileges men as men (not kinsmen; Pateman 1988), patriarchal connectivity privileges men and elders (including elder women) as kinfolk. It justifies itself in the idiom and morality of kinship rather than gender.

Women, as well as men, generally support the family system in most Middle Eastern countries, despite the disproportionate disciplining of women (and juniors). Even though specific persons often rebel, resist, and negotiate familial relations, there is surprisingly little in the way of a sustained "critique" of the family in the Middle East, from feminist or other circles (Barakat 1993, Sharabi 1988, Joseph 2002b). Given the frequent absence of systems of public support, and the common pattern of repressive states, women often find their needs better met inside rather than outside family settings (Altorki 2000). In what might be called the "pleasures of patriarchy," the kin contract is justified through love/power relations that I call care/ control—the assurance of familial care coupled with the submission to familial controls. The support given to the family system in the Middle East, despite evident gender and age inequality, is reflective of the enmeshing of the kin contract into the system of governance and is central to understanding the gendering of citizenship.

The family, in the Middle East, is supported and sanctified by religious institutions, by its special position in notions of the nation, by its legal status in constitutions and laws, and by the social and political practices that foster its enmeshment with state and civil society. The weaving of family structures, moralities, and idioms into religion, politics, law, civil society, economy, and society is crucial to the gendering of citizenship in the Middle East.

The "patriarchal connective family," embodied in the kin contract, is an undertheorized strand weaving together many of the processes that gender the legal subject in Middle Eastern states. To unravel these processes, we must analyze the ties that bind people to family, nation to family, state to family, law to family, civil society to family, and religion to family.

Family/Families and the Shaping of the Connective Citizen-Subject

Citizen-subjects are made, in the first instance, in family settings. As in most countries, multiple notions of self are supported in families in Middle Eastern societies. The differing notions of self coreside, mutually constituting each other, even though they may contradict and conflict with each other. The idea of the citizen-self as a contractual, bounded, autonomous "individual" exists legally and socially in most Middle Eastern societies. Constructs of a relational or a connective self are particularly common in many Middle Eastern countries, however. Connectivity (a culturally specific notion of the relational self theorized by many feminists; see Chodorow 1978) constitutes the self as a person with relatively fluid boundaries. Connective selves experience themselves as a part of significant others (Joseph 1993b). Relatedness, rather than boundary, autonomy, separateness, and difference, is the primary feature of the connective self. Mature connective selves are signified by the successful living-out of complex webs of interwoven relationships. Connective relationships are both functional and necessary for successful social existence in many, if not most, Middle Eastern societies (Joseph 1982b, 2000).

In Lebanon, where much of my fieldwork developing these notions has been carried out, the family system links connectivity and patriarchy in a system I have called *patriarchal connectivity*. This system (Joseph, ed., 1999) entails the production of selves with fluid boundaries organized for gendered and aged domination — supported by a culture that privileges kin structures, morality, and idioms. This form of patriarchy privileges males and elders (gender and age). Connectivity invites and requires persons to be involved with each other in shaping selves. Patriarchal connectivity supports the production of selves who respond to the involvement of others in shaping the self (and vice versa) and privileges the involvement of others by gender and age. Women and juniors expect seniors and elders to have authority in their lives (even though they may resist that authority), and seniors and elders expect to have responsibility that entails their authority toward women and juniors (even though they may not carry out those responsibilities).

Kin are central to social, political, and religious identity; economic and political security; and emotional stability in much of the Middle East. The centrality of kin (and the kin contract) is grounded in a care/control paradigm (Joseph 2000). The kin contract raises expectations that kin care for each other, provide for each other, protect each other, love each other — above all others. In return, kin are expected to privilege family and relationships over and above the self, including the respect and acceptance of the authority of males and seniors — above all others. Connectivity works within the kin contract as connective selves experience the value of the self, partly through their connection with significant others, particularly kin. The identity of the self, in connectivity, is nested within the family and significant communities (Barakat 1993, 98) — a fact that is central to the kin contract.

In the kin contract, one's primary rights and responsibilities are in relation to kin (the extended kin, not only the immediate small family). Connective or relational notions of selfhood support relational notions of rights and responsibilities (Joseph 1994), in addition to possible contractual notions. Relational rights and responsibilities imply that a person's sense of rights and responsibilities emerges from specific significant relationships (rather than being embedded in the self). Persons come to have rights by investing in relationships. Relationships also give responsibilities that are specific to those relationships. That is, within the kin contract, it is because we are siblings that we can claim rights in each other and responsibilities for each other. And those rights and responsibilities transcend any particular role or positionality that a person occupies. If a brother comes to have a government position, he is expected to act as a brother to his siblings, even in his official capacity (thus the blurring of the boundaries between kin and public domains). This fundamental principle of the kin contract contrasts with the Western liberalist formal premise that the political order is needed precisely because we are not siblings, not connected with filial or familial relationships. While this formal principle is recognized in Middle Eastern states, the kin contract subverts its operations by mediating rights and responsibilities through kin practices and relationships (real or idiomatic).[3]

---

3. I am indebted to the Oxford University Press reviewer for pointing out the need to clarify this point.

As a basis for citizenship practices, relational rights and responsibilities assume that citizens embed themselves in family and subnational communities such as religious sects, ethnic groups, and tribal groups. While citizens always have formal rights as citizens of states, citizen rights and responsibilities devolve, in part, through memberships in kin and community, though they are not completely synonymous with kin and community. That is, relational rights and responsibilities are not communal (based on an assumption of coherent corporate-like groups that act collectively) or individualist. They emerge from the concrete specific relationships each person has, the specific web of connections (a web most often grounded in kin and community). The meshing of the patriarchy, connectivity, relational rights and responsibilities, and the kin contract in the practices of citizenship in many Middle East countries means that relationships between the citizen and the state are mediated through kin, relationships, and communities, despite the existence of constitutionally and legislatively given formal rights. For women, this means that their citizen rights are often mediated through the very patriarchal structures (kin, communities, religious sects) that control (and care for) them.

Patriarchal connectivity, critical to the political workings of the kin contract, links the family system to citizenship and state in Lebanon. While my research focuses on Lebanon, numerous studies seem to indicate that various forms of patriarchal connectivity and the kin contract are operative in many Middle Eastern societies (Altorki 2000, Amawi 2000, Charrad 2000, 2001, Joseph 1999a). As such, patriarchal connectivity, relational rights, and the kin contract are key instruments in the gendering of citizenship.

Family/Families, Citizen-Subjects, and the State

The centrality of families for the making of citizens is legally recognized in many forms in Middle Eastern states, starting with state constitutions. Unlike those in most Western states, the constitutions of most Middle Eastern states identify the basic unit of society as the family rather than the individual. The fact that most Middle Eastern state constitutions identify the family as the basic unit of state membership implies that it is a person's *status* as a member of family that qualifies him or her for citizenship. Given the centrality of patriarchal connectivity, relational rights, and the kin contract in many Middle Eastern political, economic, religious, and social cultures, this implies the transportation of gendered and aged discourses and practices into citizenship discourses and practices.

Western notions of citizenship presume that relations between citizens and state transition from being status based to being contract based (Turner 1993, 5). The shift from status to contract, according to Pateman (1988, 9–10) required the "replacement of family by the 'individual' as the fundamental 'unit' of society." Turner contends that the idea of citizenship rejects the particularistic ties of family, village, or trip (1993, 5). C. B. MacPherson (1962, 262) argued that a specific form of self, the "possessive individual," was constructed by seventeenth-century political theorists as the classical citizen-subject.

Contractarianist theorists, Pateman (1988) argues, assumed that women were incapable of carrying out contractual relations. As the capacity to contract was deemed essential for citizenship, property ownership, and freedom, contractarians regarded women as secondary or indirect citizens (mediated through their husbands and fathers) at best. Contracting, property ownership, and notions of the citizen-subject are also linked in American constitutional history, according to Jennifer Nedelsky (1990). Citizen rights were based on the metaphor of bounded private property, with the rights of citizens defined as the boundaries to state authority (Nedelsky 1993). The linking of property and rights as boundaries assumed a notion of the citizen-subject as a bounded, autonomous, individualist self rooted in property ownership, and justifying the ownership of the self as property (Nedelsky 1989).

Middle Eastern states, on the other hand, generally devise themselves as the protector of the family. While many, if not most, Middle Eastern states acknowledge the idea of the social contract (Swirski 2000) or give lip service, on paper, to the idea of citizenship as a set of contractual relationships between "the individual" and the state, political practices and legal realities subordinate the citizen-subject to "the family" in most of these states. Yesim Arat (2000) suggests that the elite in Turkey use the idea of the "contract" to subsidize forms of integration to bolster their own rule. In Saudi Arabia, according to Altorki (2000), the idea of social contract is embedded in legislation but does not translate to public discourse or political practices. It is the citizen-subject embedded in relationships of kinship and community that seems to prevail in political practices rather than the citizen-subject as a self-contained, autonomous self who holds and is entitled to rights and responsibilities (Al-Mughni and Tretreault 2000, Amawi 2000, Charrad 2000, Joseph 2000).

This suggests that the head of a patriarchal family, legally constituted as the basic unit of the political community, is given rights and responsibilities over members of the family unit (the definition of which varies over time and place). For women, the linkages of connectivity, patriarchy, relational rights, and the kin contract to state politics means that women are written out of "the people" (Hatem 2000) or are seen as lacking "political personhood" (Al-Mughni and Tetreault 2000, Giacaman, Jad, and Johnson 2000, Lazreg 2000, Swirski 2000). Citizenship for women requires their dependency on men—men as kinsmen (Al-Mughni and Tetrault 2000, Giacaman, Jad, and Johnson 2000, Lazreg 1994, 2000, Peteet 1991). Women may, nevertheless, still regard the men of their families as their safety net, as many Middle Eastern states not only repress political freedoms but do not deliver on social services (Altorki 2000, Botman 1999, 107). It is not only women, however, who are not treated as "individuals" by Middle Eastern states. The relationships of male citizen-subjects to the state are also usually mediated through kin and community (Altorki 2000, Joseph 2000). Were this not so, kin and community would be far less powerful than they are. That is, it is precisely because men, as well as women, are defined in kin and communal terms that kin and community are empowered to mediate citizenship.

The privileging of men as kinsmen in citizenship laws and practices in the Middle East is seen particularly in the legal means by which citizens pass on their citizenship identities to children and spouses. In most states, citizenship in a state accrues to a person either through relations of blood (inheriting citizenship through blood descent, i.e., kinship) or land (being born on the land of the state).

Most Middle Eastern states use both land and blood criteria for granting citizenship under various circumstances. However, almost all the countries privilege blood. The privileging of blood means the privileging of kinship. All Middle Eastern countries (except Israel) uphold patrilineal forms of kinship—kin membership passed down through the father's line (Joseph 1999b). As membership in a kin community is passed down through the father's line, so membership in the state community is passed down through the father's line. That is, except for Turkey (Arat 2000), Israel (Swirksi 2000), and, to a degree, Tunisia (Charrad 2000), children may obtain citizenship through their fathers but not their mothers. Husbands may give citizenship to their foreign wives, but wives may not give citizenship to their foreign husbands, in most of the states of the region. Patrilineal descent, embedded in the specific forms of patriarchy (except Israel, where matrilineality has historically been the defining criteria of Jewry, Swirski 2000), is institutionalized and naturalized as the primary route for obtaining citizenship and a relationship with a state. All states in the region, of course, do provide means for children with unknown fathers to obtain citizenship through their citizen mothers or through birth on the land.

Middle Eastern states subsidize different family forms, but particularly the "extended" family (in Lebanon: Joseph 2000; Jordan: Amawi 2000; Saudi Arabia: Altorki 2000; Kuwait: al-Mughni and Tetreault 2000). Israel (Swirski 2000), Tunisia (Charrad 2000), and Turkey (Arat 2000) have particularly supported nuclear families, though they are found in all Middle Eastern states. Some states have challenged the control families have over their members, particularly Tunisia (Charrad 2000) and Iraq (Joseph 1982a).

Despite the variability of family forms, most Middle Eastern states constitute men as citizens through their roles as heads of patriarchal families and treat women as dependent mothers, wives, children, and siblings (Al-Mughni 1996, Arat 1996, Berkovitz 1996, Giacaman, Jad, and Johnson 1996). The Palestinian Authority has resurrected tribal patriarchy to the detriment of women (Giacaman, Jad, and Johnson 2000), defining women mainly in their familial roles and conflating them with children. Women in Israel, Kuwait, Turkey, and Lebanon are expected to put their family roles before their public roles (Al-Mughni 1996, Arat 1996, Berkovitz 1996, Joseph 1982a). Women in Tunisia and Morocco are seen as needing to be cared for and controlled (Charrad 2000, Cheriat 1996). The care/control paradigm results in the infantilization of women in citizenship terms. For example, women often must obtain the permissions of their fathers/brothers or other male guardians to marry and obtain permissions of fathers/brothers/husbands/ or other male guardians to travel or to open businesses (Altorki 2000, Amawi 2000, Hoodfar 2000, Lazreg 2000); and in some countries, the testimony of women citizens counts as half that of men (Altorki 2000, Hoodfar 2000). Until the law on testimony was changed in the early 1990s in Lebanon, for example, women could be state judges, but their testimony still counted as half that of men (Joseph 2000).

Family has been critical to the political practices of leadership in most Middle Eastern states (Altorki 2000, Amawi 2000, Charrad 2000, Joseph 2000, Tetreault and Al-Mughni 2000). Political leaders regularly bring their sons, brothers, cousins, uncles, and sons-in-law with them into positions of power within the state. Sons and brothers so regularly follow fathers and brothers as heads of political parties and state leaders that elections are often political theater (Altorki 2000, Amawi 2000, Ismael and Ismael 2000, Joseph 2000). In Syria, the constitution was re-written to change the minimum age for the presidency so Bashar Al Asad could be elected president after his father, Hafez Al Asad, died. Political leaders use their positions in the state to distribute public goods and services to their clients through family-based networks (Altorki 2000, Amawi 2000, Giacaman, Jad, and Johnson 2000, Ismael and Ismael 2000, Joseph 2000). Political leaders talk to their constituencies in family terms, speaking of the nation as a family, themselves as heads of the family, and the citizens as their children (Amawi 2000, Charrad 2000, Hoodfar 2000, Joseph 2000).

Citizens also use their families to mediate their relationships to political leaders and the state. Since allocation of state resources is often done through personalized networks, citizens' primary networks usually start with their families and lead them into the brokerage needed for the patron/client relations that often mediate state/citizen relations (Joseph 1982b). It is common for family members to inherit their client relations to political leaders from male members of their families, to vote as family seniors direct them (in order to leverage their position with political leaders), and to join or consider themselves followers or members of the same political parties or movements as their senior male kin. Citizens often depart from their families in their political identities, political relations, and po-litical actions, particularly in conditions of war (such as Lebanon's civil war), in revolution (such as in Iran and Algeria), or for the sake of specific political move-ments (such as Islamic political movements in Egypt, Algeria, and Lebanon or the Palestinian nationalist movement). But the costs of such breaks are high and are not undertaken easily.

Family remains critical to the political identities of most citizens in the Middle East. The fluidity of boundaries between government, nongovernment, and kinship has meant continuities in kin-based patriarchy in the practices of citizenship (Altorki 2000, Amawi 2000, Charrad 2000, Joseph 2002a). Since citizenship is prescribed through patrilineal descent, national identity follows patrilineal kinship in most Middle Eastern states (except Israel and Turkey). Nations are often seen as a series of patrilineal lineages, leading to the state (especially in Jordan, in the Arab Gulf states, and even in Iraq). Belonging to the patrilineal kin accords the citizen membership in the nation and the state (as well as membership in a religious community). States always take family into account in their state and nation-building projects. Family can underwrite or overshadow religion in some state-building projects, as in Lebanon (Joseph 2000), Jordan (Amawi 2000), Saudi Arabia (Altorki 2000), Tunisia, and Morocco (Charrad 2000). State building pro-jects in Turkey and Tunisia, on the other hand, have been oppositional to the family in Tunisia and Turkey (Arat 2000, Charrad 2000). The Ba'athist state-building project in Iraq tried to coopt the family (Joseph 1982a). Saudi Arabia (Altorki 2000), Lebanon (Joseph 2000), Jordan (Amawi 2000), and Morocco (Charrad 2000) assimilated family structures into their state-building projects. The Palestinian Authority breathed new life into tribal family structures in their state-building (Giacaman, Jad, and Johnson 2000).

Throughout the region, state leaders are almost exclusively male (with brief periods of female leadership in Turkey and Israel). Women in a number of Middle Eastern countries, however, have fought to gain more citizen rights and to increase women's participation in political processes. Strong women's groups in Egypt (Hatem 2000), Lebanon (Joseph 2000), Jordan (Amawi 2000), Turkey (Arat 2000), and Israel (Swirski 2000) have succeeded in rewriting some citizenship laws. Islamist women in Iran are challenging the political class governed by Islamic clerics by rereading Islamic holy texts from women-centered perspectives (Hoodfar 2000). Tunisia and Yemen have not only produced strong women's groups but at times have had relatively women-friendly regimes that have worked to increase gender equality. In Saudi Arabia, there is no constitution, which makes lobbying for changes in citizenship entirely family and tribe based (Altorki 2000). In the past few decades, there have been reverses for women in a number of countries, nevertheless (Algeria: Lazreg 2000; Egypt: Hatem 2000; Kuwait: Al-Mughni and Tetreault 2000; Iran: Hoodfar 2000). The road, clearly, is uneven, with movements in favor of and opposing women's equality gaining control of critical institutions at key moments.

Family/Families, Citizen-Subjects, and Religion

Middle Eastern states privilege families above individuals legally (Altorki 2000; Joseph 2000; Amawi 2000, Charrad 2000). They justify this by representing the family as something a priori, "prepolitical," prior to the state, sanctified by religion and God, and therefore not touchable by the state (even while they manipulate and attempt to control families; Joseph 1991, Kandiyoti 1988, 1991). The "naturalization" of family gives it a sacred aura (Yanagisako and Delaney 1995, 3), elevating family into the realm of the divine. This intertwining of family and religion entrenches the gender/age privileging of citizenship found in local patriarchies. Religious leaders further elevate family by assimilating family moralities into religious moralities. The elevation of family by religion and the simultaneous subordination of family to religion in Middle Eastern citizenship laws and practices is most pointedly seen in the widespread delegation, throughout the Middle East, of family law or laws of personal status to religious courts, what Mervat Hatem calls the "enduring alliance of nationalism and patriarchy" (Hatem 1986).

Family law (also called personal status code) regulates marriage, divorce, child custody, and inheritance. In all Middle Eastern countries (including Israel), states have given family law over to religious courts or have based civil family codes on religious laws, offering no civil alternatives to religiously based family law. Turkey (which adopted the Swiss Civil Code), Tunisia, and Yemen have civil family codes but have revised them to assuage religious clerics. It is perhaps through family law that states most profoundly gender their citizens.

All Middle Eastern countries have multiple religious communities. Most states have allowed the different religious sects to follow their own family codes (though some, like Jordan, have imposed the dominant Islamic codes on religious minorities). The plurality of legally recognized family codes has offered interesting options for men, while leaving women without a common legal framework for contesting this arena of citizen rights. While not common, men (especially Christian men) have been known to change religions in order to be able to divorce or gain the advantages of the legal codes of another religion. Such choices are much more difficult for women, who are supposed to follow the religion of their fathers and husbands. The legal pluralism creates different legal realities for women, making action on a common front of citizenship difficult. The control of women by religious/ethnic communities reinforced by the implementation of religiously based family law undermines secular notions of citizenship, not only in Turkey, which early on attempted to secularize (Arat 1996, 31), but also in Israel, where the state presents an image of secularism beneath which the realities of religious authority lurk (Swirski 2000). Lebanon, probably the most extreme case of legal pluralism in the area of family law, formally recognizes eighteen religious sects and allows them to follow their own family law. The religious sects that are not recognized by the state (Jehovah's Witnesses and Bahi'is) must either travel abroad to marry and divorce or carry out these functions in one of the recognized religious courts.

Family law, in most Middle Eastern states, gives men control over their children. Children are considered the subjects of their fathers, in general. Fathers' control over their children is seen in a number of ways. Children take the citizenship and religion of their fathers, by law in most countries. At divorce, fathers eventually obtain full custody of their children (after an initial period with their mothers, under most Islamic law). Indicative of the privileging of the father is that the family of the father has priority over the mother or her family in custody of the children when the father is dead or not available to act as the father.

Family law also gives men control over women in critical ways. In most Islamic law, divorce is a privilege of men. While women may initiate divorce under certain circumstances, this initiative is often at the cost of certain rights (to financial support from the husband, to dowry). Women are often required by religious laws to service their husbands sexually. By law or by practice, marital rape has not been recognized in most Middle Eastern states. By practice (and in some cases by law), many Middle Eastern states permit honor crimes, allowing male relatives to kill female relatives who are seen to have "dishonored" their families (usually sexually). Where honor crimes are illegal, the penalties are often lenient. In Europe, Pateman (1988, 13–4) argued, wives and children were viewed by the classical contractarians as the property of their fathers/husbands. Family law in much of the Middle East gives men property rights over their wives and children. Middle Eastern states, by deferring family law to religious courts, give legal status to the control of women by their male and elder kin.

That most Middle Eastern states have relinquished this critical arena of citizenship to religious communities reflects, in some respects, the lack of a sense of common nationhood in most Middle Eastern states. In most Middle Eastern states, subnational communities, based on religion, tribe, and ethnicity, continue to have considerable power and authority over their members, in competition with the control of states over the citizens. In some states, these subnational groups have attempted to achieve some autonomy from the state (Kurds in Iraq and Turkey) or have controlled the state

(Alawites in Syria and, for a time, Maronites in Lebanon). Some have tried to collaborate to some degree with the state (Copts in Egypt, Berbers in Morocco). Rarely, however, have these subnational communities dissolved themselves in the name of national unity, even though some states have attempted to claim the irrelevance of religion or ethnicity to citizenship (as Egypt does in regard to the Copts).

Although the definitions and boundaries of subnational communities have shifted and changed over time and rarely have communities acted collectively as communities, nevertheless, the political reality of subnational communities has persisted in most Middle Eastern states. And the burden of their survival is often laid on the backs of women. This burden is felt not only through the relinquishing of family law to religious courts by the state but also in terms of other community-maintenance responsibilities. Women are expected to be the signifiers of their communities by the clothes they wear—head scarves, full body covers (*abbayas*), face cover, or lack thereof. They are expected to marry within their communities. They are expected to have children to reproduce their communities, pass the heritage of their communities on to their children, and raise their children to support their communities' identities and boundaries. While a few Middle Eastern states have, at times, challenged subnational communities in placing this burden on women (Tunisia: Charrad 2000; Iraq: Ismael and Ismael 2000; Sudan: Hale 2000; Iran: Hoodfar 2000; Turkey: Arat 2000), most have not intervened between women and subnational communities, or have even supported the control of communities over women. Some states have even naturalized the subnational communities as the basis for state power (Lebanon: Joseph 2000; Israel: Swirski 2000). These both legalize a social reality and invent it by making membership in religious communities necessary for citizenship. Given these dynamics, women's experiences of the state have often been mediated through their communities, usually religiously defined (Arat 1996, Berkovitz 1996), further differentiating the gendering of citizenship in much of the Middle East from the contractarian, individualist notion theorized by classical liberalist philosophers.

The linkage between family and religion in the gendering of citizenship in Middle Eastern states proceeds along other lines as well. Almost all Middle Eastern religions support patriarchy. Clerics in all Middle Eastern religious sects are male. Almost all the religious institutions are themselves gender- and age-hierarchical and are invested in the authority of males and elders. Almost all religious clerics try to prevent marriage outside their own religious community, particularly policing the endogamy of women (Muslim women are not allowed to marry non-Muslim men, but Muslim men may marry non-Muslim women, for example). Religious authorities usually support the authority of patriarchs over their families. Both Muslim and Christian religions reinforce patriarchy through their institutionalization of patrilineality, assigning children to the religions of their fathers and giving fathers greater control over their children. Even in Israel, the religious authorities support familial patriarchy, despite the cultural traditions of matrilineal descent of Jewish identity (Swirski 2000). The Israeli state now recognizes descent of Jewish identity through both father and mother (Swirski 2000).

By linking family and religion, through the elevation of religious law to civil law, Middle Eastern states have reinforced not only the control of women by religious communities but also the subordination of women to the laws of patriarchy. This meshing of patriarchal family structures with religious patriarchy is one of the most significant factors leading to the gendering of citizenship through culturally specific avenues in the Middle East. The interconnections of family, religion, citizenship, and state are among the most highly contested arenas of political life in the Middle East today. From women's groups to Islamist groups, from the most secular groups to the most religious groups, family is the prize to win in the making of state and nation in the Middle East. That family has been a site of contestation in the making of state and nation—among the highest agenda items of liberal reformist movements, political Islamic movements, Islamic and secular women's movements—gives testimony to the centrality of "family" to social and political projects in the region.

Family, Women, Dangerous Connections, and the Citizen-Subject

I have suggested that the false binary of public/private and the bracketing of family from politics in the classical Western liberalist discourses of citizenship have been obstacles to understanding the gendering of citizenship in Middle Eastern states. In most Middle Eastern states, family and state are woven together; family pours into the public, and the public invades the private; religion and state cohabit spaces that absorb family into politics. Religion and state collaborate in upholding patriarchal family structures in Saudi Arabia (Altorki 2000), Israel (Swirski 2000), Iran (Hoodfar 2000), Egypt (Hatem 1986), and Lebanon (Joseph 2000). The Israeli state does not respect the privacy of the private sphere (Swirski 2000). The Palestinian state (Giacaman, Jad, and Johnson 2000), the Egyptian state (Hatem 2000), the Iraqi state (Ismael and Ismael 2000), the Saudi Arabian state (Altorki 2000), the Sudanese state (Hale 2000), and the Iranian state (Hoodfar 2000), as well as the Syrian and Libyan states, control civil society. These dangerous liaisons have meant that civil society often is not a haven for women (or men) in these regions; indeed, civil society has often not been able to protect its own autonomy, much less that of women (Joseph 1993a, 1996). The dangerous connections have meant that family can be at once a safety net and a trap. The state is both a source of protection and repression.

With tremendous insight relevant to Middle Eastern states, Carole Pateman noted that the idea of an autonomous civil society presumed the irrelevance of kinship, family, and marriage to politics and civil life. This allowed for the illusion of "civil society as a post-patriarchal social order" (Pateman 1988, 10). As I have argued here, the centrality of family to politics and the pervasiveness of patriarchy that is transported into politics by family and reinscribed onto family by politics has been a critical contributor to the gendering of social and political life in most Middle Eastern countries, including civil society. The mystifying binary of public and private masks the threads weaving together family, civil society, state, and religion into a social fabric that systematically disenfranchises women (Giacaman, Jad, and Johnson 2000).

I am not arguing that social life in Middle Eastern states is seamless, completely unbounded. There are discourses and realities of boundaries between arenas of social action. The boundaries in the Middle East are neither consistent with Western liberalist discourses of state, civil society, and citizenship nor consistent over time and place. But it is not their lack of consistency with Western notions of boundaries that leads to the disenfranchisement of women. Feminist critical analyses of the "public/private" in the West have led to the recognition of the permeability of those boundaries, their historical recency, and their close linkage with state-building projects in the West as well (Nicholson 1997, Yuval-Davis 1997). Feminists have also exposed the myth of the presumed separation between the "domestic" ("family") and government in the West (Olsen 1985). It is not the failure of boundaries between public and private in the Middle East but the institutionalization of the kin contract that has been critical to the gendering of citizenship.

I am not suggesting that boundary-making is the solution to democracy and gender equality of citizenship in the Middle East. Large-scale boundary-making has been primarily a state-making project (linked with markets and specific kinds of economies), which always implicates the transportation and transformation of power relations. It is not boundaries in and of themselves that serve the interests of women, equality, democracy, human rights, or the construction of appropriate notions of self, citizenship, and family. Boundary-making is an ongoing aspect of social life, particularly in complex societies. Rather, it is the function of those boundaries, the relations of power they bear, what they transport, what they exclude, and what they make possible.

The boundaries between arenas of social action in the Middle East are not rigid in discourse or reality, in the present or past. The porousness of boundaries between family, gender, civil society, religion, and state is neither new nor culturally unique. Indeed, it is most likely the most common state of reality across societies. The form the connections between domains of social action take changes over time and locale. There is little that is fixed, essential, either in the Middle East or the West. The point at hand, however, is the power of porousness and the political expediency of fluidity, particularly in relation to kin and state.

In order to draw attention to the centrality of family to the gendering of citizenship over a large, diverse region of the world such as the Middle East, I have glossed over issues such as the agency of actors, which are far more complex than a short essay can address. As I have pointed out in this discussion, families occur in many forms, relations between families and state are highly variable, relations within families and between families are continually under construction. Patriarchy comes in many types. There are no doubt many "social contracts" in addition to the "kin contract." Care/control, love/power, patriarchal connectivity, relational rights do not exhaust the paradigms of patriarchy, family, or kin/state relations. The agency of women and men is not compromised by the recognition of patterns. Women resist as well as comply with familial and social norms. Men reject responsibility, abuse authority as well as assimilate expectations. Families can be dysfunctional or perform. Other social factors, such as class, race, ethnicity, and tribalism, contribute to the dynamics discussed in relation to family and politics. The risks of writing about patterns are the same for any effort at disaggregating complexity and identifying continuities that lay the ground for thinking theoretically about any issue. While on the face of it such disclaimers should be obvious, the history of Orientalism and essentialist theorizing about women in general, the Middle East as a region, and women in the Middle East give merit to a reassertion of these disclaimers.

Having said that, I return to the point of this essay—that kinship is a lubricant for relationships in all social spheres in most Middle Eastern societies. Family practices, relationships, idioms, morality, and modes of operation are politically accepted and expected in political life in the Middle East. These connections between governmental, nongovernmental, and domestic spheres of social action, while in some respects providing care for women (and men), have also been dangerous for women (and men). Their power lies in their intertwining care and control, love and power, family and religion, kin and state, underwritten by the kin contract. The disenfranchisement of women from full citizenship follows not simply from the intertwining of arenas of social action, however, but from the systemic gendering and aging of social action that is subsidized by the mutually constitutive relationships between patriarchal family systems and politics. The enmeshing of arenas of social action is contractual. It is a contract, a social contract, a kin contract. Pateman (1988, 2) contended that the "contract is the means through which modern patriarchy is constituted" in the West. I would suggest that the kin contract is the critical means for constituting political patriarchy in most Middle Eastern states, with its predictable consequence, the gendering of citizenship.

Bibliography

Al-Mughni, Haya. 1996. Women's Organizations in Kuwait. *Middle East Report*, no. 198, vol. 26, no.1: 32–5.

Al-Mughni, Haya, and Mary Ann Tetreault. 2000. Citizenship, Gender and the Politics of Quasi States. In *Gender and Citizenship in the Middle East*, ed. Suad Joseph, 237–60. Syracuse, N.Y.: Syracuse University Press.

Altorki, Soraya. 2000. The Concept and Practice of Citizenship in Saudi Arabia. In *Gender and Citizenship in the Middle East*, ed. Suad Joseph, 215–36. Syracuse, N.Y.: Syracuse University Press.

Amawi, Abla. 2000. Gender and Citizenship in Jordan. In *Gender and Citizenship in the Middle East*, ed. Suad Joseph, 158–84. Syracuse, N.Y.: Syracuse University Press.

Arat, Yesim. 1996. On Gender and Citizenship in Turkey. *Middle East Report*, no. 198, vol. 26, no. 1: 28–31.

———. 2000. Gender and Citizenship in Turkey. In *Gender and Citizenship in the Middle East*, ed. Suad Joseph, 275–86. Syracuse, N.Y.: Syracuse University Press.

Barakat, Halim. 1993. *The Arab World: Society, Culture and State*. Berkeley: University of California Press.

Benhabib, Seyla. 1992. *Situating the Self: Gender, Community and Postmodernism in Contemporary Ethics*. Cambridge, England: Polity Press.

Berkovitz, Nitza. 1996. Women and the Women's Equal Rights Law in Israel. *Middle East Report*, no. 198, vol. 26, no. 1: 19–21.

Botman, Selman. 1999. *Engendering Citizenship in Egypt*. New York: Columbia University Press.

Charrad, Mounira. 1990. State and Gender in the Maghrib. *Middle East Report*, no. 163, vol. 20, no. 2: 19–24.

———. 2000. Becoming a Citizen: Lineage Versus Individual in Tunisia and Morocco. In *Gender and Citizenship in the Middle East*, ed. Suad Joseph, 70–87. Syracuse, N.Y.: Syracuse University Press.

———. 2001. *States and Women's Rights: The Making of Postcolonial Tunisia, Algeria, and Morocco*. Berkeley: University of California Press.

Cheriat, Boutheina. 1996. Gender, Civil Society and Citizenship in Algeria. *Middle East Report*, no. 198, vol. 26, no. 1: 22–6.

Chodorow, Nancy. 1978. *The Reproduction of Mothering: Psychoanalysis and the Sociology of Gender*. Berkeley: University of California Press.

Collier, Jane F., Bill Maurer, and Liliana Suarez-Navaz. 1995. Sanctioned Identities: Legal Constructions of Modern Personhood. *Identities* 2, 1–2: 1–27.

Cott, Nancy. 1995. Giving Character to Our Whole Civil Polity: Marriage and the Public Order in the Late Nineteenth Century. In *United States History as Women's History: New Feminist Essays*, ed. Linda Kerber, Alice Kessler-Harris, and Kathryn Kish Sklar, 107–24. Chapel Hill: University of North Carolina Press.

Deleuze, Gilles. 1997. The Rise of the Social. In Jacques Donzelot, *The Policing of Families*, ix–xxvii. Baltimore: Johns Hopkins University Press.

Donzelot, Jacques. 1997. *The Policing of Families*. Baltimore: Johns Hopkins University Press.

Doumani, Beshara, ed. 2003. *Family History in the Middle East: Household, Property and Gender*. Albany: State University of New York Press.

Elshtain, Jean Bethke. 1982. *The Family in Political Thought*. Amherst: University of Massachusetts Press.

Giacaman, Rita, Islah Jad, and Penny Johnson. 1996. For the Public Good? Gender and Social Citizenship in Palestine. *Middle East Report*, no. 198. vol. 26, no. 1: 11–7.

———. 2000. Gender and Citizenship Under the Palestinian Authority. In *Gender and Citizenship in the Middle East*, ed. Suad Joseph, 137–57. Syracuse, N.Y.: Syracuse University Press.

Gran, Peter. 1996. Organization of Culture and the Construction of the Family in the Modern Middle East. In *Women, the Family and Divorce Laws in Islamic History*, ed. Amira El-Azhary Sonbol, 64–78. Syracuse, N.Y.: Syracuse University Press.

Hale, Sondra. 1996. *Gendering Politics in Sudan: Islamism, Socialism and the State*. Boulder, Colo.: Westview Press.

———. 2000. The Islamic State and Gendered Citizenship in Sudan. In *Gender and Citizenship in the Middle East*, ed. Suad Joseph, 88–106. Syracuse, N.Y.: Syracuse University Press.

Hatem, Mervet. 1986. The Enduring Alliance of Nationalism and Patriarchy in Muslim Personal Status Laws: The Case of Modern Egypt. *Feminist Issues* 6, 1: 19–43.

———. 2000. The Pitfalls of the Nationalist Discourses on Citizenship in Egypt. In *Gender and Citizenship in the Middle East*, ed. Suad Joseph, 33–57. Syracuse, N.Y.: Syracuse University Press.

Hoodfar, Homa. 2000. Iranian Women at the Intersections of Citizenship and the Family Code. In *Gender and Citizenship in the Middle East*, ed. Suad Joseph, 287–313. Syracuse, N.Y.: Syracuse University Press.

Hunt, Lynn. 1992. *The Family Romance of the French Revolution*. Berkeley: University of California Press.

Ismael, Jacqueline S., and Shereen T. Ismael. 2000. Gender and State in Iraq. In *Gender and Citizenship in the Middle East*, ed. Suad Joseph, 85–214. Syracuse, N.Y.: Syracuse University Press.

Joseph, Suad. 1982a. The Mobilization of Iraq Women into the Wage Labor Force. *Studies in Third World Societies* 16: 69–90.

———. 1982b. The Family as Security and Bondage: A Political Strategy of the Lebanese Urban Working Class. In *Towards a Political Economy of Urbanization in Third World Countries*, ed. Helen Safa, 151–71. New Delhi: Oxford University Press.

———. 1991. Elite Strategies for State Building: Women, Family, Religion and State in Iraq and Lebanon. In *Women, Islam and the State*, ed. Deniz Kandiyoti, 176–200. London: MacMillan.

———. 1993a. Gender and Civil Society: An Interview with Suad Joseph with Joe Stork. *Middle East Report*, no.183, vol. 23, no. 4 (July–August): 22–6.

———. 1993b. Connectivity and Patriarchy Among Urban Working Class Arab Families in Lebanon. *Ethos* 21, 4 (December): 465–84.

———. 1994. Problematizing Gender and Relational Rights: Experiences from Lebanon. *Social Politics* 1, 3 (fall): 271–85.

———. 1996. Gender and Citizenship in Middle Eastern States. *Middle East Report*, no. 198, vol. 26, no. 1: 4–10.

———. 1997. The Public/Private—The Imagined Boundary in the Imaged Nation/State/Community: The Lebanese Case. *Feminist Review* 57 (autumn): 73–92.

———. 1999a. Women Between Nation and State in Lebanon. In *Between Women and Nation: Transnational Feminisms and the State*, ed. Norma Alarcon, Caren Kaplan, and Minoo Moallem, 162–81. Durham, N.C.: Duke University Press.

———. 1999b. Descent of the Nation: Kinship and Citizenship in Lebanon. *Citizenship Studies* 3, 3: 295–318.

———. 2000. Civic Myths, Citizenship and Gender in Lebanon. In *Gender and Citizenship in the Middle East*, ed. Suad Joseph, 107–36. Syracuse, N.Y.: Syracuse University Press.

———. 2002a. Civil Society, The Public/Private, and Gender in Lebanon. Pp. 167–189 in *Social Constructions of Nationalism*, ed. Fatma Muge Gocek. Albany: State University of New York Press.

———. 2002b. The Family as Politics. Presented at the American University in Beirut, May.

———, ed. 1999. *Intimate Selving in Arab Families: Gender, Self and Identity*. Syracuse, N.Y.: Syracuse University Press.

———. 2000. *Gender and Citizenship in the Middle East*. Syracuse, N.Y.: Syracuse University Press.

Kandiyoti, Deniz. 1988. Bargaining with Patriarchy. *Gender and Society* 2, 3: 274–90.

———, ed. 1991. *Women, Islam and the State*. London: Macmillan.

Lazreg, Marnia. 1994. *The Eloquence of Silence: Algerian Women in Question*. New York: Routledge.

———. 2000. Citizenship and Gender in Algeria. In *Gender and Citizenship in the Middle East*, ed. Suad Joseph, 58–69. Syracuse, N.Y.: Syracuse University Press.

Lister, Ruth. 1997. *Citizenship. Feminist Perspectives*. New York: New York University Press.

Macpherson, C. B. 1950. *Citizenship and Social Class and Other Essays*. Cambridge: Cambridge University Press.

———. 1962. *The Political Theory of Possessive Individualism*. London: Oxford University Press.

Nedelsky, Jennifer. 1989. Reconceiving Autonomy: Sources, Thoughts and Possibilities. *Yale Journal of Law and Feminism* 1, 7: 7–36.

———. 1990. Law, Boundaries, and the Bounded Self. *Representations* 30: 162–89.

———. 1993. Reconceiving Rights as Relationship. *Review of Constitutional Studies* 1, 1: 1–26.

Nicholson, Linda. 1997. The Myth of the Traditional Family. In *Feminism and Families*, ed. Hilde Lindeman Nelson, 27–42. New York: Routledge.

Okin, Susan Moller. 1989. *Justice, Gender and the Family*. New York: Basic Books.

Olsen, Frances E. 1985. The Myth of State Intervention in the Family. *Journal of Law Reform* 18, 4 (summer): 835–64.

Ong, Aihwa. 1996. Cultural Citizenship as Subject-Making: Immigrants Negotiate Racial and Cultural Boundaries in the United States. *Cultural Anthropology* 37, 5 (December): 737–62.

Pateman, Carole. 1988. *The Sexual Contract*. Stanford: Stanford University Press.

Peteet, Julie M. 1991. *Gender in Crisis. Women and the Palestinian Resistance Movement*. New York: Columbia University Press.

Reiter, Rayna R. 1975. Men and Women in the South of France: Public and Private Domains. Pp. 252–82 in *Towards an Anthropology of Women*, ed. Rayna R. Reiter. New York: Monthly Review Press.

Schneider, David M. 1984. *A Critique of the Study of Kinship*. Ann Arbor: University of Michigan Press.

Sharabi, Hisham. 1988. *Neopatriarchy: A Theory of Distorted Change in Arab Society*. New York: Oxford University Press.

Stevens, Jacqueline. 1999. *Reproducing the State*. Princeton: Princeton University Press.

Swirski, Barbara. 2000. The Citizenship of Jewish and Palestinian Arab Women in Israel. In *Gender and Citizenship in the Middle East*, ed. Suad Joseph, 314–44. Syracuse, N.Y.: Syracuse University Press.

Turner, Bryan. 1993. Contemporary Problems in the Theory of Citizenship. In *Citizenship and Social*, ed. Bryan Turner, 1–18. London: Sage.

Voet, Rian. 1998. *Feminism and Citizenship*. London: Sage.

Yanagisako, Sylvia, and Carol Delaney, eds. 1995. *Naturalizing Power: Essays in Feminist Cultural Analysis*. New York: Routledge.

Yuval-Davis, Nira. 1997. Women, Citizenship and Difference. *Feminist Review* 57 (autumn): 4–27.

9

Citizenship and Faith

AMINA WADUD

This chapter proposes an important corollary between the idea of citizenship, in the context of a civil society of the modern nation-state, and the idea of moral agent (*khilafah*) in the context of Islamic theology as built upon in its primary sources. The corollary examines the relationship between the two in order to construct a faith-based synthesis. In the context of the nation-state, Muslim women having been working toward reforms to establish full and equal citizenship for Muslim women, despite the absence of historical precedent in the Islamic tradition. The benefit of this essay is that it demonstrates how modern Muslim civil societies can mediate between the Islamic tradition and secular constructions of rights and reforms. It offers a profaith legitimation for reforms based on textual authentication in the context of the Muslim women's movements. Foundational to this analysis is the contextual idea of nation-state within the broader global agenda of colonialism, as it has come to replace the idea of empire. As I shall show, this transition has not been fluid. Reconciling opposing ideas between Islamic political thought in the context of a theocratic empire and the post-Enlightenment idea of the secular nation-state is pivotal to understanding how the concepts of citizen and *khilafah* are related.[1]

Because of the invasion of colonialism, the reality of the nation-state is a global phenomenon, whether compatible or incompatible with the cultures of traditional society. In the case of Islam, reconciling incompatibilities has required rigorous

---

1. This essay introduces many concepts that are considered fundamental or basic to Islam within the field of Islamic studies. Those seeking additional information on understanding the basics can refer to any number of introductory works on Islam. Some recommended titles are Fazlur Rahman, *Islam*, 2nd ed. (Chicago: University of Chicago Press, 1979); Karen Armstrong, *Islam: A Short History* (New York: Modern Library, 2000); Frederick Mathewson Denny, *An Introduction to Islam*, 2nd ed. (New York: MacMillan, 1994); Sachiko Murata and William Chittick, *The Vision of Islam* (New York, Paragon House, 1994); John Esposito, *Islam the Straight Path*, 3rd ed. (New York, Oxford University Press, 1998); Akbar S. Ahmed, *Discovering Islam: Making Sense of Muslim History and Society* (New York, Routledge, 1993).

intellectual reconstruction in the way we understand Islam's primary sources and the way we understand the history, development, and implementation of *shari'ah*, the system of law that grew out of these sources after intense juridical consideration. The benefits of modern civil society are not self-evident unless they are examined against the integrity of an authentic Islamic identity. Instead of haphazard grafting, we aim for a dynamic reconciliation into a system for a moral society that recognizes the benefits of modern civil society while yet sustaining Islamic traditions without succumbing to the consequence of patriarchal interpretations that marginalized women's public and private roles.

Islam

The word *islam* comes from a triliteral root S-L-M that means "peace." In this case, it is peace attained by living in complete harmony with the entire universe. Such harmony, Islam holds, can only be achieved by surrender to the will of the Creator of the universe and all that is within it, *Allah*, Arabic for One God: the Unique, the Unified, and the Unifier. This is known as *tawhid*, the most fundamental basis for all of Islamic thought. In its simplest form, *tawhid* is monotheism. But monotheism here is not a static depiction of a domineering godhead removed and remote from human hearts and affairs, distant from the ebb and flow of the phenomenological realm with its constant growth and change. It is the life force or essence of all creative action and interaction and is occasionally manifest through to us in the ordinary, mundane realm. According to the Islamic tradition, the most significant and exquisite form of this manifestation is in human speech: revelation.

Although Judaism, Christianity, and Islam share the fundamental belief in revelation as God's self-disclosure in the form of human speech, there are radical distinctions between their concepts of revelation. This chapter focuses on Islamic conceptions of revelation and presumes that readers will acknowledge that the distinctive relationship of revelation, text, and history as based upon the Islamic specifics are pivotal in Islamic reconstructions and reform. As a historical movement, Islam began with the first word of revelation sent to the Prophet Muhammad in the early part of the seventh century just outside of Makkah, in a cave where he would go on retreat for spiritual meditation. The process of revelation continued over a period of twenty-three years and left behind a substantial text, the Qur'an.

The Qur'an

A brief history of the text and its significance demonstrates its primacy as a tool for transformation in thought and action. Islam could be described as the religion of the book. In the context of medieval theological discussions about "logos," Islam never took this to mean anything except the "word" of revelation. While early Christian theologians were developing the foundational notion of "the word made flesh," Muslim theologians deliberated over the same dialectal issues of permanence and temporality, immanence and transcendence, while sustaining the words of the revealed text itself as the reference point, instead of incarnation.[2] For my purpose, it is sufficient to emphasize that just as there could be no Christianity without Christ, there could be no Islam without the book, the Qur'an.

In Islam, a primordial contract (*mithaq*) or covenant between the Creator and created humans includes the promise of guidance to humankind (20:123)[3] in explicit and implicit forms. Implicit guidance is all of the Creation itself: nature. Indeed, the Qur'an says, even in our own selves there are signs (that point to the existence of one God; 51:20–21). Explicit guidance, in the form of revelation, comes from God directly to certain select persons among humankind, who are obliged to disseminate that message by embodying the principles within it through living example, and by announcing its content aloud. Islam actually recognizes thousands of persons selected for this task, including Adam, Abraham, Moses, Jesus, and Muhammad. However, it also recognizes that for various reasons of historical interruption, the words of the message have never been preserved intact as they were revealed, only recorded later by second and third hand. Thus the notion of the continuity of the message itself—believe in one God, do justice on the earth, in addition to the literary history of the Qur'anic revelation and preservation[4]—makes the Qur'an distinctive and definitive.

The message of the Qur'an is paramount. In Qur'anic cosmology the purpose for human creation is explained, "Verily I will create a *khalifah* on the earth" (38:26).[5] A *khalifah* is a trustee, a vice-regent, or an agent. All humankind is assigned as trustees of God *on the earth*. Although challenged to live in surrender (in *islam*) with all of the Creation, the human *khalifah* is assigned and empowered to act fully and freely as an independent agent accountable for all choice in actions. A tension holds together the distinctive dual nature of the moral being: free, yet morally responsible for all choices and accountable for the consequence of the actions taken. It should go without saying, but for the consequences of omissions, agency is a characteristic of every human, irrespective of race, class, age, nationality, or gender. More to the point, each woman is created as a *khalifah* with the moral responsibility to act as agent before Allah in the Creation.

For the first thirteen years of the revelatory experience, the Prophet Muhammad remained in Makkah, where he faced a certain amount of hostility and only managed to bring into Islam a minority of significant followers. In the year 622, the Prophet accepted an invitation to migrate to Madinah and established a living community there under the guidance of the Qur'anic worldview. He would

2. "We Muslims believe that The Qur'an is the Word of God, revealed to the Prophet Muhammad through the medium of a human language." Muhammad Asad, foreword to *The Message of the Qur'an*, translated and explained by Muhammad Asad (Dar al-Andalus, Gibraltar: Kazi, 1980), p. iv.

3. All references to the Qur'an will be followed by the chapter number and verse number in parentheses.

4. Ahmad Von Denffer, *Ulum al Qur'an: An Introduction to the Sciences of the Qur'an* (Leicester, England: The Islamic Foundation, 1985), pp. 31–52.

5. Furthermore, the Qur'anic story of Creation does not start with a male person, extract a female person, blame a female temptress, or start life on earth with a fall from grace, and it has no trace of original sin.

become both a spiritual and political leader. This year is known as *al-hijrah* and marks the beginning of the Muslim calendar (AH). The next ten years of revelation reflect a more concrete focus on the establishment of a just social order as both reflected in universal terms and established in specific historical context. It was during this ten-year period that the Qur'an would make clear its mandate to eradicate discrimination against women. The Qur'an deals with an extensive number of social justice issues, such as treatment and freedom of slaves, fair business dealing, fair judgments between disputing parties, social and financial contracts, ethics of war, treatment of children, and conditions of communal relations. However, there are more explicit passages in the Qur'an that are directed toward social reforms specifically addressing the well-being of women, as individuals, members of the family, and members of society than there are passages on any other social justice issue.

In this period it was shown what it was like to live Islam as a complete way of life in one social cultural milieu. This goal (to live Islam as a complete way of life) has remained as both an obligation and a moral imperative for Muslims and within Islamic cultural and political contexts since the time of Madinah, which is often considered ideal. However, the question of the interpretation of that ideal has been interrogated at various times in Muslim history, not the least of these being the present complex time of history in which we find ourselves. While the Prophet himself was alive, his presence was of irreplaceable significance because of his task as both spiritual and political leader. This role was irrevocably linked to his experience as the "mouthpiece" for revelation. He was entrusted to relay the revelations as they were received and to attest to their perfect preservation for posterity. This was achieved by both written and oral means throughout his lifetime—a legacy that would be carried out after his death, until we have before us today exact duplicate copies of the revelation as he received it, uninterrupted by later speculations or editorials. This is why the Islamic notion of revelation differs from the other revelatory traditions. There is a continuous historical link in both written and oral form to the living experience of revelation directly to the Prophet Muhammad. All copies of the Qur'an are therefore identical, and translations are accepted not as text but only as interpretation.[6]

Sunnah

The second task incumbent upon the Prophet as spiritual leader was to embody the essence of that message in his behavior. "If you want to know the prophet's

6. As Muhammad Asad says regarding translation, "I do not claim to have 'translated' the Qur'an in the sense in which, say, Plato or Shakespeare can be translated. Unlike any other book, its meaning and its linguistic presentation form one unbreakable whole. The position of the individual words in the sentence, the rhythm and sound of its phrases and their syntactical construction, the manner in which a metaphor flows almost imperceptibly into a pragmatic statement, the use of the acoustic stress not merely in the service of rhetoric but as a means of alluding to the unspoken but clearly implied ideas: all this make the Qur'an, in the last resort, unique and untranslatable." *The Message*, p. v.

behavior," said his young wife A'ishah, "his behavior was like the Qur'an." He embodied the Qur'anic ethos. This is known as the *sunnah* of the Prophet, or his normative behavior. The significance of this was most blatantly apparent following his death. After all, according to Islam, prophets are only humans—albeit select humans—chosen for a unique task. Although they are morally infallible, they are neither divine nor immortal. As long as the Prophet was alive, questions about right actions were addressed directly to him. After his death, not only would such questions continue to arise but, as the community spread and its members' experiences evolved into even more unprecedented circumstances, more complex questions would arise. This required some means for addressing them appropriately within an Islamic framework. As a consequence of this requirement, methods for reflecting upon the Qur'anic ethos and the Prophet's normative practices were developed into distinct disciplines. The discipline most closely related to praxis was known as *shari'ah*, or Islamic law. Historically, this came to mean the pragmatic and intellectual development of a fine-tuned juridical system with methods of jurisprudence and legal theories that are related to them, which are called *fiqh*.

Shari'ah

During the early part of the Abbasid period, (132–650 AH/749–1258 CE) the second Islamic empire, a complexity of dynamic, multifaceted juridical formulations took shape, culminating in the codification of a complete system of law for all aspects of behavior: ritual, personal status, family, criminal, and public interactions.[7] From this legal movement that began shortly after the death of the Prophet to its conclusion two to three centuries later, four Sunni schools and one major Shi'ah school were established. They are still in use, representing the oldest continual legal system in application in world history. The area where Islamic law maintains its greatest control today is in personal status or family laws. Paradoxically, this simultaneously reflects the Qur'an's explicit concern with the status of women, whether in the family or as individuals, as well as reflecting the place most in need of progressive legal reforms.

Law is significant to the process of change, especially in the context of Islamic history. It encompasses every aspect of people's lives. Islam is perceived as a comprehensive system concerned with the total human well-being, in this life and the next. Consequently, the Islamic worldview is developed along a two-pronged system of *orthodoxy*: right thoughts, right beliefs, truth or faith; and orthopraxis: right practice or good deeds. *Shari'ah* as an intellectual discipline has held dominion over praxis. The *shari'ah* system is further divided into two subcategories of actions: *ibadah* and *mu'amalah*. *Ibadah* refers strictly to ritual worship. Although progressive Muslim thinkers are also calling for ritual reforms in the conceptualization

---

7. See Abdullahi An-Na'im, *Towards an Islamic Reformation: Civil Liberties, Human Rights and International Law* (Syracuse, N.Y.: Syracuse University Press, 1990), pp. 16–9, for a concise summary of the limits and techniques for this period of legal codification and canonization.

of absolute male hegemony over public ritual leadership, I leave that aspect of the discourse aside here. The subcategory that is given the greatest detailed consideration and development in *shari'ah* is *mu'amalah*, or social relations. The bulk of *shari'ah* is focused on how to establish just relations within society.

The primary sources for the construction of *shari'ah*, I reiterate, include the Qur'an and *sunnah* as divine sources. However, using the Qur'an for *shari'ah* meant using the interpretations and opinions of the jurists. Likewise, using the *sunnah* was not conceptually static. At one time it meant following the living example; then it meant taking clear advice from the prophet's companions about norms or regarding customary practice. Later, the corpus of material known as *ahadith*—for "statements," "reports," or "traditions"—was canonized by a rigorous collection methodology. Then direct reference to this material sufficiently served as official designation of normative practice. It is important to emphasize here that while Muslims accept the divine nature of both Qur'anic revelation and Prophetic behavior as the embodiment of that revelation, operationalizing the two into juridical codes for the purpose of practical implementation involves human mediation. Since men (in this case literally male persons) developed all of *shari'ah* as a matter of history, then all of *shari'ah* can be contested by other knowledgeable persons. This is distinctive from the traditional and current fundamentalist attitude that *shari'ah* is divine and must therefore simply be followed literally. More specifically, injustice that results from the implementation of historical *shari'ah* should be contested.[8] Developing legitimacy and rationale for such contestation, as well as developing the exact methods, are major tasks of modern Islamic reform, including, but not exclusive to, gender reform.

In addition to the necessary yet fallible human mediation between the divine sources of the law and the codifications drawn from them, two other sources of *shari'ah* were derived as logical extensions of a rational process (or *ijtihad*). One is *qiyas*, or analogical reasoning, and the other is *ijma*, or the consensus of the jurists. *Qiyas* relies upon an explicit textual and/or juridical precedent as a clear basis for arguing for or against an unprecedented but analogous situation. For example, alcohol is explicitly prohibited in the Qur'an, including passages presenting the *legis rationale* regarding the negative circumstances surrounding alcohol consumption and its effects. A reasonable analogy was made between this use of alcohol and illegal drugs on the basis of *qiyas*; therefore, drugs are also prohibited in Islam. *Ijma* relates to an agreement drawn between prominent jurists over the best decision regarding an unprecedented situation without such clear and explicit analogous textual reference. They took several juridical arguments into consideration and weighed the benefits of each against the others. However, when the

---

8. The beginning of contesting laws in the context of Islam is what Khaled Abou El Fadl, *Speaking in God's Name: Islamic Law Authority and Women* (Oxford: Oneworld, 2001), calls a "conscientious pause" (p. 33). If one finds inconsistency even with one's understanding of God and God's message one has a moral obligation to pause and reflect. After this reflection, I propose, one has another moral obligation: to try and change or reform the laws in accordance with one's understanding of the highest moral ideal (p. 213).

consensus had been reached, the opinions confirmed by this consensus became permanent, fixed, and binding. Looking at these methods briefly, it seems evident that there are spaces for reform in the application of all four of these sources of the law.

Of specific importance to my discussion on law, agency, and citizenship are the opinions of the early Islamic jurists regarding the subject of "rights." It is the correlations between traditional juridical discourse and modern human rights discourses, which are primarily secular, that indicate the possible directions that can be followed in order to understand and act upon such matters as women's rights, human rights, rights of the ruled, and rights of citizens. Rights in Islamic jurisprudence stem from the word *haqq*, as reality, or truth that can also be used to mean right, claim, or duty, depending on the context. A "right" is the competence or capacity conferred upon an individual or collective entity without reciprocal duty. As such, human beings can be bearers of rights. Three primary kinds of rights are differentiated: rights of God, with a revealed imperative; rights of persons, which are seen as world affirming; and dual rights, a hybrid of the two. Rights of God refer to things like the mandatory ritual practices. Rights of persons are secular and civil and refer to individual and social interests. In enforcement terms, one party has a claim, and another has an obligation. As such, rights are construed as having reciprocal obligations. Furthermore, they can be mandated within the confines of public policy in civil society, and created by means of a political process. Yet civil and devotional rights are both accorded the same moral status in Islam.[9]

The *shari'ah* conceptualization of governance, based upon the idea of an empire, makes the ruler the legitimate authority assigned to organize and orchestrate obedience to the *shari'ah*. He reigned over ruled subjects whose responses were limited to obedience and acquiescence, as a reflection of their duties before Allah. In this system, subjects were defined in accordance with their status. Status was not equal between ruler and ruled or between various members of the ruled. Believers, that is, Muslims, had a higher status than nonbelievers or members of other religions. Believing men had a higher status than believing women.

Citizenship in the Law and the Notion of Nation-State

With regard to this essay, *shari'ah* relegated women to an inferior status within its notion of a ruled society and recognized no space for the consideration of reforms in that status. While no single step can simply reconcile discrepancies between *shari'ah* and modern systems of civil society, as envisioned by the idea of a nation-state, for example, it is the interface between these two systems—Islamic *shari'ah* and the nation-state—that encapsulate the problem: Muslim women between citizenship and faith. As a matter of faith, ultimately this is a discussion of Muslim

---

9. Ebrahim Moosa, "The Dilemma of Islamic Rights Schemes," *Journal of Law and Religion* 15, 1 and 2 (2000–20001): 191–2.

women's full human dignities, because Islamic law claims it was designated to achieve full human dignity under the demands of both social justice and the protection of the social, moral, and spiritual well-being of human beings. However, due to factors discussed earlier, it fell short in many important ways. As mediators, Muslims did not and do not now always act in accordance with Islam as the ideal toward which Muslims aspire. Yet that ideal remains a basis for the construction and governance of Islamic society.

While problems arise from the reductionist approach of merely accepting medieval constructions of law and interpretations of texts as final and absolute, modern Islamic reforms do not intend to remove that foundational basis altogether and unconditionally embrace modern secular discourses on human rights and other concerns as absolute and necessarily universal either. "Islamic rights discourse has an entirely different genesis and pedigree compared to secular human rights discourse." Rights are culturally constructed, and in "each ethical and moral culture there is not only a sense of *what* rights mean, but also *how* rights are created."[10] There are still conceptual distinctions between Islamic perspectives on the meaning of human rights and secular "universal" standards, as codified in such international documents as the Universal Declaration of Human Rights (UDHR). Such documents imply a consensus over the meaning of both "universal" and "human rights," despite broad areas of conflict between traditional cultures and secular modern ones. Furthermore, the addition of the 1979 International Convention on the Elimination of All Forms of Discrimination against Women was necessary to address gaps in the UDHR with respect to women's full human rights concerns, and practical strategies to implement those concerns were even further addressed by a subsequent platform for implementation. In other words, just giving the denotation "universal" at the conclusion of certain international deliberations does not guarantee its universality. "There is a heated debate whether human rights are universal or a Western concept and whether concomitantly they are universally valid or not. . . . The genesis of a moral claim may condition its validity, but it certainly does not determine it."[11]

The concept of *citizen*, as we have come to understand it today, is articulated in post-Enlightenment terms, transformed into global perspective by the establishment of the modern nation-state. The modern nation-state is pluralistic and diverse, dealing with an interdependent world, a world system of economic development (whether good or bad) with various political, strategic, and security concerns. "Human society needs some form of authority/government which has the necessary powers to maintain law and order and regulate political, economic, and social activities."[12] To avoid corruption and abuse of power and to safeguard the public good, the government must be regulated by a clearly defined and strictly applied set of rules that is formally described as a "constitution." An important feature of the nation-state construct is the relationship between the government, or

10. Moosa, "Dilemma," p. 188.
11. Moosa, "Dilemma," p. 189
12. An-Na'im, *Towards an Islamic Reformation*, p. 70.

the state, as a powerful and dominant entity and the individual upon whom is conferred citizenship. The citizen, as an individual, is entitled to claim certain rights and obligated to fulfill certain duties. She claims these rights on the ground of being human; hence the term *human rights*.

Muslim Nation-State versus Islamic State

As an outcome of colonialism, modern Muslim civil society operates within the nation-state construct. Although Islam always had a notion of a just social order and of protecting human dignities, simply conflating the idea of citizen as understood in post-colonialism and incorporated into international documents in the 20th century with the idea of citizen from traditional societies, and then forcing these new concepts through the *shari'ah* construction of constitutionality, with its under-standing of the relationship between individual members of society and the ruler, points to the problems of haphazard grafting. For while the historical formulation of the *shari'ah* was intended to address the rights and responsibilities of the governance and the citizen/subject,[13] the idea of an Islamic state is not compatible in all ways with the secular nation-state idea. The convergences and overlaps should not cam-ouflage significant areas of incongruity when evidence indicates the two systems are not mutually self-supporting. In particular, strengths and weaknesses with respect to gender must be ferreted out as they bear upon citizenship and justice.

In the Islamic state, with its exclusive view of citizenship and the rights of the individual citizen, equality of women and men was not envisioned. Furthermore, women's access to public office and public life was precluded by the socialization of women through a process of conditioning women into a helpless, dependent existence. In addition, the lack of infrastructure to support an independent lifestyle for a woman as an alternative to her dependency role has made it impossible for women to live wholesome, autonomous lives.

The patriarchal presumptions that premodern Islamic jurisprudence made with respect to women affect their civic and personal liberties. Even today, Islamic jurisprudence still holds that women do not acquire legal and moral majority in certain transactions and therefore require the guardianship of males. Yet, while women lack the capacity to contract marriages independently, they simultaneously have full control over their wealth and in managing all their financial affairs. This demonstrates some of the internal inconsistencies within *shari'ah* constructs.

Imperatives to Change and Reconstruction Methodologies

Islamic thought is open to revision and reconstruction by receiving fresh inspira-tion from modern thought and experience, according, for example, to Iqbal, of

---

13. This is also true for the status of non-Muslims in an Islamic state, although this essay does not critically consider this in detail.

Indian origin, one of many prominent modernist thinkers who wrote in the middle part of the twentieth century.[14] However, that reconstruction must reflect our own indigenous and authentic approach to the spirit and best traditions of our faith as we face the sweeping challenges posed to us today, intellectually, politically, economically, and ethically. To achieve this reconstruction, emphasis is placed on methodology, the way things have been developed within the tradition and the way things honor that tradition, while simultaneously acknowledging constraints or shortcomings within it vis-à-vis the realities of today. Islamic authenticity and legitimacy are maintained in such a way as to respond to our needs and aspirations in today's world. This is fundamental to the issues confronting Islamic thought and reform today.

In order to construct alternative versions of legitimate social structures using Islamic concepts and techniques as understood and implemented by Muslims today, Muslims must rethink both our heritage and our current complexities. For legal reconstruction, for example, Muslim progressives have proposed three options. One option is to rely on established jurist traditions as authoritative canon and use an eclectic approach, picking and choosing from their variations. The results of this method is not only arbitrary but also fails to remove the bias against women and non-Muslims within Muslim society. A second option is to use the primary sources without consideration of canonical tradition. Even as this option lacks credibility, failing to register enough popular or specialist support, it also disrupts the honor and integrity of Islamic tradition and continuity, either assuming a historical void or arrogantly proposing that one operation in time, the present, is necessarily privileged over all operations in times before it. The third, more tenable option is to combine the two: to consider the canon while yet providing creative interpretation that interrogates both the sources and the epistemological presumptions of traditional jurisprudence in light of current hermeneutical investigations.[15]

For example, Tunisia was able to formulate a legal reconsideration of the permissibility of polygamy and institute a policy restricting marriage to a monogamous form using the textual reinterpretation strategy. One verse from the Qur'an (4:3) permits the continuation of the existing practice of polygyny, but only if the practice observes the limitations and conditions it describes. First, it limited the number, whereas the previous practice had put no limits on quantity, and it limited the conditions under which a man may take on another wife, but, most important, it required justice in this practice. Throughout the development of the *shari'ah*, the jurists gave pragmatic interpretations of the meaning of justice. Their measurements were the ones that could be determined by the courts and used as the basis for adjudicating between parties who brought the matter of unjust treatment to the courts for resolution or, for some women, in order to dissolve the marriage.

Coincidentally, another verse of the Qur'an (4:129) states: "You will not be able to deal equally [using a verb form of the Arabic word for *justice*] between your wives..." Interpretations of this verse of course vary, with the jurist tending to

---

14. As referenced by Moosa, "Dilemma," p. 187.
15. Moosa, "Dilemma," p. 195.

emphasize the latter part of the verse that says "but do not turn away [from one] altogether" to permit the continuation of polygyny, despite the inability to actually achieve justice between wives.

The Tunisian government argued that verse 4:129 actually sets up a precedent for monogamy as the just norm and that the Qur'an's conditional acceptance of polygyny meant that it was intended to be phased out over time. As such, polygyny is not permissible under the law in Tunisia. In this case, intra-Islamic justification for the reform was given by reinterpretation of the primary source. Certainly many reforms in inequitable laws and practices have been codified in other Muslim countries, but the rationale is often based on extra-Islamic justifications. In response to these, many Muslim citizens will argue that it is their Islamic right or duty to continue such practices, even when some consider them to be unjust.

Muslim progressive thinkers take into account the sociological, economic, and political transformations that have occurred in Muslim societies and bring these into dialogue with the tradition to reinvent the means for relating in ways authentically Islamic to new contexts. Colonialism has transformed traditional societies from being status oriented, which determined a body of reciprocal obligations, duties, and responsibilities, to being contract oriented as to the means of exchange, operating with a written constitution wherein the individual is seen as a discrete entity that exercises independent authority. In the contract model of modern civil society, the notion of a political subject in a personal government is replaced by the notion of citizen in an impersonal state, in order to limit the powers of the rulers and to subject them to the scrutiny of the citizenry or its elected officials.[16]

Faith and Ethics: A Reconciliation

I return here to the Qur'anic concept introduced earlier, *khalifah*, as moral agent. I propose an ethical and theological basis for a just social order in the context of the modern Muslim nation-state, especially as relates to gender. To begin with, I agree with the necessity of moving Muslim political and legal systems toward establishing social relationships on the basis of a contractual relationship, because it supports the ontology of the creation of the human being as agent or trustee for Allah on the earth. The Qur'anic ideal points toward a cooperation between Allah, Creator of all the worlds, and humankind, creatures entrusted with each other and the earth. This is a three-pronged contract: God to human, human to God, and human to human. The moral agent, as conceived here, rests in the tension between the covenant (*amanah*) and service (*ibadah*).

Agency does not denote free rein and self-aggrandizement but empowerment and responsibility, operationalized in reciprocal terms with others, in the context of one's circumstance, in order to arrive at truth, justice, honor, and human dignity. We are responsible for the choices we make at every juncture, and we will be held accountable via the ultimate judgment for all of our choices, such that hopefully

---

16. Moosa, "Dilemma," p. 214.

we are morally inclined toward the choices that facilitate the completion of our trust. Ultimately, that trust is binding between self, God, and other. Only with all three aspects of this formula can the proper balance be sustained. Just as the agent-servant paradigm in the Qur'an with regard to the Ultimate and the human being sets up the understanding of both unlimited choice in human free will, so also does it set up the expectations of using that will freely toward right service, not as a limit but as a moral choice.

We are given a certain capacity through agency, which we are meant to understand as a gift to be utilized in the service of Allah; therefore, it is actually a matter of moral maturity or responsibility. There is a reciprocal relationship in the Qur'an between capacity and responsibility. The greater one's capacity, the greater responsibility one is charged to fulfill. As a reminder and affirmation, nothing in the Qur'an or *sunnah* restricts agency for reasons of gender. For while agency is not limited to state or national legislation alone but reflects a transcendental order affecting the quality of the entire being, nothing relieves the agent—not even state sanctions—from the responsibility of completing the duty of justice. This juxtaposition between faith and civil order was so eloquently addressed by Martin Luther King, Jr., in his "Letter from a Birmingham Jail," in which he articulated his nonviolent acts of civil disobedience as part of his belief in a just God. Furthermore, Malcom X shifted the articulation of his struggles for the complete human dignity of African Americans away from civil rights discourse into the global arena of human rights discourse. He fought to reclaim the loss of human rights that resulted from the systemization of racism in America. In other words, as a moral duty to God, one must act in society and within or against existing political structures and codes toward freedom, truth, justice, and dignity.

Progressive Muslim women and men are articulating such an overarching claim against the eradication of full human agency, as stressed by the Qur'an against historical patriarchal discourse and text that reduced women to subject through an epistemology of inferior status and incapacity. The paradigmatic formula for this articulation is at the core of Islam's self-identification and rests on that three-pronged relationship: Allah to human, human to Allah, and human to human. This is none other than operationalizing the fundamental principle of *tawhid*, which at its primal level means oneness of God. In its social construction *tawhid* works as follows.

Not only is Allah one, unique, but also Allah is pervasive. Augustine's articulation most closely resembles the mechanism for imagining the unimaginable. "God is a circle the center of which is everywhere, the circumference of which is nowhere." Indeed, in recognition of the current sphere of human understanding, this notion must extend into a three-dimensional perceptual reality—as a sphere in the universe: the globe, or our world. From the center of the circle or sphere, according to the Sufis, the mystics of Islam, an unlimited projection of rays or spokes extends outward toward the unbounded circumference, to represent a relationship of proximity between all Creation and therefore human creatures and the Ultimate, in the role of Creator (*tashbih*). Coexisting with the image of extending rays is another image, a series of concentric circles emanating from the center, not touching each other, to represent the uniqueness of the sacred other: "*Laysa ka mithlihi shay'*," says the Qur'an. Allah is not like any "thing" in Its creation (*tanzih*). Only by coordination of the two images can the central paradigm and overarching principle in the Islamic worldview of *tawhid* be expressed: the complete harmony and unicity of the Creator, unique within Itself, unifying all Creation, as the cause of all unity within Itself and an expression of Its harmony with all else.

In the context of social interactions (or *mu'amalah*, according to the *shari'ah* categories of praxis) *tawhid* is the base term for the moral achievement of *mu'awadah*, reciprocity. Reciprocity is a guiding principle within many spiritual, religious, and philosophical moral orders up to the present. Its various articulations, such as *Do unto others as you would have them do unto you*, have an Islamic equivalent in the Prophet's *hadith*: "One of you does not believe until he or she wants for another as for self."[17] I have formulated the *tawhid* construct to encapsulate this reciprocity.

Allah is pervasive and the highest conceptual term in the Islamic worldview. Allah is unique.

Allah

self   other

Humanity is created as part of the inherent duality of Creation. Therefore, in the relationship between any two humans, juxtaposition vis-à-vis the inherent nature of duality (whether opposites or conceptual pairs) must be reflected. However, unless this juxtaposition is viewed on the horizontal plane (transcendentally), reciprocity fails, and hegemony prevails. Self is over other. Allah's pervasiveness and highest moral standing, in addition to Its unifying property vis-à-vis all of Creation, is the key term for reconstructing every juxtaposition back onto a new horizontal axis marked metaphysically by our conceptualization of the "place" of Allah in this construct. This would prevent one human from ever exercising privilege or priority over another.

In the model below, where "self" appears to be above "other" on a vertical axis, the conceptualization of the composition is incomplete and suspended without the proper placement of the highest essence, Allah, to complete it.

self
   Allah (if missing creates the appearance of hierarchy)
other

That such an articulation was not categorically represented in *shari'ah* or in Islamic ethical theory is no surprise. The same exclusionary patriarchal readings were in effect when theories and principles of ethics were being formulated and discussed, as in the development of *shari'ah*. However, it is here, at this time and

---

17. I have edited this statement from its original, more literal articulation to one that is gender inclusive.

place of history, that the patriarchal bias can be corrected toward a more inclusive and egalitarian formation of ethical theory as a necessary prerequisite and a principle toward legal reform. Yet those addressing the issue of gender reform today are doing little or no work in the area of ethics. Men wrote all of the references I found, and none of them explicitly addressed gender. According to Majid Fakhry, "an ethical theory is a reasoned account of the nature and grounds of right actions and decisions and the principles underlying the claim that they are morally commendable or reprehensible."[18] Such a theory then provides a "justification and appraisal of moral judgment as well as the discrimination between right and wrong actions or decisions."[19]

In Islam, "we start from the premise that the [Qur'an] and the traditions embody the original core of the Islamic ethical spirit."[20] Therefore, we start with the idea that what is constructed as right and wrong in Islam is based on the Qur'an and *sunnah*. From the perspective of my discussion of the faith-based term *moral agency*, the responsibility of acting on the earth to fulfill moral agency involves acting in accordance with the guidance about right and wrong given in these two primary sources. As previously discussed with regard to citizenship between secular and Islamic systems, the purpose of the historical construction of Islamic law or *shari'ah* was to fulfill that end: to construct a system that reflects the "justification and appraisal of moral judgment as well as the discrimination between right and wrong actions or decisions."[21]

Constructing a moral system is a noble effort indeed. Suffice it to say that there could be no Islamic society without such an effort. Indeed, I am proposing that it is foundational to legal reconstruction of a moral social order in Islam. Yet morality cannot be legislated. Although social systems are premised upon certain moral understandings, and the intent behind all legal systems is to complete the establishment of a moral order—however conceived and based upon whatever sources—the fulfillment of such a goal cannot be completed by the mere establishment of rules or laws. The Qur'an embodies the whole of the Islamic ethos and is the source "around which the whole of Muslim moral, religious and social life revolves," yet it "contains no ethical *theories* in the strict sense."[22] An ethical theory "is a reasoned account of the nature and grounds of right actions and decision and principles underling the claim that they are morally commendable or reprehensible. ... To be complete, an ethical system must deal adequately with these aspects of moral inquiry in an articulate and coherent way."[23] Once again this stress on the definition of ethical concepts reconfirms the significance of the interpretive process and confronts the dilemma of human formulation, because human beings are the agents responsible. "Let there be among you a community [of people] who

18. Majid Fakhry, *Ethical Theories in Islam* (Leiden: Brill, 1991).
19. Fakhry, *Ethical Theories*, p. 1.
20. Fakhry, *Ethical Theories*.
21. Fakhry, *Ethical Theories*.
22. Fakhry, *Ethical Theories*.
23. Fakhry, *Ethical Theories*.

invite unto all that is good [*khayr*], and enjoin the doing of what is right [*ma'ruf*] and forbid the doing of what is wrong [*munkar*]" (3:104).

While you cannot legislate a person into a state of moral excellence, one advantage of civil society is its ability to legislate a system of checks and balances with regard to certain manifestations or representations of moral qualities and to construct a system of legislation with means to enforce, including punishments should voluntary fulfillment fail. But that system is also viewed as human made, put at the service of the ideas of moral agency, as interpreted by humans themselves. The inherent fluidity of such a system in the case of Muslim traditionalists is both challenged by and contained within its dependence on active engagement with the source texts of the Islamic tradition. But as times change, so does our capacity to understand the divine will and our need to revise the methodologies of human implementation accordingly. No single decision at any one time and place, with its peculiarities and circumstances, will necessarily prove final and decisive for all.

In addition, civil society—even Muslim civil society—bears the mark of cultural, historical, and regional context. Although inspired perhaps by a consensus over the primary sources, historically, the development of Muslim civil society has reflected the cultural nuances of the peoples who are implementing it. I suggest certain interrelationships between certain concepts—moral order, moral agent, civil society, and citizen—in order to collect in their juxtaposition some of their merits and limitations.

Civil society intervenes on behalf of the well-being of its citizenry. In the context of those societies defined as Islamic or Muslim, civil society claims to orchestrate the Islamic moral order on behalf of the Muslims and non-Muslims within. Ideally, people in Muslim civil societies are agents attempting individually and collectively to establish the moral order in accordance to the Qur'anic mandate. Since there is no singular social order that can be said conclusively to designate or represent the Qur'an and the *sunnah*, then of necessity, there will be a dynamic relationship between citizen and civil society. The responsibility of the citizen, in the form of the individual, and selected interest groups, as well as larger organizations and ministries, is to interact on behalf of achieving the moral order ordained by the Qur'an and *sunnah*. This should be an inevitable facet of Muslim civil society.

Although there is no hint anywhere in the primary sources that the responsibility to establish what is good, and to forbid what is evil, has been restricted from any mature person for reasons of race, class, or gender, the development of Islamic ethical theories, *shari'ah*, and other disciplines all engaged in the process of intentional or unintentional reinscription of gender disparities affecting the theories developed and codes concluded. In particular, in legal terms, the moral agent is conceived as a metaphysical reality for both women and men but not the basis of social political agency. Social and political agency was restricted to the male person in these theories.

If not predicated explicitly upon the male person, then, often the agents referred to are developed while obscuring their actual references to males and giving a "superficial appearance [that] can easily lead to the impression that they are inclusive of women." However, when a gender identification is given, it not only refers to the male person but also relegates women to "restricted opportunities" within such theories.[24]

Some examples from Islamic ethical theory will suffice as demonstration: "Apart from knowledge or consciousness, the most fundamental precondition or ground of human responsibility is that of freedom."[25] Although one of the primary characteristics of moral agency is freedom, in Islamic intellectual developments, discussions of moral theory are explicitly allowed to the free male. The female is made subservient to another system, called "family," and her role and function as agent is restricted by the terms of her participation in the family. Although this essay renders a different interpretation of Islam's primary sources to conclude that women must be considered full and equal human beings by virtue of the Qur'anic notion of agency, the development of Islamic law and the customary practices of many Muslim societies reflect the idea of woman's agency relative to her roles and status in the extended patriarchal family. Consequently, a simultaneous moralizing discourse using the word "honor" is constructed to give the impression that the woman's subsidiary roles in the family actually identify her as a moral being. However, without characterizing the woman's agency as autonomous vis-à-vis God, and with characterizing it as dependent upon her roles and status in "family," the moral role she is given can be taken away by violations such as rape.

Furthermore, family is often not included as a unit of society worth consideration on par with the public agent, moral agency, ethical theory, civil society, or leadership in the moral order discussed. Rather, family relies heavily upon the voluntary participation of its members. When these members were part of an integral and integrated extended family network, many of the pressures created by the modern movement toward nuclear families were dispersed between women situated in a larger, female-centered network of support. In the absence of that support, more pressure falls upon individual women and men in this new conjugal relationship, and these pressures have in fact increased the disadvantages for the woman, as well as subjected her to an increase in problems such as domestic violence.

Power is another term that bears significantly on the understanding of moral agency in the form of capacity—although with notable concern regarding the differences between *power to* and *power over*. *Power to* is the condition of human capacity and, as understood in the Islamic legacy of moral agency, imparts power or capacity to human beings within a unique covenant between the individual and the divine. However, in the early Islamic discourse over ethical theory and civil society, human empowerment is always directed toward independent male power and most often to power as exercised over others. Females are relegated to a status of subjects to male agency, with "power or capacity being a prerogative of man [*sic*] as a free agent."[26] Women as individuals in such moral theory are not considered full agents

24. Susan Moller Okin calls this "false gender neutrality," in *Justice, Gender and the Family* (New York: Basic Books, 1989), p. 11.
25. Fakhry, *Ethical Theories*, p. 19.
26. Fakhry, *Ethical Theories*, p. 21.

but are incorporated into explicit consideration of family and as extensions of men's agency.

Despite the regulation of these historical interpretations and the codification of these developments about the citizen, the *sunnah* reinforces the Qur'anic thesis of the primacy of righteousness or piety (*taqwa*) over outward attitude or appearance. The Prophet stated, "Allah will not look at your bodies or forms, but at your hearts." The focus is moved away from gender as a feature of disparity. Likewise, the famous statement of the Prophet about "all actions being judged on the basis of their intentions" situates the locus of intention in the heart and not between the legs.

Although the *ahadith* of the Prophet did "not give us a definition of what the good and the evil referred to really are, we can clearly infer from it the express identification of goodness with conformity to the dictates of Islam or the Koran [*sic*]."[27] In the Qur'an, "who ever does good, whether male or female and is a believer" shall be rewarded (3:195). Such an emphasis challenges the gender disparity that developed in the Islamic intellectual legacy and ethical theory.

More important, as I hope I have demonstrated here, gender disparity was an underlying characteristic in the development of Islamic *shari'ah* historically, which was the means for establishing the basic moral rights and wrongs, as well as the checks and balances to maintain them in the context of Muslim civil society. This *shari'ah* construction of woman can only grant the female person a deviant status, insufficient for the completion of her *khilafah* before Allah: the ultimate purpose of her humanity. As a result, she is either denied the avenues for fully completing her duties before Allah, or she is a utility for the fulfillment of male agency.

If agency is not subject to civil society, as discussed earlier, and civil society is insufficient for achieving the moral order, then it behooves women as agents, with the support of men who also respect their full moral responsibility as agents, to take inspiration from the spirit and ethos of the Qur'an and the *sunnah*, in order to pragmatically construct a civil society truly reflecting the moral order of Islam. Resisting the unfair treatment of women in the context of Muslim societies is part of the moral duty of every Muslim woman and man and represents one aspect in completion of moral agency. In fact, moral agency defines the role women and men should play in society. Since a society, even an Islamic one, has the potential to represent or repress the moral order as ordained by the Qur'an, whenever civil circumstances fall short, then the means for facilitating the successful reforms of that social order toward the moral ideal involves the full participation of its citizens. Here citizens are agents, acting on the society, and not mere subjects acted upon by an unjust rule. This was a missing element in the development of *shari'ah* where the law referred to women as subjects to be acted upon and not as actors deciding how to utilize our own agency.

Whenever society defines the role of a woman in any way short of the completion of her agency, then it is the duty of all moral agents to resist and reform that

27. Fakhry, *Ethical Theories*, p. 24.

society. In the context of civil society, she can avail herself of the means of that society as a citizen in order to fulfill her role as agent. There is a reciprocal relationship then between citizenship and agency—with the understanding that the ultimate goals are dictated in the Islamic sources even if the history of Muslim cultures has never been privileged to successfully complete those goals because of such diverse understandings and forms of implementation as Islam spread into diverse patriarchal social, cultural, and historical spaces. In these times, as we gain greater clarity about the relationships between citizens and agents, we can correct the historical flaw in Islamic legal development concerning a premise: the construction of laws to legislate over the lives of full moral agents requires the participation of the agents themselves.

Finally, and yet foremost, moral agency, as a matter of faith, is neither contained nor enhanced by any existing or previously construed social systems. Although moral agency may have been the goal, it requires continual effort to sustain such a moral imperative to maintain social justice as it pertains to women and men. The ways in which traditional Muslim societies and Islamic law have denied women's full agency is incongruent with the achievement of a just social order as sought after in the Qur'an and by the Prophet. In other words, irrespective of our citizenship status, as a matter of faith we are obligated to implement the equality inherent in the *tawhidic* paradigm, fundamental to our religious system. It is a moral imperative incumbent upon all agents in Islam. Ultimately, I use this as the basis for justifying alternative interpretation of *shari'ah's* primary source, the Qur'an, the sacred text of Islam. That the Qur'an has been exclusively interpreted by men for over fourteen centuries and we have no record of women's perspectives on the text until the latter part of the twentieth century indicates a tremendous gap in our intellectual legacy, the filling of which has begun in earnest as part of progressive Islamic reform.

The tendency toward patriarchal interpretations rather than more egalitarian meanings of the primary sources is one of the major focus points in today's reform movements. This essay actively engages in the juxtaposition between text and interpretation in order to construct a hierarchy of meaning where the deeper inner spirit of the faith system and the understanding of Islam vis-à-vis women's agency on earth is given priority over the utilitarian and subservient codification of her status according to the development of *shari'ah* historically. My intention is not merely rhetorical. I seek to create substantive justifications for the implementation of legal reforms at the actual level of social praxis and policy-making that more closely reflect the egalitarian framework of Islam's sacred text.

10

Women's Education

A Global Challenge

Martha C. Nussbaum

She mixes the cowdung with her fingers. It is gooey, smelly; she deftly mixes it with hay; and some bran; then she tries to stand up on the slippery floor of the cowshed and skids; slowly she regains her balance, goes outside with her basket and deftly pats cowdung cakes on the walls, on tree-trunks. . . . When dry her mother uses them for cooking. . . . She does a myriad other kaleidoscopic activities. The economy would not survive without her—at least not the economy of the poor: the girl child.

While she is doing all this what is her brother doing? Studying and getting his books ready for school.

The girl child thus remains outside education.

> Viji Srinivasan, director of Adithi (Patna, Bihar, India)
> in its monthly newsletter

The right to education flows directly from the right to life and is related to the dignity of the individual.

> Supreme Court of India, *Unnikrishnan J. P. v. State of*
> *Andhra Pradesh* (AIR 1993 SC 2178)

Women's Literacy: A Typical Day in an Activist's Life

It is late afternoon in the Sithamarhi district of rural Bihar, in northeastern India. Bihar is an especially anarchic state, with corrupt government, problematic infrastructure, and few services for the poor. Roads are so bad that even a Jeep cannot go more than twenty miles per hour; thus it has taken us two days to go what must be a relatively short distance from the capital city of Patna to this area near the Nepalese border. We arrive to find little in the way of public education, but a lot of activity provided by a local branch of the Patna-based nongovernmental organization

Adithi, founded and run by Viji Srinivasan, whose dynamic organization is one of the most influential advocates for women's education in this difficult region.[1]

The girls of the village, goatherds by day, are starting school. They come together in a shed, all ages, to attend the Adithi literacy program. In some regions of India, most notably Kerala, state government has been highly effective in promoting literacy for both boys and girls. Here in Bihar, state government, run from jail by the demagogue Laloo Prasad Yadav, fails to deliver essential services to the poor, so most education for the rural poor is pieced together in this way.[2] Viji and I sit on the ground to watch the class, which, like the one-room schoolhouses I read about as a child in stories of the American West, covers all levels and subjects at once, with about fifteen students. Somehow, it all seems to work, through the resourcefulness and responsiveness of the teachers, themselves poor rural women who have been assisted by Adithi's programs.

Viji, who has worked in women's development for almost forty years, began to run Adithi in 1988. It currently helps more than 25,000 women and children in rural Bihar. After the math and the reading comes drama: the girls proudly present for Viji and me a play they have improvised and that they recently performed for their entire village, about a young man who refuses to demand a dowry when he marries. (Dowry is a major cause of women's poor life chances in India, both because it defines a girl child as a drag on family resources and because it can later be used as the occasion for extortionate demands for more, frequently involving domestic violence and even murder.) The girls play all the roles; one big tough girl, whose six-foot stature gives surprising evidence of good nutrition, takes special pleasure in acting the young man's villainous father, greedy for dowry. (This area of rural Bihar has a female-to-male ratio of 75 to 100, giving strong indication of unequal nutrition and health care; girls in school do better because their families expect that they may bring in an income.) At last, young love and good sense triumph: the couple get married and go their own way, and no money changes hands. Even the groom's

---

1. Adithi had to begin by creating teaching materials. India has 385 or so langauges, seventeen official, and many with no written traditions. The poor are often simply unable to obtain an education if their only language is one in which education is not offered.

2. Laloo Prasad Yadav's wife Rabri Devi was running the state officially, given that he had been jailed for corruption (a grain/bribery scandal). Shortly after this time, a state of national emergency was declared in Bihar, and the state was put under the direct governance of the national government for a month or two, not long enough to effect any real change. I cannot resist adding one point connected to my earlier writing. In several articles, most recently "Human Capabilities, Female Human Beings" (Nussbaum 1996), I criticized an article by the anthropologist Frédérique Marglin that attacked the practice of smallpox vaccination in India on the grounds that it had eradicated the cult of Sittala Devi, the goddess to whom one prays in order to avert smallpox. I can now announce that Sittala Devi is alive and well in Bihar. Indeed, she flourishes under the patronage of Laloo Prasad Yadav, who believes that she cured him of a liver ailment. I have seen her beauteous shrine in a slum in Patna, surrounded by the signs of Laloo's neglect of his civic duties. Laloo's record is not unmixed, however. As of January 2005, as Railways Minister in the new government led by Manmohon Singh and Sonia Gandhi, he has been responsible for the telling inquiry into the incident at Godhra that precipitated the genocidal violence against Muslims in Gujarat in 2002. The inquiry, chaired by a Justice of the Supreme Court, showed that the incident, in which 58 Hindus died in a burned railway carriage, was a tragic accident and not a planned Muslim assault.

parents say that this way is better. The girls giggle with pleasure at the subversive thing they have cooked up. One little girl, too young for the play, sits by the window, her hair lit up by the setting sun. On her slate she draws a large and improbable flower. "Isn't she wonderful?" Viji whispers with evident zest.

Since my practice is to follow activists around, observing what they do, I usually do not see villages in which activists have not been active. So I usually do not see the most depressing things. But I know that for every village like this one, there are ten where girls have no education at all, no employment options, no opportunity to criticize the institutions that determine the course of their lives. In the nation as a whole, female literacy is still under 50 percent.[3] And the sex ratio, a good index of the worth in which female life is held, has been plummeting, from 92:100 in the 1990 census to around 85:100 now.[4] Those are aggregate figures and official statistics. Here in this particular region of Bihar, a head count by Adithi has found the astonishing figure of 75:100. Talking about this to Viji, I ask, "How do you sustain hope in a situation like this, when you can see that even if you do some good in one place there are so many more places that you haven't influenced?" She says, "I just try to focus on what my organization can do here and now. That is the way I keep on."

Women's education is both crucial and contested. A key to the amelioration of many distinct problems in women's lives, it is spreading, but it is also under threat, both from custom and traditional hierarchies of power and from the sheer inability of states and nations to take effective action.

In this chapter, I shall try to show, first, exactly why education should be thought to be a key for women in making progress on many other problems in their lives. Second, I shall describe the sources of resistance to educating women and argue that objections from the side of traditionalism are misplaced and incoherent. (Here I shall draw on my experience with women's development groups in India.) Finally, I shall argue that if women's education is to be fostered around the world, two things must happen that are now not sufficiently happening. First, nations, and states within nations, must make women's education a high-priority matter and devote a good deal of their resources and energies to it. Second, wealthy nations, their concerned citizens, and their corporations must all commit resources to the effort.

In the process, all concerned should recognize that promoting economic growth is not a sufficient way to promote education for women. Development theorists who focus only on maximizing economic growth, assuming that growth alone will provide for other central human needs, are very likely to shortchange female

3. The rate is 45.5 percent, according to the 2000 census; the male ratio is 68.4 percent. (For data here and elsewhere, see UNDP 2001.)

4. Even the 1990 figure was the lowest since the census began to be taken early in this century. It is estimated that when women and men receive equal nutrition and health care, the sex ratio should be around 102 or 103 women to 100 men. The recent sharp decline can be attributed to the new availability of techniques for determining the sex of the fetus, and a resulting increase in sex-selective abortion. These techniques are illegal, but they are available more or less everywhere.

education. In their comparative field studies of the Indian states, Amartya Sen and Jean Drèze have shown that growth-oriented policies do not improve the quality of education, particularly female education, in the absence of additional focused state action (Drèze and Sen 1995).[5] Thus states such as Gujarat and Haryana that have done well in fostering economic growth often do quite poorly in basic education;[6] and Kerala, whose economy has not grown well, can boast 99 percent literacy for both boys and girls in adolescence, against a background of 35 percent female and 65 percent male literacy for the nation as a whole.[7] In Kerala, intelligent state action has delivered what NGOs like Adithi currently try to provide in states such as Bihar, where the public sector has not assumed the challenge of female education. And indeed it is very important to insist that development is a normative concept, and that we should not assume that the human norms we want will be delivered simply through a policy of fostering economic growth. As the late Mahbub ul Haq (the leading development economist and former director of the United Nations Development Programme [UNDP]) wrote in 1990, in the first of the *Human Development Reports* of the UNDP, "the real wealth of a nation is its people. And the purpose of development is to create an enabling environment for people to enjoy long, healthy, and creative lives. This simple but powerful truth is too often forgotten in the pursuit of material and financial wealth" (UNDP 1990, 1).

Mentioning the *Human Development Reports* gives me a way to respond, in a preliminary way at least, to a perpetual question: What is the use of theory, when we can see that what makes women's lives better is courageous activism of the Viji Srinivasan type? Now one might respond, first, with a plea of personal competence. Some people are good activists; others are not. If theory is what one can do, and professionally does, then one might as well try to see how theory might make a positive contribution to the lives of women. I believe, however, that the examples of Sen and ul Haq point the way to a stronger defense of theory.

Good theories are an important part of getting a hearing for such moral arguments in the international arena. Before the "human development" paradigm was crafted by ul Haq, drawing on Sen's ideas, the development paradigm was focused exclusively on economic growth. The quality of life was measured by looking only at gross national product (GNP) per capita, an approach that is totally inadequate to analyzing the problems women face in the developing world (Nussbaum and Sen 1993). Having a new explicit theory of what real development consists in, and putting that forward in reports that packaged information in a new way and ranked nations in a new way, was not a totally original contribution, for of course advocates for the poor had been saying just such things for years. But the theorization of such insights was a big part of enabling the new "human development" paradigm to capture the attention of governments, development agencies,

---

5. The field studies are published in Drèze and Sen 1996.
6. Bihar is not doing well either economically or in its record on health and education.
7. The democratically elected Marxist government has allowed labor unions to force wages very high, which has caused jobs to move to neighboring states. Many Keralan men are forced to look for employment outside the state.

and, increasingly, agencies such as the World Bank. The "capabilities approach" to the measurement of the quality of life (which Sen and I have developed in different ways) needed to be brought down to earth and made easily accessible for policy-makers and bureaucrats: this was the tremendous contribution of ul Haq, who had a keen instinct for what would "work" politically and what would be too fussy or complex.[8] But the background theoretical ideas needed to be there to be scrutinized, and these ideas continue to be a source of further work and of argument against the still-dominant economic growth paradigm. It is only because the work has some degree of theoretical sophistication that it is increasingly being used by economists who consult in international agencies and by philosophers who develop its implications further.[9]

Our world is increasingly dominated by the profit motive, as multinational corporations and global markets increasingly leach sovereignty away from national governments. The dominant economic paradigm encourages continued insensitivity to the situation of the world's poorest people, and to the special disadvantages suffered by women—not because economists are by nature bad people but because they see things through the lens of a bad theory (which, of course, might have insensitivity somewhere behind it, or maintaining it in place). This paradigm, and the practices it supports, should be contested. Consumer protests and protests in the streets are one crucial part of that critical process, but good theory is another part that is not without value. It is not as though we could ever remake the world so that it was simply run by the wisdom of people such as Viji Srinivasan. It is run by think tanks, corporations, bureaucrats, and politicians, and these people typically use some formal model of what they are pursuing. If they have no "human development" paradigm and no writings expressing the importance of women's education and other goals stressed by that paradigm, they will use the existing paradigm, and they will focus exclusively on growth. So those of us who do not have Viji Srinivasan's creativity, stamina, local knowledge, and physical courage may still have a task that we can undertake that could possibly be of some use, when sufficiently attentive to the complexities of experience.

Education and Women's Capabilities

Despite a constant focus on women's education as a priority in global discussions of human rights and quality of life, and in the efforts of activists of all sorts and many governments, women still lag well behind men in many countries of the world, even at the level of basic literacy. In many countries, male and female literacy rates are similar. These include virtually all the countries that the *Human Development Report* 2001 of the UNDP identifies as countries of "high human development," because most of these nations have close to 100 percent literacy, at

8. For some differences between Sen's version of the capabilities approach and my own, see Nussbaum 2003b.

9. As, for example, in Alkire 2002.

least as measured by data supplied by the countries themselves (UNDP 2001).[10] But relative male-female equality can also be found in many poorer nations, such as Trinidad and Tobago, Panama, Russia, Belarus, Romania, Thailand, Columbia, Venezuela, Jamaica,[11] Sri Lanka, Paraguay, Ecuador, the Dominican Republic, South Africa, Guyana, Vietnam, Botswana, and Lesotho.[12]

There are, however, forty-three countries in which male literacy rates are fifteen percentage points or more higher than the female rate. Since the *HDR* lists 162 nations, this means more than one fourth of the nations in the world. These nations include India, Syria, Turkey, Pakistan, Nepal, Bangladesh, Nigeria, Sudan, and, in general most, though not all, of the poorer nations of Africa.[13] (China's gap is 14.5 percent, so it barely avoids being part of the group of forty-three.) In absolute terms, women's literacy rates are beneath 50 percent in India, Bangladesh, Pakistan, Nepal, Egypt, and the preponderant number of the nations listed in the "low human development" category.[14] Some of the lowest rates are as follows: Pakistan at 30 percent, Nepal at 22.8 percent, Bangladesh at 29.3 percent, Yemen at 23.9 percent, Senegal at 26.7 percent, Gambia at 28.5 percent, Guinea-Bissau at 18.3 percent, Burkina Faso at 13.3 percent, and Niger at 7.9 percent.

If we now turn to secondary education, the gaps are even more striking. Moreover, as is not generally the case with basic literacy, the gaps are actually growing: in twenty-seven countries the secondary school enrollment of girls declined between 1985 and 1997. And this happened, as the *HDR* stresses, during a time of rapid technological development, in which skills became ever more important as passports to economic opportunity (UNDP 2001, 15). Finally, although data on university enrollments of women are not presented in the HDR, it is evident that in many nations women form a small fraction of the university population.

Why should we think that this matters deeply? Isn't all this emphasis on literacy an elite value, possibly not relevant to the lives that poor working people are trying to lead? In the 1980s, Rajeev Gandhi came to Harvard to deliver a large public lecture about the achievements of his administration. Questioned by some Indian students about why he had done so little to raise literacy rates, he replied, "The common people have a wisdom that would only be tarnished by literacy."

10. Countries in this group that show a striking male-female disparity (more than five percentage points) include Singapore, Hong Kong, Brunei Darussalam, Bahrain, and Kuwait. Lest we think that the "Arab States" are systematically depriving women: the United Arab Emirates (UAE) and Qatar show a higher literacy rate for women than for men. The sheikh of the UAE is a vigorous supporter of female education and is also opening a coeducational liberal arts university that recently offered a position to one of my graduate students who specializes in feminism and environmental ethics.

11. Jamaica, although relatively poor (78 on the Human Development Index), actually shows 90.3 percent female literacy and 82.4 percent male literacy.

12. In Lesotho, women allegedly have 93.3 percent literacy, as against only 71.7 percent for men, so there is really a large gender gap, but in the atypical direction.

13. Kenya, which barely gets into the "medium" rather than "low human development" group, does unusually well on education, with 74.8 percent literacy for women, 88.3 percent for men.

14. The most striking exception at the bottom of the Human Development Index is Zambia, with 70.2 percent female literacy, 84.6 percent male literacy.

Why was this answer so ill received by the Indians in the audience, and (more important) why was it a bad answer?

First of all, let us get rid once and for all of the idea that literacy is a value that is peculiarly "Western." Women all over the world are struggling to attain it, and some of the biggest success stories in the area of literacy are non-Western stories. Kerala, for example, raised literacy rates to virtually 100 percent for both boys and girls—by virtue of intense government concern, creative school designing, and other things that I shall later discuss. That is a staggering achievement, given Kerala's poverty, and it is supported with joy and energy by girls and women.

We can add that most women in developed countries do not have to struggle to become literate: it is foisted upon them. So we do not really know how deeply we value it, or whether we would in fact fight for it, the way women in India and other developing countries do every day, often at risk to safety and even life. But perhaps we can see even more clearly why literacy is not a parochial value if we begin to ponder the connections between literacy and other capabilities for which women are striving all over the world.

If there was a time when illiteracy was not a barrier to employment, that time has passed. The nature of the world economy is such that illiteracy condemns a woman (or man) to a small number of low-skilled types of employment. With limited employment opportunities, a woman is also limited in her options to leave a bad or abusive marriage. If a woman can get work outside the home, she can stand on her own. If she is illiterate, she will either remain in an abusive marriage for lack of options, or she may leave and have nothing to fall back on. (Many sex workers end up in sex work for precisely this reason.) While in the family, an illiterate woman has a low bargaining position for basic resources such as food and medical care, because her exit options are so poor and her perceived contribution to the success of the family unit is low.[15] Where women have decent employment options outside the home, the sex ratio tends to reflect a higher valuation of the worth of female life.

Literacy is of course not the only key factor in improving women's bargaining position: training in other marketable skills is also valuable, though literacy is more flexible. Property rights that give women access to credit and programs that give them credit even in the absence of real property are also highly significant.[16]

Because literacy is connected in general with the ability to move outside the home and to stand on one's own outside of it, it is also connected to the ability of women to meet and collaborate with other women. Women may of course form local face-to-face networks of solidarity, and they ubiquitously do. But to participate in a larger movement for political change, women need to be able to communicate through mail, e-mail, and so forth.

More generally, women's access to the political process is very much enhanced by literacy. We can see this very clearly in the history of the *panchayats*, or local village councils, in India. In 1992, India adopted the Seventy-Second and Seventy-Third Amendments to the Constitution, giving women a mandatory

15. See Sen 1991.
16. See Agarwal 1994, 1997.

33 percent reservation in the *panchayats*.[17] (Elections take place by rotation: in each cycle, a given seat is designated as a woman's seat, and the woman's seat shifts from cycle to cycle.) This move, of course, had intrinsic significance. Increasing women's literacy by itself would not have produced anything like a 33 percent result, as we can see from the United States, where women still hold only 13 percent of seats in Congress. But in order for this result to be truly effective, making women dignified and independent equals of males, literacy has to enter the picture. According to extensive studies of the *panchayat* system by Niraja Jayal and Nirmala Buch, women are persistently mocked and devalued in the *panchayats* if they are illiterate. (Jayal and Buch note that illiterate men do not suffer similar disabilities.)[18] Women often campaign as stand-ins for husbands who can no longer hold their seats—and their independence is greater if they are literate, able thus to have greater independent access to information and communications. As a woman seeks to contest a nonreserved seat (sometimes running against her own husband), her chances are clearly enhanced if she can move as a fully independent actor in society, with access to communications from memos to national newspapers.[19] Literacy is clearly crucial in this transition. Buch finds that one of the biggest changes brought about by the new system is a greater demand on the part of women for the education of their daughters—so that they can take their place as equals in the new system. While this finding shows us that we should not push for literacy in isolation from other values such as political participation—for here it is the fact of greater participation that drives the demand for literacy, not the reverse—it does show us that the two are allies.

On the plane of national and international politics, it is very difficult indeed for an illiterate woman to enjoy full participation. India makes it easy for illiterate people to vote, by using party symbols instead of words on ballots; national elections have a remarkably high voter turnout, including many illiterate women and men. But, obviously enough, a person who can read the newspapers has a much fuller and more independent voice than one who cannot. (In most of rural India, electricity is sporadic, often available only at odd hours of the night. Thus television is no solution. There are many television sets that are purely decorative.) As actual participants in national legislatures and in international gatherings such as human rights meetings, illiterate women are obviously very likely to be left out. Even if at times their voices are heard, they cannot participate fully as equals in meetings that involve the circulation of draft upon draft of a human rights document.

Even in professions where literacy is not crucial to the employment itself, it proves crucial to the politics of employment, as women need to band together, often transnationally, to fight for better labor standards. A fine example of this fact

17. See Nussbaum 2004a.
18. See Buch 2000; Jayal 2000; I am also greatly indebted to Zoya Hasan (2000).
19. See "Sex, Laws, and Inequality: What India Can Teach the United States" (Nussbaum 2002b), where I discuss one such case, and the history in general. (*Caveat lector:* the publishers removed reference to teaching the United States from my title when they showed it on the cover of the journal, calling it simply "Sex, Laws, and Inequality: India's Experience.")

is Women in the Informal Economy Globalizing and Organizing (WIEGO), an international group of female home-based workers (hawkers and vendors, craft laborers, etc.) who have organized for better working conditions. This group does reach out systematically to illiterate women; but again: it is obvious that participants in the international meetings of this organization, where draft resolutions are discussed, are overwhelmingly likely to be educated women.

Literacy is crucial, too, for women's access to the legal system. Even to bring a charge against someone who has raped you, you have to file a complaint.[20] If your father or husband is not helping you out, and some legal NGO does not take on your case, you are nowhere if you cannot read and write—and, indeed, more than that. For you need an education that includes basic knowledge of the political and legal process in your own nation. Many NGOs in India spend a lot of time helping uneducated women bring their complaints, and individual educated women often do this as a kind of voluntary public service. But, obviously enough, more such work could be done if more people could do it!

These concrete factors suggest some less tangible connections. Literacy (and education in general) is very much connected to women's ability to form social relationships on a basis of equality with others and to achieve the important social good of self-respect. It is important, as well, to mobility (through access to jobs and the political process), to health and life (through the connection to bodily integrity and exit options)—in short, to more or less all of the "capabilities" that I have argued for as central political entitlements.[21]

Especially important is the role that female education has been shown to have in controlling population growth. No single factor has a larger impact on the birth rate: for as women learn to inform themselves about the world, they also increasingly take charge of decisions affecting their own lives. And as their bargaining position in the family improves through their marketable skills, their views are more likely to prevail.[22]

So far I have focused on the role played by education in supporting other capabilities. But learning has a more subtle value as well, as a cultivation of powers of thought and expression that might otherwise go neglected. Such neglect of a human being's mental space is especially likely in lives that are given over to heavy physical labor and the added burden of housework and child care. The girls in Bihar were learning useful skills, but they were also learning to value their own humanity. The pride and confidence of their stance as they performed the play, their happy giggles as they told us how they first shocked, then influenced, their village—all this shows us that what is at stake in literacy is no mere skill but human

---

20. Called, in India, "First Information Reports" (FIRs), these documents must be initiated by the victim: thus in India law-enforcement agencies all on their own typically do not initiate criminal prosecution.

21. See Nussbaum 2000, 2003b. For the list of capabilities, as published in Nussbaum 2000, see the appendix to this essay.

22. See Sen 1996. Presented as a working document at the Cairo Population meeting, Sen's essay strongly influenced their conclusions. For a more general discussion of women's bargaining position and the factors affecting it, see Agarwal 1997.

dignity itself and the political and social conditions that make it possible for people to live with dignity. A young widow in an adult literacy program in Bangladesh told the activist Martha Chen that her mother questioned the value of the class. She replied: "Ma, what valuable things there are in the books you will not understand because you cannot read and write. If somebody behaves badly with me, I go home and sit with the books. When I sit with the books my mind becomes better" (Chen 1983, 202).[23] The feeling of a place of mental concentration and cultivation that is one's own can only be properly prized, perhaps, if one has lacked it. There is something in sitting with a book, this young woman was saying, that makes her feel more herself, less willing to be pushed around by others.

Thinking about the intrinsic value of basic education makes us see that what should be promoted—and what good activists typically promote—is not mere rote use of skills; it is an inquiring habit of mind and a cultivation of the inner space of the imagination. The girls in Bihar did not just drill on their sums and write letters on their slates. They gave plays, sang, and told stories. They used imagination to address their predicament, and this use of the imagination was woven into the entire educational process. This is typical of the approach of good NGOs in this area—unless their efforts are blocked by entrenched social forces. One day in January 2000, I went with the activist Sarda Jain to visit a girls' literacy project in rural Rajasthan, several hours from Jaipur. This is the region of India in which child marriage (illegal) is the most common. Large groups of girls are married off at ages four or six. Although they do not live with their husbands until age twelve or so, their course in life is set. Their parents must keep them indoors or watch over them constantly to guard their purity, so that they can't really play outside like little boys. In addition, the parents know that these girls won't support them in their old age—they already "belong" to another family. So their development and health are typically neglected. The program I was visiting, run by an NGO called Vishaka, gives basic literacy and skills training to girls between the ages of six and twelve, that is, before they go to live with their husbands, and while they are doing either domestic work or goatherding.[24] On this particular day, the girls from many different villages were coming together for testing in a large group. Sarda said to me, "I don't want to see the sums on their slates, I want to see the look in their eyes." The girls duly appeared—all dolled up in their women's finery, unable to move freely, faces partly covered. The expected presence of strangers had made their parents costume them so as to assume their role as wives. They were physically unable to dance. Sarda was profoundly disappointed, for she interpreted the demeanor and appearance of the girls as a sign that all their training was merely skin deep and

---

23. Rohima, the woman in question, also emphasizes the way in which literacy has increased her general mental concentration and understanding.

24. Vishaka is famous in India because it was the plaintiff in one of the landmark sexual harassment cases (*Vishaka v. Rajasthan*, discussed in Nussbaum 2002b and in Nussbaum 2004b). The Vishaka case is not the one I call "problematic": it is a promising example of the creative use of international documents in crafting domestic law. The Supreme Court held, in this case, that the guidelines on sexual harassment in the Convention on the Elimination of All Forms of Discrimination against Women (CEDAW) were binding on the nation through its ratification of the treaty.

would not survive in their new lives as married women, as an inner shaping of their mental world.

My argument about the role of education in developing central human capabilities in no sense implies that without education women do not have selves worthy of respect, or basic human dignity. We may acknowledge that the absence of education involves a blighting of human powers without at all denying that the person who has been so blighted retains a basic core of human equality that grounds normative claims of justice. Indeed, in the capabilities approach, it is precisely the presence of human dignity that gives rise to a claim that core human capacities should be developed, as an urgent issue of justice. Thinking about how to reconcile the recognition of dignity with the recognition that life's accidents can deform and deeply mar human powers is a very difficult matter, one that political philosophy has not yet resolved in a fully satisfactory way.[25] But it does seem clear that we can respect basic human capacities (what I elsewhere call "basic capabilities") without denying that the failure to support them (by nutrition, health care, education, etc.) can blight them in a serious way, by denying them a full development that is essential to the person's ability to live a live worthy of human dignity. The uneducated woman is likely to be a woman whose human powers of mind have been seriously underdeveloped, in just the way that the starving and powerless workers whom Marx describes in the *Economic and Philosophical Manuscripts* ([1848] 1982) are cut off from the fully human use of their faculties.

So far, I have focused on basic literacy—and with much reason, given the depressing statistics about women's literacy in the developing world. And basic literacy already opens up many options for women, as well as having intrinsic value as a cultivation of mind and thought. But one should emphasize that most job opportunities require far more than basic literacy. So does most active participation in citizenship and politics. Secondary education is a more difficult goal by far for women than primary education, since it is at this time that girls who have managed to go to school are often taken out of school to do housework or to get married. University education is the most difficult of all, because it usually requires going away from home, and the sacrifices involved are more readily made for boys than for girls. But the reality of politics in developing countries suggests that university-educated women are far more likely to be able to influence debates at a national level, as well as to have access to the most influential and higher paying jobs.

Women from poor rural areas face particularly great obstacles in seeking a higher education. A new University is currently being founded to address this need. The Asian University for Women (AUW) will be located in Bangladesh under a land grant arrangement from the national government. It will seek out female students from all over South Asia, preferring students from poor and rural areas and focusing on nations that have a weak higher education structure, such as Pakistan, Bangladesh, and Nepal, although it will also include women from India, Sri Lanka, and possibly Indonesia and Malaysia. It will be modeled on the liberal arts

25. See Nussbaum 2002b, 2002c.

college, as we know it in America; that is, two years will be spent pursuing a wide variety of subjects thought to constitute a "liberal education," and then two will be spent in a major subject, connected to job opportunities, and culminating in the equivalent of a European or Indian M.A. The major subjects are largely in the sciences and social sciences (computer science, public health, etc.), but the "humanities," much neglected in Asian higher education generally, will play a central role. Thus the required curriculum will probably include an emphasis on public debate and critical thinking, the study of the major world religions and cultures, and a large role for the arts.[26] (These ideas have deep roots in Bengali educational traditions, and particularly in the thought and educational practice of Rabindranath Tagore.) All these subjects will be introduced not as abstract elite refinements but as deeply interwoven with the experiences, traditions, and problems of developing nations. The language of instruction will (inevitably) be English, but, through intensive language training prior to the start of regular enrollment, much effort will be taken not to disadvantage women who have not had much exposure to English in their high school education.[27] Faculty will be drawn from young Asian and also non-Asian scholars all over the world. The project itself is Asian in inspiration but also fully international; most of the members of the Board of Advisors are from Asia, though there are a few outsiders.[28]

The mission of AUW will inevitably be controversial, especially for its commitment to single-sex education. Many development thinkers are skeptical about encouraging the segregation of women. I myself believe that in an era of gross inequalities, single-sex institutions perform a very valuable function, helping women achieve confidence and overcome collective action problems that exist in their home settings. I also applaud the choice of the liberal arts format, which will

26. The curriculum planning group, as of June 2003, consisted of Savitri Goonesekere, former chancellor of the University of Colombo in Sri Lanka and one of the redactors of CEDAW; Ayesha Jalal, prominent Pakistani historian who writes on the history of India; Fran Volkmann, former acting president of Smith College; and myself. In January 2003 we held a meeting at Visva-Bharati University in Santiniketan, West Bengal, India—the university founded by Rabindranath Tagore, together with his famous Santiniketan school. Leading female educators from Bangladesh and India were present and advised us on the future of the University. Those especially active (and likely to be involved in future planning) were Jasodhara Bagchi, head of the Women's Commission in the state of West Bengal and founder of the first program in Women's Studies in India (at Jadavpur University in Calcutta) and Roop Rekha Verma, former vice-chancellor of the University of Lucknow and chair of Philosophy and Women's Studies at that university. (For some of my own educational ideas, see Nussbaum 1997.)

27. Or who have been badly taught. In India there is a huge class gap here: the children of the upper middle class typically go to "English medium" schools (private, often Roman Catholic), where they gain native-speaker fluency in English. In the regular public schools, instruction is mechanical and does not impart real fluency.

28. The founder and guiding spirit is Kamal Ahmad, originally from Bangladesh, educated at Harvard, currently working for a law firm in London; Asian members of the board of advisors have included, at various times, Corazon Aquino, Fazle Hasan Abed from the Bangladesh Rural Advancement Committee, Mohammed Yunus of the Grameen Bank (Bangladesh), the feminist lawyer Asma Jehangir (Pakistan), and others from India, Indonesia, and Japan. Mark Malloch Brown from the UNDP has also been involved at various stages, as have Mary Robinson of the UN, Henry Rosovsky of Harvard, and Alice Huang of the California Institute of Technology.

promote an education focused on the needs of citizenship and the whole course of life rather than simply on narrow preprofessional learning. This format, too, permits explicit study of the history and problems of women and a focus on their experience in developing countries. Women's studies has proven enormously difficult to integrate into the European model, where students enter university to pursue only a single subject.[29]

The problems of educating women in the developing world are enormous, as my data show. And yet education for women is crucial to women's other opportunities and entitlements, as well as being of great intrinsic value.

Resistance to Women's Education

If all this is so, why should women's education encounter any resistance at all? Why shouldn't the whole world agree that it is an urgent priority? Of course, at this point we encounter resistance of an obvious sort from entrenched custom and power. I have stressed that women's education is revolutionary; it is a key to many other sources of power and opportunity. It is therefore not at all surprising that people who resist extending these other sources of power and opportunity to women typically oppose women's education, or at least its extension. Sometimes this opposition takes an extreme form, as it did in Afghanistan under the Taliban. Often it takes a less extreme form, but it is real enough.[30]

Sometimes this type of opposition is masked by benign neglect. Thus many states that pay lip service to women's education and may at some level really think it important are simply not willing to do much to bring it about. India has been very slow to translate the equality of opportunity that its Constitution guaranteed women in 1950 into actual policy aimed at making these opportunities real. Some part of this is sheer mismanagement and inefficiency, aided by widespread corruption in local government. But there can be no doubt that there are many people involved in politics in India who really do not want more educated women, in employment or in politics.

Resistance to female education is increased when its proponents push for real education, by which I mean an overall empowerment of the woman through not just literacy and numeracy but also the cultivation of the imagination and a mastery of her political and economic situation. Obviously enough, the sort of education

---

29. Hence a growing interest in liberal arts education in Europe as well: for example, the European College of Liberal Arts in Berlin and the University for Humanist Studies in Utrecht. But the concept is being discussed all over, from Sweden to Italy. Whether these discussions will inspire real change depends largely on whether faculty will become willing to teach undergraduates in small groups and really pay attention to them. Thus AUW, drawing as it will on Asians educated in the liberal arts system (*inter alios* and *alias*), is initially better placed than are the huge European universities, where professors rarely have serious contact with undergraduates.

30. On the history of this resistance in Bengal, a region marked by early progressive efforts to educate women, see Bagchi 1997. Bagchi describes the way the language of purity and nationalism was used to oppose women's literacy.

I am favoring in this essay is far more threatening than mere literacy and numeracy, and to that extent it faces a tougher struggle.

Sometimes, however, resistance comes from sheer economic necessity. Thus, many individual parents who have no objection to educating girls and boys on a basis of equality may be able to afford to educate only one of their children (in the sense that they will need to keep some at home to do the housework or send some out to do unpaid work such as herding or even wage work). In many cultural circumstances, existing employment opportunities dictate that the one educated must be a boy because his overall employment opportunities are greater and education is a necessary passport to these.[31] So the neglect of female education may be a matter of survival for parents in many parts of the world. This sort of resistance must be addressed, and I shall get to that point in my next section.

So far, however, we have not dealt with anyone who uses a plausible normative argument to oppose female education as a goal. I shall therefore turn to such an argument. For want of a better name, let us call it the Rajeev Gandhi argument. Put a little more elegantly than he put it, this argument says that the world contains many cultures. Many are nonliterate. These nonliterate cultures should not be held in contempt. They, and the artistic and other human achievements they have made, should be respected. But literacy radically transforms such cultures. For example, oral poetry does not survive the advent of widespread literacy. So pushing for universal literacy is tantamount to destroying sources of value.[32]

In response to this argument, I must make two points from the outset. First, cultures are not museum pieces to be contemplated; they are lives of human beings to be lived. So it is inappropriate to romanticize any aspect of culture that either contains misery and injustice in itself or is linked to misery and injustice. Thus, when Frédérique Marglin romanticizes the lives of *devadasis*, child temple prostitutes, on the grounds that they preserve beautiful traditions of dance, this seems a misplaced nostalgic reaction that objectifies the misery that such girls suffer, taken from their families at a very young age and subjected to sex without consent.[33] Illiteracy itself may already be such a misery and injustice intrinsically, at least for many women in many places. This is especially likely to be true when not going to school is replaced by long hours of grinding labor, not by any other type of cultivation of mind and imagination; and this is typically the case for women who do not go to school. Oral poets are usually either males or highly educated leisured females. Illiteracy, moreover, is strongly linked, as I have already argued, to other forms of injustice: domestic violence without exit options, unequal political and employment opportunities.

31. Interestingly, although this is the most common situation for poor parents in India, it is not so for the Muslim minority. Muslim men typically have poorer job opportunities than do Hindu men, because of both poverty and discrimination. Muslim parents do not press hard for the education of boys where they believe that the boy's job opportunities are in low-paying jobs that do not require education. In this situation, parents frequently continue the education of their daughters and send their sons out to work.

32. This argument has the general form of arguments about the preservation of traditional cultures in rural India by Frédérique and Stephen Marglin (1990).

33. See F. A. Marglin 1985. For a different view of *devadasis*, see Omvedt 1983.

Second, cultures are not monoliths. They do not contain a single set of norms and a single normative tradition. They contain real people, jockeying for power and opportunity. Women are often at odds with the norms that are well known as "the norms" of "the culture." The cultural argument, basing its case on the values enshrined within a culture, should not fail to note these tensions.[34] But then what we have on our hands will probably be much more complicated than a choice between the value of educating women and the value of traditional poetry and art: for we must include the resistance of women to tradition as one of the values that is also internal to the culture. In general, these internal tensions and disagreements make it very hard to use existing culture as any source of norms. The appeal to culture is thus in danger of falling into utter incoherence: for what is appealed to is in tension with other elements of itself.

We can add to this point the fact that very often, powerful groups within a culture who are resisting change attempt to brand the internal demand for change as foreign in order to discredit it. This has been a persistent phenomenon in the history of women's attempts to become educated. Jasodhara Bagchi records that nineteenth-century women's education programs in Bengal, although led by internal reformers, were branded as "English" and "Western" by traditionalists. This happens all the time around the world. Chen quotes a woman in the literacy project run by the Bangladesh Rural Advancement Committee as saying, "They [male village leaders] say we will become Christian and English people will take us away. We are ruining the prestige of the village and breaking *purdah*. If we can get food, we will become Christian." To this already sarcastic characterization of the opponent this woman adds, "We do not listen to the *mullahs* any more. They also did not give us even a quarter kilo of rice. Now we get ten maunds of rice [i.e. because the women are earning incomes]" (Chen 1983, 176). We obviously should not be misled by the fact that opponents of a movement for change name it Western. If it is there in the culture, it is in it, no matter whether it is new or old, traditional or antitraditional. We may often be inclined to say that literacy is more a part of the culture of rural women in India and Bangladesh than it is of our own, in the sense that they choose it, fight for it, grab hold of it, where none of us has ever done any such thing.

What about the fact, though, that women themselves sometimes voice a reluctance to becoming educated? Bagchi records in her 1997 book that one fourth of the school-age girls she surveyed in West Bengal thought that women should have less education than men. "When we asked them why they felt so, the answers we received all pointed to the fact that from childhood most girls had been conditioned to believe that men were superior to women and boys to girls" (Bagchi 1997, 105). Such views are typical examples of "adaptive preferences," preferences that have simply adjusted to traditional norms and opportunities; it is not clear that public policy should take them into account. These girls know their options and opportunities: so, as Jon Elster says, why desire the grapes that are out of reach?[35]

---

34. See Nussbaum 2000, chap. 1.
35. For discussion of the whole issue of adaptive preferences, and the views of Elster and Sen, see Nussbaum 2000, chap. 2. Sen discusses this question in many writings; one good example is Sen 1991.

There are other possibilities when girls express a reluctance to become educated. The girls studied by Bagchi are still living at home, so even if they have a strong desire for education, they may be unwilling to voice it. A third possibility is that they have a genuine nonadaptive preference for less or no education but that it is not fully informed: they do not know, for example, how much their political and employment opportunities will be limited by not becoming educated. A fourth possibility is that they have a genuine, fully informed preference for little or no education, but that it is a rational response to other inequalities in their lives: they may think, what point is there in going to school when I am going to be married off at age ten and denied any chance to leave the house thereafter, and when being educated may make my husband and my in-laws more likely to abuse me?[36] A fifth possibility is that they don't want to go to school because it seems difficult and no fun. Many children have such preferences, although we rarely consider them fully informed. Finally, there may be cases in which an individual girl or woman (more convincingly, a woman), surveying all of the possibilities in life, concludes that education is not for her, not a constituent of the life that she would wish to lead.

How should we respond to these different types of resistance on the part of women themselves? It seems to me that where we are dealing with children, we should not honor such preferences. The debate over compulsory primary and secondary education has been a long and difficult one in the history of most nations, but by now there is an international consensus that education has the status of a fundamental human entitlement and that the only way to secure it to people is to make education compulsory for children of certain ages. This has proven the only way to surmount the resistance of parents and other adults, who would like, say, to use these children for labor inside the house or outside it. It has also proven the only way to get children themselves to see what the value of an education is for them. And we typically don't think it objectionable to make children go to school when they don't want to. Indeed, we would think ill of either parents or governments that said that there shall be public education only for children who actually want to go to school and only when they have this preference. I see no reason why we should think otherwise about children in other countries. Indeed, it seems quite condescending to say, "Of course we require education of our own Western children, because we think their minds are terrible things to waste; but it is not so big a deal when it is those Indian or Pakistani or Bangladeshi minds." It seems just right that the Indian government is thinking of making the right to compulsory primary and secondary education a fundamental right of all citizens.[37]

If compulsory primary and secondary education were ever securely implemented, there would be no question about how to treat illiterate adult women. But

---

36. For one example of such abuse, see Tagore (1913) 1990. Similarly, Gary Becker argues (1995) that both women and African Americans "underinvest" in their "human capital" as a rational response to the discrimination that they actually suffer in employment. Women's preference for veiling, where it exists, typically falls in this category, for it is often described as a rational response to the way men actually treat them, though it might not be the woman's preference if that bad state of affairs were not in place.

37. See Mehendale 1998.

for the foreseeable future, there surely is such a question. Obviously enough, it is wrong to dragoon a woman, working or otherwise, into schooling that she refuses. On the other hand, however, it seems possible to err in the opposite direction, expecting that women will come demanding schooling if they want it, and not taking cognizance of the problems of ill-informed and adaptive preferences, to say nothing of resistance from husbands, the difficulties of a working life with children, and so forth. So it seems right to work hard to design programs for adult women that are compatible with their working day, attractive, and thoughtful about how to deal with the resistance the women may encounter. The most successful literacy programs for rural adult women typically include a large element of social bonding and consciousness raising, because in this way women gain many benefits over and above literacy: emotional solidarity, collective action to overcome shared problems, courage in facing opposition. Successful literacy programs also typically link education to programs of economic empowerment (through credit and labor organization) that are more attractive to husbands than their wives' education may be. Many women who do not initially favor literacy may join a group for the other benefits it offers, or even for education for their daughters, and then come upon the pleasures and advantages of education subsequently.

For such reasons, the most successful programs are always grounded in the local region and sensitive to the local scene. As I have mentioned, the language problem by itself makes this necessary: rural women may not speak any language that literate activist organizers speak. Typically, therefore, the headquarters of an organization is in a major city, for example Patna, Bihar's largest city, but its field offices enjoy considerable autonomy and operate by recruiting successful graduates of the program as new employees. Regular visiting from the center is important to oversee and coordinate activities and also to protect the local leaders from intimidation and help solve any legal and political problems that arise.[38] Activist leaders typically go to bat for their local field organizations with political leaders, courts, and employers. They also attempt to forge good relationships with influential organizations and businesses in the urban center, another strategy through which they exercise influence.

Solving the Problem

The worldwide crisis of female education has multiple dimensions. In part, it is a problem of poverty and cannot be stably solved without raising the living standard of the poor in each nation. In part, the data indicate, it is a separate problem,

---

38. *Vishaka v. Rajasthan* (see n. 24) arose out of a sexual assault against field workers working for Vishaka in a rural area. Adithi is currently dealing with the prosecution of one of its rural leaders, in the very area that I visited, for murder. A local landowner, unhappy about the sharecropping women's newfound solidarity and aggressiveness, alleged that his aunt had been fatally poisoned by an Adithi local field coordinator—on the grounds that the aunt had died some time after leaving that woman's house. Although it is perfectly obvious to any unbiased person that this is a preposterous charge, local law enforcement is very corrupt, and the organs of the deceased woman, crucial for the resolution of the case, have been impounded by the pathologist, who refuses to release his report to the defense. Literacy activism is full of such perils.

whose solution requires special, focused action. Action aimed at raising the education level of women and girls has, in turn, several distinct elements. Both nations and states within nations must get involved; and rich nations must support the efforts of poorer nations.

To see the importance of intelligent state action, we need only consider the case of Kerala, frequently discussed in the development literature.[39] A relatively poor state in India, it has nonetheless achieved 99 percent literacy for both boys and girls in adolescent age groups. Several factors play a role here. The history of matrilineal property transmission and matrilocal residence makes female life take on from the start a greater worth in the eyes of parents than it seems to have in many parts of the nation. Thus, while the sex ratio in the nation as a whole is plummeting, as a result of access to sex-selective abortion, and has now reached the alarming figure of 85 women to 100 men (see earlier), the sex ratio in Kerala is 102 women to 100 men, just what demographers say one should expect if equal nutrition and health care are present. Education for women, moreover, is a tradition with a long history in Kerala. In the seventeenth century, Jesuit missionaries began campaigning for literacy for both boys and girls, and this influence had an important effect.

But these historical factors are only a part of the story. For much of its history since independence, Kerala has had a democratically elected Marxist government that successfully pursued an ambitious plan of land reform, crucial to the empowerment of the poor, and that has pushed hard for both health services and education. Some of the techniques the government has used to increase literacy—besides aggressive campaigning in every region—are the provision of a nutritious school lunch for children, which offsets much of the lost income for parents who depend on child labor, and flexible school hours, which allow working children and children who help their parents in the home to enroll in school.

There is no reason in principle why these excellent ideas cannot be followed elsewhere. (Indeed, a Supreme Court decision late in 2002 has now ordered all states to adopt Kerala's program of providing a nutritious school lunch, and there is evidence that this directive is being implemented.) All too often, what happens is that local officials are corrupt and take the education money without establishing schools; or teachers are corrupt and take government money without showing up.

National governments are also a large part of the solution. Sen and Drèze show dramatically how India and China diverged after India's independence. The two nations had similar literacy rates in 1947; fifty-five years later, China has 76.3 percent adult literacy for women and 91.7 percent for men, by contrast to India's 45.4 percent and 68.4 percent.[40] Another useful contrast is Sri Lanka, a nation geographically and ethnically close to India, which by now has achieved adult literacy rates of 89.0 percent for women and 94.4 percent for men. Clearly one of the key failures of Nehru's plan for the new nation was an insufficient emphasis on basic education. This fact is now generally recognized.

39. See Drèze and Sen 1995; and, in the companion volume of field studies, see the field study of Kerala by V. K. Ramachandran.
40. These are data for 2000, cited in UNDP 2002, 223–224.

Adithi in the past has received much of its funding from the national government, which funds a few programs of its own but also helps the NGOs that do so
much of the work in rural areas. Recently, however, the Hindu right-wing government has taken a most unfortunate turn. Although basic literacy for the poor is a
crying need and also a key to the nation's economy, the minister of human resource
development, Murli Manohar Joshi, a very ideological Hindu fundamentalist, has
focused most of his energy on an expensive attempt to rewrite school textbooks to
"Hinduize" them, removing references to bad acts of Hindus in history (such as
violence against Muslims), removing the evidence that Hindus ever ate beef, and so
forth. In the process he has carried on an aggressive campaign against leading historians (for example Romila Thapar, one of the most distinguished living scholars of India's history), charging them with being subversives for simply wanting to
write the truth. His actions have been challenged by a petition currently before
the Supreme Court.[41] Among the many things that are wrong with Joshi's policy,
not the least is the fact that it represents a major diversion of both energy and funds
away from the problem of basic literacy. This is very likely no accident, given that
raising the fortunes of the poor, a large proportion of whom are either Muslim or
lower caste, may not be high on Joshi's personal agenda in any case.

So that is an example of how not to solve the problem at the national level.
How to solve it? Struggling against the corruption of state and local governments,
funding special programs in areas where state government is not delivering services, funding NGOs like Adithi—all these measures, taken in the past, have a
track record of at least some success. Another key issue is the removal of school fees
for textbooks, uniforms, and so on, which often make it impossible for the poor to
attend nominally free state-run schools. All these measures must be coupled with
more aggressive enforcement (which in some regions just means more than none)
of laws against child marriage and dowry and, again, funding of NGOs who do
good work on these problems. In other nations, similarly, governments need to
figure out what particular factors are blocking girls and women from being educated and then to design policies to address the problem.

Courts can clearly play a role here. In 2002, India placed compulsory primary
and secondary education in the Fundamental Rights section of the constitution,
following the Supreme Court case cited in my epigraph, which said that it was one.
Such a decision does not go far in the absence of suitable legislation and implementation, but it can provide a nudge to policymakers, as it did in this case,
giving strong support to the legislative push for a new constitutional amendment.[42]

---

41. For just a few of the recent discussions of this controversy, see Dhavan 2001, M. Hasan 2002,
Times of India 2002a and b, *Hindustan Times* 2002.

42. The Court is referring to an interpretative tradition according to which article 21 of the Constitution (the analogue of our Fourteenth Amendment), which stipulates that no person may be deprived
of "life or liberty" without due process of law, should be interpreted broadly, so as to include within the
concept of life the idea of a life with human dignity. This tradition has therefore also held that the right
to life includes the right to livelihood. Comparable to the developments described here is the U.S. history
of education of children with disabilities: court cases in the early 1970s led to the Education for All
Handicapped Children Act of 1972 and the Individuals with Disabilities Education Act in 1997.

The enormous worldwide problem of female education cannot, however, be solved by domestic policies in each nation alone. Adithi's projects in the Sithamarhi district alone have received support from Swiss and Dutch development agencies. In general, women's literacy projects in India receive assistance from a wide range of international development agencies, prominently including those of Sweden, Norway, and the Netherlands. International charities such as OXFAM (with its branches in various countries), UNICEF, and others play a role. Because U.S. charitable donors cannot receive a tax deduction for a donation directly to a group such as Adithi, umbrella charities have sprung up in the United States that focus on specialized funding of literacy projects in India. (No doubt the same is true of other nations.)

Well-intentioned donors must be vigilant, for many India-related charities in the United States are fronts that funnel money to Hindu/right organizations that engage in anti-Muslim violence.[43] The India Development and Relief Fund (IDRF), which claims to have various attractive purposes, is actually a front organization for the RSS (Rashtriya Swayamsevak Sangh, the paramilitary right-wing organization loosely connected to the governing Bharatiya Janata Party). One of the front organizations on the Indian side, a recipient of IDRF money, is actually called Sewa Bharati, a name that is similar to that of the Self-Employed Women's Association (SEWA), one of the most impressive NGOs working on women's issues. There are many other such cases. United States money is behind the recent genocide of Muslim men and the mass rapes of Muslim women in the state of Gujarat: in evidence presented to the U.S. Commission on International Religious Freedom, Najid Hussain, a professor at the University of Delaware, estimated that nine of every ten dollars used to foment religious violence in Gujarat came from the United States.[44] Some such donors know what they are doing: unfortunately, many wealthy Indian-Americans are staunch supporters of such causes. But there is reason to believe that much of the money is given in ignorance. Kanwal Rekhi, chair of The IndUS Entrepreneurs (an organization of South Asian businesspeople), wrote in the *Wall Street Journal*, "Many overseas Indian Hindus, including some in this country, finance religious groups in India in the belief that the funds will be used to build temples, and educate and feed the poor of their faith. Many would be appalled to know that some recipients of their money are out to destroy minorities (Christians as well as Muslims) and their places of worship" (Rekhi and Rowan 2002).[45] I recommend either giving directly to some Indian NGO that one knows well (and forfeiting the U.S. charitable deduction) or giving to OXFAM, which does not make India a particular focus but which does good work wherever it operates and does enough in India to make those who care particularly about that nation content.

Today overall, as is the case with world poverty and need generally, the nations of the developed world are doing too little to support the education of the world's

---

43. For discussion of this problem, with references, see Nussbaum 2003c.

44. For data see references in Nussbaum 2003c and A. K. Sen 2002.

45. The authors suggest that Vajpayee should label such causes terrorist and thus strike a blow against this covert funding of violence.

women. The United States clearly stands out as one that is doing remarkably less than it can and should. President Clinton showed a surprising level of knowledge and involvement on this particular issue: his visit to India deliberately highlighted the issue of women's literacy, and the groups he chose to visit in Rajasthan and elsewhere were well chosen, in a way that favorably impressed Indian thinkers and activists. But in the absence of a much larger budgetary commitment to foreign aid, his efforts to attend to the problem will not go far.

Delicate questions arise concerning how far one may promote a political agenda in another nation. Where there is no democratically accountable government in place, it seems reasonable enough to suppose that "nation-building" may take the overall empowerment of the people as its focus, a goal toward which the education of women is an extremely central strategy. Where, as in the case of India, there is a democratically accountable government in place, the nations of the developed world have different choices. They may simply give to the national government on the theory that this is the democratically elected surrogate for the people, and it should not be bypassed. But in the case of India today, that would both be a rather inefficient way of promoting women's literacy (given that the national government does little of the educating in rural areas) and, at present, insofar as such money would ever support education in the first place (nuclear bombs are a project dearer to the heart of the leaders of the nation), it would be a way of lending support to Joshi's policies, which it is not too bold to call blatantly racist, as well as violative of the free speech of historians.[46] By contrast, Clinton's attempt to highlight the good work of NGOs working with women seems to me perfectly acceptable, posing no delicate issue of paternalism, since the cause is so widely supported and so urgent. United States government funding for these same NGOs, which already receive funds from many world governments through their official development agencies, seems to me also perfectly acceptable. The development agencies of nations that devote a substantial portion of their budget to these ends are constantly in the business of making value judgments, like any grant-giving agency; they review proposals, and inevitably they have some goals (in this case, women's literacy) that they want to support and others (the Hinduization of textbooks) that they might not want to support. Although it seems to me that it would be wrong to send troops to India or even to impose economic sanctions on India for its violations of free speech in education, giving money to NGOs for women's education rather than to the national government for nuclear bombs and the Hinduization of textbooks seems to me perfectly reasonable, and a way of supporting women and the rural poor against national forces that do not fully represent their aspirations.[47] Although I believe that we should make a rather strong distinction between the justification of a political value and its implementation outside our national borders, refusing actively to implement much of what we think that we can morally justify out of respect for national sovereignty, women's literacy is a value

---

46. His attempt to glorify and whitewash the Hindu past is part and parcel of the most sinister attempts to foment violence against Muslims.

47. See my discussion of some of these matters in Nussbaum 2001.

with enormously strong popular support (and indeed, the national government itself strongly backs it, though its ways of doing so are extremely odd), so there seems to be no reason why we should not judge that certain NGOs pursue that goal more effectively and acceptably than the national government.[48]

The primary point to be made is that the nations of the developed world, and their individual citizens, are doing much, much too little to address this problem. So, too, I must now add, are the multinational corporations that increasingly determine the course of policy in the developing countries where they do business. To such corporations, we may make two arguments in favor of devoting substantial resources to education, and particularly female education, in the regions where they operate. First, we may make an efficiency argument. Money invested in education, we say, is money well spent. An educated workforce is a more productive and stable workforce. Women who are educated contribute to the economic development and the political stability of the entire region.[49] Kerala, for example, does not have the interreligious violence that is now sweeping over Gujarat, a state that has promoted economic growth while largely neglecting education and other areas of "human development."[50]

We may also, let us hope, link to this efficiency argument a moral argument. Using part of one's profits to educate the next generation is the decent thing to do. This is not an idea utterly alien to the American rich, as the history of U.S. colleges and universities shows. Is it too much to hope that we may prevail on the rich who are rich because of the work of people in developing nations to make a similar commitment to the well-being of the children of their workers?

The issue of women's education is both urgent and complex. But it has long been the neglected poor relation of the international development world, ignored by many of the most powerful thinkers and actors in this field in favor of the single goal of economic growth, which by itself delivers little to the poor of developing nations.[51] Even when politicians and activists are sensitive to the predicament of the poor, they have often neglected this issue in their own way, preferring to focus

---

48. On justification and implementation, see Nussbaum 2003a.

49. Buch 2000 shows that women's presence in *panchayats* has increased expenditure on health, especially child health, and other aspects of the welfare of the poor, as contrasted with other goals that might contribute less to the long-term security and well-being of the region.

50. I do not mean in any way to blame the Gujarat genocide on the local poor, since it is clearly fomented at the national level, with assistance from state government. But I do believe that a more highly educated local population might possibly have mounted more effective resistance earlier against the genocidal measures, and might also, well before that, have selected a state government that would focus more on the welfare of the poor and less on Hinduization. There is also an indirect point: any government that would make female education a top priority (as in Kerala) is unlikely to be the sort of government that would also make genocide and mass rape top priorities. It is no surprise that the current chief of police in the state of Gujarat—called out of retirement in the Punjab to "restore law and order"— is none other than K.P.S. Gill, defendant in the landmark sexual harassment case described in Nussbaum 2004b. Having put many innocent Sikhs to death in the Punjab, and having made a second career as a champion of sexual harassment, he now presides over murder and rape.

51. See the analysis in Drèze and Sen 1995.

on issues such as health and democratization, which appear less culturally controversial. I have argued that women's education is extremely urgent, indeed a key to women's empowerment. There are no good arguments against making it a top priority for development in this century. Theoretical analysis and good normative models have a valuable role to play in establishing these facts in the corridors of power.

Appendix: The Central Human Capabilities
(version as in Nussbaum 2000)

1. *Life.* Being able to live to the end of a human life of normal length; not dying prematurely, or before one's life is so reduced as to be not worth living.

2. *Bodily Health.* Being able to have good health, including reproductive health; to be adequately nourished; to have adequate shelter.

3. *Bodily Integrity.* Being able to move freely from place to place; to be secure against violent assault, including sexual assault and domestic violence; having opportunities for sexual satisfaction and for choice in matters of reproduction.

4. *Senses, Imagination, and Thought.* Being able to use the senses, to imagine, think, and reason—and to do these things in a "truly human" way, a way informed and cultivated by an adequate education, including, but by no means limited to, literacy and basic mathematical and scientific training. Being able to use imagination and thought in connection with experiencing and producing works and events of one's own choice, religious, literary, musical, and so forth. Being able to use one's mind in ways protected by guarantees of freedom of expression with respect to both political and artistic speech, and freedom of religious exercise. Being able to have pleasurable experiences and to avoid nonbeneficial pain.

5. *Emotions.* Being able to have attachments to things and people outside ourselves; to love those who love and care for us, to grieve at their absence; in general, to love, to grieve, to experience longing, gratitude, and justified anger. Not having one's emotional development blighted by fear and anxiety. (Supporting this capability means supporting forms of human association that can be shown to be crucial in their development.)

6. *Practical Reason.* Being able to form a conception of the good and to engage in critical reflection about the planning of one's life. (This entails protection for the liberty of conscience and religious observance.)

7. *Affiliation.*
   A. Being able to live with and toward others, to recognize and show concern for other human beings, to engage in various forms of social interaction; to be able to imagine the situation of another. (Protecting this capability means protecting institutions that constitute and nourish such forms of affiliation, and also protecting the freedom of assembly and political speech.)

   B.   Having the social bases of self respect and nonhumiliation; being able
          to be treated as a dignified being whose worth is equal to that of others.
          This entails provisions of nondiscrimination on the basis of race, sex,
          sexual orientation, ethnicity, caste, religion, and national origin.
 8.   *Other Species.* Being able to live with concern for and in relation to
       animals, plants, and the world of nature.
 9.   *Play.* Being able to laugh, to play, to enjoy recreational activities.
10.   *Control over One's Environment.*
   A.   *Political.* Being able to participate effectively in political choices
          that govern one's life; having the right of political participation,
          protections of free speech and association.
   B.   *Material.* Being able to hold property (both land and movable
          goods), and having property rights on an equal basis with others;
          having the right to seek employment on an equal basis with others;
          having the freedom from unwarranted search and seizure. In work,
          being able to work as a human being, exercising practical reason
          and entering into meaningful relationships of mutual recognition
          with other workers.

Bibliography

Agarwal, Bina. 1994. *A Field of One's Own: Gender and Land Rights in South Asia.*
    Cambridge, England: Cambridge University Press.
——. 1997. "'Bargaining' and Gender Relations: Within and Beyond the Household."
    Feminist Economics 3(1): 1–51.
Alkire, Sabina. 2002. *Valuing Freedoms: Sen's Capability Approach and Poverty Reduction.*
    Oxford: Clarendon Press.
Bagchi, Jasodhara. 1997. *Loved and Unloved: The Girl Child in the Family.* Calcutta: Stree.
Becker, Gary. 1995. "Nobel Lecture: The Economic Way of Looking at Behavior." In *The
    Essence of Becker,* ed. Ramón Febrero and Pedro S. Schwartz. Stanford: Hoover
    Institution, 633–58.
Buch, Nirmala. 2000. *From Oppression to Assertion: A Study of Panchayats and Women in
    M.P., Rajasthan and U.P.* New Delhi: Centre for Women's Development Studies.
Chen, Martha A. 1983. *A Quiet Revolution: Women in Transition in Rural Bangladesh.*
    Cambridge: Schenkman.
Dhavan, Rajeev. 2001. "Textbooks and Communalism." *Hindu,* November 30.
Drèze, Jean, and Amartya Sen. 1995. *India: Economic Development and Social Opportunity.*
    Delhi: Oxford University Press.
——. 1996. *Indian Development: Selected Regional Perspectives.* Oxford: Oxford University
    Press.
Elster, Jon. 1985. *Sour Grapes: Studies in the Subversion of Rationality.* Cambridge:
    Cambridge University Press.
Hasan, Mushirul. 2002. "Agenda of Rewriting Textbooks Jeopardises the Study of History."
    Indian Express, February 6.
Hasan, Zoya. 2000. "Women's Reservations and the 'Politics of Presence.'" Paper presented
    at the annual meeting of the American Philosophical Association, Eastern Division,
    New York, December 28, 2000.
Hindustan Times. 2002. "HRDline Propaganda." February 25.

Jayal, Niraja Gopal. 2000. "Gender and Decentralization." Unpublished manuscript, Centre for the Study of Law and Governance, Jawaharal Nehru University, New Delhi, India.

Marglin, Frédérique Apffel. 1985. *Wives of the God-King: The Rituals of the Devadasis of Puri.* Delhi: Oxford University Press.

Marglin, Frédérique Apffel, and Stephen A. Marglin, eds. 1990. *Dominating Knowledge: Development, Culture, and Resistance.* Oxford: Oxford University Press.

Marx, Karl. (1848) 1982. "Economic and Philosophical Manuscripts." Trans. T. B. Bottomore. In *Marx's Concept of Man,* ed. Erich Fromm. New York: Continuum, 87–196.

Mehendale, Archana. 1998. "Compulsory Primary Education in India: The Legal Framework. *From the Lawyers Collective* 13(4): 4–12.

Nussbaum, Martha. 1996. "Human Capabilities, Female Human Beings." In *Women, Culture and Development,* ed. Martha Nussbaum and Jonathan Glover. Oxford: Oxford University Press, 61–105.

———. 1997. *Cultivating Humanity: A Classical Defense of Reform in Liberal Education.* Cambridge: Harvard University Press.

———. 2000. *Women and Human Development: The Capabilities Approach.* Cambridge, England: Cambridge University Press.

———. 2001. "India: Implementing Sex Equality Through Law." *Chicago Journal of International Law* 2(1): 35–58.

———. 2002a. "'Mutilated and Deformed': Adam Smith on the Material Basis of Human Dignity." A lecture in memory of Tamara Horowitz, presented at the University of Pittsburgh, April 5. Unpublished, part of a book in progress entitled *The Cosmopolitan Tradition,* under contract to Yale University Press.

———. 2002b. "Sex, Laws, and Inequality: What India Can Teach the United States." *Daedalus* (winter): 95–106.

———. 2002c. "The Worth of Human Dignity: Two Tensions in Stoic Cosmopolitanism." In *Philosophy and Power in the Graeco-Roman World: Essays in Honour of Miriam Griffin,* ed. Gillian Clark and Tessa Rajak. Oxford: Oxford University Press, 31–49.

———. 2003a. "Women and the Law of Peoples." *Politics, Philosophy, and Economics* 1(3): 283–306.

———. 2003b. "Capabilities as Fundamental Entitlements: Sen and Social Justice." *Feminist Economics* 9(2–3): 33–59.

———. 2003c. "Genocide in Gujarat." *Dissent* (summer): 61–9.

———. 2004a. "India, Sex Equality, and Constitutional Law." In *Constituting Women: The Gender of Constitutional Jurisprudence,* ed. Beverly Baines and Ruth Rubio Marin. Cambridge: Cambridge University Press, 174–204.

———. 2004b. "The Modesty of Mrs. Bajaj: India's Problematic Route to Sexual Harassment Law." In *Directions in Sexual Harassment Law,* ed. Catharine MacKinnon and Reva Siegel. New Haven: Yale University Press, 633–71.

Nussbaum, Martha, and Amartya Sen. 1993. Introduction to *The Quality of Life,* ed. Martha Nussbaum and Amartya Sen. Oxford: Clarendon Press, 1–8.

Omvedt, Gail. 1983. "Devadasi Custom and the Fight Against It." *Manushi* 4 (November–December): 16–9.

Rekhi, Kanwal, and Henry S. Rowen. 2002. "India Confronts Its Own Intolerance." *Wall Street Journal,* May 21.

Sen, Amartya K. 1991. "Gender and Cooperative Conflicts." In *Persistent Inequalities: Women and World Development,* ed. Irene Tinker. Oxford: Clarendon Press, 123–49.

———. 1996. "Fertility and Coercion." *University of Chicago Law Review* 63(3):1035–62.

Sen, A. K. (not the same person as Amartya K. Sen). 2002. "Deflections to the Right." Speech. Available online at: http://mail.sarai.net/pipermail/reader-list/2002-August/001653.html.

Tagore, Rabindranath. (1913) 1990. "Haimanti." In *Women, Outcastes, Peasants, and Rebels: A Selection of Bengali Short Stories,* trans. Kalpana Bardhan. Berkeley: University of California Press, 84–96.

Times of India. 2002a. "History Joshi Wants to Censor." February 24.

———. 2002b. "History Row Goes to SC." February 23.

United Nations Development Programme (UNDP). 1990. *Human Development Report.* Oxford: Oxford University Press.

———. 2001. *Human Development Report 2001: Making New Technologies Work for Human Development.* Oxford: Oxford University Press.

———. 2002. *Human Development Report 2002: Deepening Democracy in a Fragmented World.* Oxford: Oxford University Press.

Index

Ackelsberg, Martha, 94
Adithi, 189–191, 204 n.38, 206–207
Afghanistan, U.S. war with, 28–31
    repackaged as humanitarian intervention, 28
    rhetoric of women's rights, 28
Agacinski, Sylviane, 45–48
    and dominant version of *parité*, 47–48
Alarcón, Norma, 120
Anzaldúa, Gloria, 114–115, 117–118, 124
Arab Families Working Group (AFWG), 150 n.1
arenas of citizenship, 106–108
Asian University for Women (AUW), 198–200
assimilation, 113
Auclert, Hubertine, 38
autonomy, 8

Bagchi, Jasodhara, 202–203
Bangladesh Rural Advancement
    Committee, 202
battered women, 55–62
    and advocacy groups, 59
    and cultural intimidation, 57
    and judicial intimidation, 59–62
    and legal representation, 57–59
    and linguistic intimidation, 57
    and spatial intimidation, 56
de Beauvoir, Simone, 38
Benhabib, Seyla, 72, 151–152
Bombay Forum Against Oppression of
    Women, 105
"borderlands." *See* Chicana feminism
Brown, María Rivera, 83
Buch, Nirmala, 195
Bush, George W., 15, 22–23, 28
Bush, Laura, 28–29
Butler, Judith, 48

Camden, Habiba, 81
care, 131–132, 142–144. *See also* care crisis; care
    work
    as fundamentally public, 144
    as masculine or feminine, 142–143
    as not private, 142
care crisis, 7, 132–139
    and American political system, 138–139
    and care workers, 133–135
    and globalization, 133–135
    and immigration, 137
    and "pink-collar ghetto," 134
    problems with privatization, 137–138
    response through privatization, 135–136
    response through socialization, 136–137
    and second wave of feminism, 133
    and Third World women, 135
    and unjust institutions, 133
care movement, 141–143
care work, 7, 132–144
    and citizenship, 139–144
    and governmental responsibility, 7
    and illegal immigrants, 7
    as imported commodity, 135
    as masculine or feminine, 142–143
    privatization of, 7
    as subject to exploitation, 135
    and Third World women, 135
    and women, 7
Chen, Martha, 197, 202
Chicago Abused Women's Coalition, 60
Chicana feminism, 112–126
    and the American Southwest, 115, 123
    and borderlands, 114–115, 123
    commitment to coalition politics, 125–126
    as different from white feminism, 124–125